Popular Fiction and Social Change

Popular Fiction and Social Change

EDITED BY
CHRISTOPHER PAWLING

MACMILLAN

© Rosalind Brunt, Bridget Fowler, David Glover,
Jerry Palmer, Martin Jordin, Stuart Laing,
Adrian Mellor, Christopher Pawling 1984

First published 1984
Reprinted 1985

Published by
Higher and Further Education Division
MACMILLAN PUBLISHERS LTD
Houndmills, Basingstoke, Hampshire RG21 2XS
and London
Companies and representatives
throughout the world

Printed in Hong Kong

British Library Cataloguing in Publication Data
Pawling, Christopher
Popular fiction and social change.
1. Popular fiction – England – History
I. Title
820'.9   PR149.P6
ISBN 0–333–34319–0
ISBN 0–333–34320–4 Pbk

Contents

Notes on Contributors

ROSALIND BRUNT is a senior lecturer in the department of Communication Studies at Sheffield City Polytechnic, where she specialises in the fields of mass communications and women's studies. She has co-edited, with George Bridges, *Silver Linings: Some Strategies for the Eighties* and, with Caroline Rowan, *Feminism, Culture and Politics*.

BRIDGET FOWLER lectures in sociology at the University of Glasgow, where her teaching includes a course on the sociology of literature. The chapter which she has contributed to this volume is a revised version of an article which first appeared in the *British Journal of Sociology* in March 1979.

DAVE GLOVER is a senior lecturer in the School of Applied Social Studies at Humberside College of Higher Education, where his teaching includes courses on mass communications. He is the author of a number of articles in the field of cultural studies and of *The Sociology of the Mass Media*.

MARTIN JORDIN is a senior lecturer in the department of Communication Studies at Sheffield City Polytechnic where he specialises in the sociology of literature. His research has concentrated on the relationship between the arts and the state.

STUART LAING lectures in English in the School of Cultural and Community Studies at the University of Sussex. He has published articles on pre-war literature, including one on the popular novelist, Philip Gibbs, in *Literature and History*, and has just completed a number of pieces on the post-war novel and the conditions of literary production for a forthcoming volume on the period 1945–70.

ADRIAN MELLOR is a senior lecturer at Liverpool Polytechnic, where his teaching includes a course on the sociology of literature. His publications include a chapter on 'Writers and the General Strike' (with C. Pawling and C. Sparks) in M. Morris (ed.) *The General Strike* and several essays in the *Student Encyclopedia of Sociology*, edited by Michael Mann.

JERRY PALMER lectures on sociology and cultural studies at the City Polytechnic in London. His publications include an essay 'Thrillers: The Deviant Behind the Consensus' in *The Politics of Deviance*, I. Taylor and L. Taylor (eds) and *Thrillers: Genesis and Structure of a Popular Genre*.

CHRISTOPHER PAWLING is a senior lecturer in the department of Communication Studies at Sheffield City Polytechnic where he teaches courses on the sociology of literature. His publications include 'Writers and the General Strike' (with Adrian Mellor) and an article on George Orwell and the Documentary in *Literature and History*.

Introduction: Popular Fiction: Ideology or Utopia?

CHRISTOPHER PAWLING

Popular Fiction and Literary Criticism

Although there has been a growth of interest in popular fiction over the last few years, one could not claim that it has been established in schools or colleges as a central component of literary studies. The English lecturer who proposes a course in this area may well be told that it would be difficult to find space on the timetable for such a 'minor' field of study, although the same objections do not seem to apply when one of his/her colleagues suggests yet another option in seventeenth-century poetry. A course dealing with popular genres such as science fiction or thrillers is, apparently, a luxury which the department cannot afford. 'It would be nice if we had the time, of course, but . . .' Such entrenched resistance is not wholly surprising. Most intellectual disciplines harbour conservative as well as innovative tendencies. Once a field of study has been established within an academic institution it will attract a community of teachers and scholars who have a vested interest in its continuity and growth. Adherents to the discipline tend to work within its intellectual paradigms, taking them as given rather than exploring the boundaries of their subject in a critical manner. Literary criticism is no exception to this rule. Moreover, since it is not a discipline which is characterised by a strong interest in' theory, its self-definition relies heavily on what is absent from the field, as well as what is included within its boundaries. The identity of English Literature as an intellectual discipline is, in part, dependent on a 'significant other' – popular literature or 'paraliterature' – whose absence from the conventional syllabus is crucial in helping to constitute the dominant literary culture. As Marc Angenot comments, 'paraliterature occupies the space outside the literary enclosure, as a forbidden, taboo, and perhaps degraded product', against which the 'self' of literature proper is forged.[1]

To the disinterested, non-literary specialist the neglect of those texts which have captured the interest of wide sections of the reading public must seem a little strange. For, in as much as the discipline lays claim to a position in the human sciences, literary criticism should be looking forward to the moment when it is able to account for the whole of literary culture, and not just that segment which has been canonised within the academic institution. We would do well to heed Darko Suvin's warning that, 'a discipline which refuses to take into account 90 per cent or more of what constitutes its domain seems to me not only to have large zones of blindness but also to run serious risks of distorted vision in the small zone it focuses on (so-called high lit.)'.[2]

There are some indications that attitudes are changing and that popular fiction is beginning to be accepted as a serious area of study. The last few years have witnessed the emergence of new interdisciplinary courses, such as Cultural Studies or Communications (in Britain this development has taken place largely outside the universities which are much more rigidly discipline-orientated than their American counterparts) where the prejudice against studying popular literature is, theoretically, much less marked. Once one begins to examine literature as a 'communicative practice' with social and historical roots, then one cannot afford to ignore those fictional worlds which command the widest public. Moreover, it has become increasingly clear that the analysis of popular narrative can provide a crucial link between the field of literature and other aesthetic modes of communication such as film and television.[3]

However, it would be foolish to assume that popular fiction has been accepted into the academic fold on a permanent basis. In a period of educational contraction, the principle of 'last in, first out' may well be operated by those who feel happier with a more traditional approach to literature and, consequently, welcome the opportunity to jettison those 'illegitimate' areas which have been added to the curriculum since the 1960s. Clearly, those teachers who are committed to the preservation and expansion of courses in popular literature have an urgent task ahead of them. They must be able to convince the more sceptical of their colleagues that this is not a 'soft option', and that it has been able to generate a serious body of theoretically informed criticism. Those who are not acquainted with the subject still find it difficult to accept that the 'reading' of a thriller or romance could be anything other than the most straightforward exercise in comprehension. Accordingly, they may assume that the study of popular fiction involves a simple process of familiarisation with a number of 'second-rate' novels and question the logic of devoting valuable time to such a seemingly peripheral activity.

The Encounter with Sociology

From the outset it has to be recognised that much of the secondary work on popular literature is untheorised and eclectic (anyone who has consulted one of the main 'house journals' in the field – the American *Journal of Popular Culture* – will know what I mean by this description). This is partly due to the fact that the tangential relationship of popular culture to the traditional concerns of both sociology and literary criticism has inhibited the development of an integrated approach to the subject. Instead, the prospective student has been faced with either (a) empirical surveys of the production, marketing and consumption of popular fiction which deliberately eschew any consideration of the meanings embodied within the texts themselves (e.g. the work of Escarpit in France)[4], or (b) analyses which use the tools of literary criticism to give an 'internal' account of the themes embodied within the text or genre, but are unwilling or unable to make connexions between the literary artefact and the social context in which it 'moves and has its being'.[5] The net result of such a dichotomy is that it splits literature into a 'socio-historical *external context*, and the pure and undefiled still centre of the literary text which is left to an unholy alliance of technical description and ideologizing impressionism' (Suvin).[6]

In the main, where sociologists have actually examined the texts of popular culture they have dealt with them as direct bearers of ideology. So the early 'content analysis' produced interesting data on the images of social identity which were reproduced in the fictional 'discourse' of magazine fiction (see especially the work of Berelson on the presentation of minority Americans in the mass periodicals of the late 1930s and early 1940s)[7] but had nothing to say about the relationship between ideology and the *fictional* elements in the text (narrative strategies, etc.). Like all forms of cultural creation, popular fiction both reflects social meanings/mores and, perhaps more importantly, *intervenes* in the life of society by organising and interpreting experiences which have previously been subjected only to partial reflection. Thus, to 'understand' popular fiction is to examine it as a form of cultural production and as a *process of meaning creation* which offers a particular way of thinking and feeling about one's relationship to oneself, to others, and to society as a whole.

Genre Analysis

It is here that genre analysis is so important, as it allows us to dispense with the notion that popular novels are simple repositories of sociological data. Once we examine individual genres such as the thriller or women's romance we can see that they generate particular rules or norms of expectation which are crucial factors in the reader's acceptance or rejection of the text. As Fredric Jameson has noted, 'Genres are essentially contracts between a writer and his [sic] readers; or rather, to use the term which Claudio Guillen has so usefully revived, they are literary *institutions*, which like other institutions of social life are based on tacit agreements or contracts'.[8] The work of the Formalists and Structuralists (Propp, Todorov, Eco, etc.)[9] has been devoted to an investigation of the rules which govern these literary 'contracts', concentrating on those features which mark out one genre from another. For example, it is clear that the narrative of the thriller offers a form of 'pleasure' (the thrill of uncertainty which is generated by the opposition between security and adventure) which is different from that of women's romance (see Jerry Palmer's contribution to this volume of essays). Thus we need to account for that 'relative autonomy' of the narrative which helps to define the boundaries of different genres and the work of the Formalists/Structuralists has been crucial in this regard. However, we also have to remember that these genres do not exist in a vacuum, but that they circulate in specific social, cultural and historical contexts (a fact which the Formalists and Structuralists tend to forget). Therefore the chapters in this book which are grouped under the heading of genre analysis have concentrated on those historical features which demarcate our popular genres from those of other societies, rather than seeing them as reworkings of universal 'archetypal' structures.[10]

Narrative and Ideology: Macherey and Goldmann

One of the most important breakthroughs in 'cultural reading' has been the realisation that the links or 'mediations' between the text and society are present in that text itself, as well as existing externally in the form of norms, world visions, etc. Starting with Lévi-Strauss in 'The Structural Study of Myth',[11] a number of researchers have examined the way in which the narrative process in primitive myths serves an ideological function in resolving conceptual contradictions inherent in those societies. Lévi-Strauss' analysis is important in putting the emphasis, not only on *what* the myth says, but on *the way* that it says it. Ideology is present in both the form and content of the myth as text, and the narrative itself provides a crucial link between the 'external' reality of social experience and the 'internal' meaning which is derived therefrom. Fredric Jameson has commented that this allows us to view narrative as 'a "form of reasoning" about experience and society' which is 'of equal dignity to the various types of conceptual thought in service in daily life'.[12] If one accepts this contention, then the examination of narrative in contemporary mythologies such as the romance can provide a crucial point of entry into the world of 'lived ideology' (see, for example, Bridget Fowler's chapter in this volume).

Arguably the most convincing and elaborate demonstration of what such an analysis should look like is Pierre Macherey's long essay, 'Jules Verne: The Faulty Narrative'.[13] Macherey reverses the mode of procedure which normally operates in the sociology of literature, by starting with an analysis of the internal logic or 'problematic' of the text before moving on to a reconstruction of the ideological 'field' which lies behind the narrative. Instead of matching the text against an external 'world vision' Macherey examines the way in which that text works on the raw material of ideology to produce a new 'reality', a fictive world with its own form of 'reasoning'. Macherey argues that the demand for self-consistency in the creation of this fictive world forces the author to test out certain ideological propositions which form the basis of the literary 'discourse'. The narrative may thus reveal any contradictions inherent in those assumptions/myths governing the motives and actions of the characters. Often these contradictions are then simply suppressed through various 'magical resolutions', but in certain cases the whole narrative may be 'flawed' if the author refuses this escape route and pursues the contradictions to the point where they threaten to destabilise the text.

Thus, Verne's story, *The Mysterious Island*, begins with what looks like a straightforward celebration of 'bourgeois' science as a group of castaways use science and engineering skills to establish their version of 'civilisation' on the island. However, the self-confidence of this opening narrative is undermined by their discovery of the mysterious Captain Nemo, who has turned his back on society and who represents a return to that 'heroic' stage in bourgeois history when scientific enquiry was supposedly untainted by social relations. This 'ideal' image of science is finally rejected by Verne, and Nemo is presented as an anachronistic figure whose illusions end in his own destruction and that of his beloved island. Nonetheless, the tragedy of Nemo has the effect of undermining the image of an all-conquering science and highlighting contradictions within the intended 'project' of the text. Verne's story does not offer a *conscious* interrogation of the 'bourgeois' image of science but Macherey's reading reveals a flaw in the narrative – the textual equivalent of a geological fault or slippage – which allows us to gain access to the repressed meanings or 'political unconscious' (Fredric Jameson) of the narrative.[14]

The influence of Macherey's approach on this book is most visible in Martin Jordin's analysis of the 1950s science fiction novel *Wolfbane*. In a case-study which is very reminiscent of Macherey's dissection of *The Mysterious Island*, Jordin shows that the narrative of *Wolfbane* does not just *reproduce* given ideological assumptions about the role of science in society but that it also puts that ideology to work, 'testing, defining and reconstructing it in the process of interpreting the changing content of . . . historical experience'. According to Jordin, *Wolfbane* reverses the usual 'order of priority' which had governed the narrative of the SF formula by implying that science must first be liberated from its service to an irrational social order before it can become an instrument of human progress. (SF had more commonly projected the idea that scientific 'progress' would inevitably produce a more free and equal society.) This reversal of the 'logic' of the formula may be attributed to a number of socio-political developments (Jordin argues that, *inter alia*, this period saw the increasing subordination of the readership of SF, largely the scientific middle class, to the needs of the corporate economy). However, like Macherey, Jordin is concerned with emphasising the 'relative autonomy' of the text, seeing it as a site of 'ideological struggle' and therefore not just a *reflection* of external social processes. Thus his account of *Wolfbane* concentrates on the way in which the narrative '*constructs*, rather than reflects, an ideological position, in seeking to give perceptions of historical reality ideological consistency and coherence'.

Of all the contributions Martin Jordin's is, as I have already commented, the one which most closely resembles Macherey's approach, and I must be careful not to give the impression that other contributors would necessarily go along with the Machereyan emphasis on immanent textual analysis. Indeed, if one reads through the essay on science fiction by Adrian Mellor it is clear that he leans much more towards that position in literary theory which is associated with the work of Lucien Goldmann.[15] Mellor concentrates on the way in which science fiction *expresses* the 'world vision' of its readership, on its *relative* autonomy, rather than treating it as a relatively *independent* entity. Thus, whereas Jordin's analysis of *Wolfbane* emphasises the disillusionment with science as part of a creative interrogation of ideology *within* the text, Mellor would stress that the flight from science reflects a process of fragmentation which is already detectable outside the text, in the developing 'world-vision' of the 'educated middle class'. One must be wary of oversimplifying the division between these two approaches as both writers would accept the notion of 'relative autonomy' as being central to cultural analysis. In part the difference arises from a contrasting focus of attention, rather than a fundamental theoretical conflict – Mellor is interested in constructing an overall picture of SF as a genre, whereas Jordin concentrates on the narrative mechanics of one moment of change and therefore is bound to privilege the more 'autonomous' features of the text. Nevertheless, a comparison of the two chapters shows that the authors are committed to rather different modes of procedure, even though they share the same basic philosophy.

The Popular/Elite Dichotomy: Lowenthal and Cawelti

Thus it would be wrong to imply that Macherey is somehow the guiding hand behind this collection of essays. However, his writings do offer some general propositions about the relationship between popular and élite literature which provides a link between our separate contributions. Here I am thinking in particular of the way in which he breaks with 'established' literary criticism in his refusal to divide the sphere of literature between 'Literature' (an autonomous realm which is somehow free from ideology), and 'popular' or 'mass' literature (supposedly a direct reflection of ideology and therefore not amenable to the sophisticated analysis which is given to 'canonic' texts). Macherey is exceedingly suspicious of such simplistic oppositions, as the following quotation shows:

> Are texts literary in themselves, by their own intrinsic characteristics which distinguish them from non-literary texts? I think one must say that a text is literary because it is recognized as such, at a certain moment, under certain conditions. It may not have been so recognised before, and it may not be after. I did a lot of work on Jules Verne, at a time when no-one spoke of him; now he has become an *author*, and everyone does his or her book on Jules Verne. He has been returned to 'French Literature'; he is explained in class. But

when I worked on him, he was not even a minor author; this
was not 'Literature'.[16]

As Macherey remarks, perhaps the most interesting feature of
his work on Verne is the way in which it highlights the
relativity of literary value, and the need to problematise
categories such as 'popular' and 'high' literature. The fact that
Verne has been added to the curriculum since Macherey
published his research shows that the 'canon' is a historical
construct, rather than a fixed entity, and that it is open to
revision. Hence the importance of Macherey's challenge to the
a priori assumption that a science fiction story by someone who
was 'not even a minor author' was unworthy of detailed
consideration at the 'literary' level.

Thus we need to challenge the assumption that there is one
mode of analysis which is appropriate for the study of popular
fiction and another which is suitable for 'real' literature. This
sort of dichotomy soon leads to a 'reductionist' approach
where, to quote Tony Bennett, 'non-canonized texts are
necessarily collapsed back into the conditions of production from
which they derive'.[17] So we get studies of popular fiction which
are limited to an account of the marketing strategies employed
in promoting bestsellers. Or we are given a rudimentary
account of the role of 'mass' fiction as a component of the
'culture industry', whose sole function is the reproduction of
'false consciousness'. Consider the following quotation from
Leo Lowenthal's book, *Literature, Popular Culture and Society*:

. . . since the separation of literature into two distinct fields of
art and commodity in the course of the eighteenth century,
the popular literary products can make no claim to insight
and truth. Yet, since they have become a powerful force in
the life of modern man, their symbols cannot be overesti-
mated as diagnostic tools for studying man in contemporary
society.[18]

Although Lowenthal claims that he is attaching some importance to the study of popular literature, he reduces it to a
'symptom' of social change. Moreover, it is not made clear why
commodity production should only have an adverse effect on

this form of literary production. Whilst one is not denying that
the emergence of a market economy has profound implications
for the relationship between author and reader, it seems naïve
to claim that literature as 'art' is somehow immune from this
process.

Even a sensitive critic such as John Cawelti, whose *Adventure,
Mystery, and Romance* is one of the seminal studies of popular
fiction, tends to argue that it is *intrinsically* more ideological than
its 'élite' counterpart. For Cawelti, 'formulaic' fiction has the
function of reproducing cultural consensus, in contrast to
'mimetic' (élite) fiction which confronts us with the problematic and contradictory 'reality' of our world: 'the mimetic
element in literature confronts us with the world as we know it,
while the formulaic element reflects the construction of an ideal
world without the disorder, the ambiguity, the uncertainty and
the limitations of the world of our experience'. Thus Cawelti
views formulaic literature as an 'artistry of escape' which
achieves widespread popularity because it provides security
and consolation for the reader – 'the tensions, ambiguities and
frustrations of ordinary experience are painted over by magic
pigments of adventure, romance and mystery'.[19]

The first thing to note about this model is that it attempts to
defend popular fiction by assigning it to the realms of escape
and distraction. Thus, Patrick Parrinder is perfectly correct in
arguing that there is no place in Cawelti's scheme for 'a
literature of genuine innovation, or for one of informal "underground" education'.[20] Such a function is reserved for 'mimetic'
literature which is by its very nature less 'formulaic' and,
hence, more original. This approach begs a number of
important questions. For example, there is the too easy
assumption that, because popular fiction is predominantly a
generic form of literary production it is *necessarily* also 'conventional' in an artistically conservative sense. But this is to ignore
the fact that *all* literature is concerned with the manipulation of
narrative expectations in some way, and that the most
avant-garde form of literary subversion inevitably sets up
generic patterns after a while. Even an arch modernist such as
Theodor Adorno has recognised that formulae (which he terms
'stereotypes') are an essential element in the organisation and
anticipation of experience, and he argues that 'no art can

entirely dispense with them'.[21] Instead of just making the equation, popular = formulaic, it would be more prudent to ask how, and under what conditions, specific literary genres ossify and lose their creative potential, whilst recognising that this is a question which applies to both popular and élite fiction.

A second, and related, point concerns the way in which Cawelti's approach tends to privilege the consensual role of popular culture. Thus he argues that the function of formulaic literature is to manage social tension and promote cultural stability by assimilating new interests into 'conventional imaginative structures'. For example, the black-oriented action stories of the early 1970s, such as *Shaft*, use a traditional formula – the 'hard-boiled' thriller – but fill it with a new content. Thus, the new black self-consciousness of that period is able to find expression in 'conventional forms of fantasy not significantly different in their assumptions and value structures from the sort of adventure stories that have been enjoyed by American audiences for several decades'.[22]

It is not hard to see that Cawelti's 'functionalist' theory has its origins in mainstream American sociology. Following in the tracks of writers such as Talcott Parsons and Edward Shils, Cawelti sees American culture as the embodiment of a set of 'core' values which gradually spread outwards to the periphery of society and eventually embrace 'marginal' groups such as the black minorities. The problem with this model is that it takes certain values for granted and assumes that culture is a homogeneous entity, rather than seeing it as a site of struggle which is marked by contradictions. In other words, the 'functionalist' approach tends to overlook the effect of power relations on the production and reproduction of cultural meanings. If we return to the example of the 'Black Action' stories it is clear that, whilst they make the black man into the initiator of action, they also tend to glorify a 'machismo' image, with the result that the cultural 'integration' of the male section of the black community takes place at the expense of the woman, who experiences a double subordination.

In many ways Cawelti's approach is a direct reversal of the position adopted by Lowenthal. Whereas the latter condemns popular fiction as a purveyor of 'false consciousness', the former tends to extol this consensual function in a rather uncritical manner. One must be careful not to oversimplify Cawelti's work, as the case-studies in *Adventure, Mystery, and Romance* tend to belie the overall theory put forward in the first two chapters, adopting a more dialectical approach to the relationship between popular fiction and ideology. Nevertheless, Cawelti does seem to place a premium on the harmonising, normative function of formulaic narrative whereas, to quote from Martin Jordin's chapter on *Wolfbane*, 'when we look at the ideological conflict within each text, it becomes clear that it is also potentially *subversive* of that consensus'.

Popular Fiction and 'Common Sense': the Influence of Gramsci

Even the most banal of narratives may help to shed light on the material reality which lies behind the ostensibly unified, conflict-free world of ideology. Thus Rosalind Brunt's chapter on Barbara Cartland's romance stories highlights a contradiction in the narrative, between the intended 'message' which focuses on the role of woman as a transcendent, spiritual being, and the actual process of narration which concentrates on the more mundane reality of 'love and marriage'. The main narrative threatens to undermine the romantic message by highlighting the historical 'necessities' which lead women to pursue men and to turn love into an 'economically rational career'. Hence the repeated references to the importance of virginity as a commodity which secures the heroine an economic place in the world through a 'good' marriage. All in all, Cartland's novels reveal a clear-eyed view of women's involvement in a patriarchal commodity market which sits uneasily with her romantic idealism. Although there is always a celebration of the 'spiritual' union of marriage at the end of the novels, this concluding message is effectively 'tacked on' to a narrative whose impulse is towards a materialist account of gender relations.

Rosalind Brunt's account of Cartland's work is interesting because it breaks with simple functionalist analysis (whether Marxisant, à la Althusser or non-Marxist, à la Cawelti), in focusing on the *contradictions* in the texts. Her feminist reading of Cartland alerts us to the way in which the author's conscious intentions are partially subverted at an unconscious level by a material reality which weighs heavily on the narrative, and cannot simply be wished away by the 'magical resolutions' at the end of the text. (Similarly, Bridget Fowler, when discussing the romance stories of the 'thirties', comments on the emergence of 'structures of feeling' which are 'dissonant with the ideological recuperation of the ending'.) However, although Cartland's novels can be interpreted in a manner which renders them potentially subversive of the author's overt intentions, that does not mean that they generate an 'alternative' view of female identity. Indeed, they reproduce values which are explicitly opposed to those of the women's movement and there can be no doubt that Cartland opposes any move towards greater social and cultural equality for her sex.

Cartland approaches her readers on the terrain of what Gramsci has termed 'common sense' (i.e. that area of 'negotiated' meanings which forms the 'spontaneous philosophy' or 'structure of feeling' of society's subordinate groupings, and which occupies the space between hegemonic ideology and material reality).[23] Through Cartland's narratives women come to know what they already 'know' from daily experience – that they are 'naturally' subordinate to men and that they must operate in a different, 'feminine' manner if they are to succeed as women. Thus, by recognising themselves in the form of identity which Cartland offers, women are socialised into existing gender relations. One is effectively enclosed within a circular narrative which says: 'This is so, isn't it?' The heroine may have to decide between alternative courses of action (e.g. whether to marry for love or money), but this choice is bound by the parameters of common sense (there is no suggestion that the heroine should not marry at all). At the same time, the reproduction of ideological categories through common sense notions of the woman's role can only be accomplished by addressing an important material aspect of her situation – her dependence on marriage as a route to economic security.

I want to spend a little more time on Gramsci's notion of common sense, as it may help us to gain some insight into the contradictions of that world of 'lived ideology' which lies behind popular fiction. Gramsci describes common sense philosophy as being 'strangely composite', since it contains

'Stone Age elements and principles of a more advanced science, prejudices from all past phases of history at the local level and intuitions of a future philosophy which will be that of a human race united the world over'.[24] Here Gramsci highlights that dialectic between ideology and utopia which is so crucial to the constitution of popular fiction. Thus if we return to Cartland's romance stories we can see that they contain 'Stone Age elements' (the fascination with the aristocracy, for example) and 'intuitions' of a Utopian future free from contradictions. Clearly in Cartland's work the 'Stone Age' traces predominate, and this is a characteristic of most 'mass formulaic' literature in what Gramsci terms 'normal times'. However, at the moments of intensified political and cultural struggle the balance begins to tip the other way and common sense adopts a more Utopian outlook, so that there is an active popular demand for literature which embodies alternative values.

Popular Fiction: Ideology or Utopia?

This seesawing dialectic between ideology and utopia is a particular concern of the last three chapters in our book, where we focus on the relationship between popular fiction and cultural politics at certain key moments in the post-war period. We open this section with Stuart Laing's piece on *Room at the Top* and an examination of the 'morality of affluence' in the late 1950s. Laing argues that John Braine's novel evoked such a popular response because it addressed contemporary debates and latent anxieties about the direction in which British society was moving at that time (in particular, the fear that an old world of 'authentic' values, associated with the pre-war working-class, was on the verge of extinction). Braine's novel of the 'working-class hero' does not just reflect the preoccupations of that moment as he makes his own intervention in the debate about affluence by offering an alternative 'reality' based on the hero's relationship with Alice. However, this utopian vision of a haven in the midst of the 'rat race' is crushed with Alice's death and the novel finally surrenders to a cynical acceptance of the present and the inevitability of 'affluence'.

The fatalism of *Room at the Top* corresponded to a marked lack of popular struggle for 'alternative' political and cultural goals.

Thus its tone was that of a *moral* critique, echoing the politics of CND and other predominantly middle-class pressure groups of that time which were, as Laing comments,· attempts to make society live up to its stated ideals, rather than movements with a concrete vision of the 'just society'. By contrast, the middle 1960s witnessed the emergence of a 'counter-culture' which placed far more emphasis on the transformation of existing social relationships as a prerequisite of political change. This could hardly be counted as a 'mass' movement in the classic sense of the word, since it was largely confined to the middle class. However, it did have a populist outlook which was expressed in a number of ways, not least the rejection of cultural divisions and the celebration of popular art as an arena of cultural struggle.

David Glover's chapter concentrates on that 'moment' in the 1960s when certain writers of fantasy, notably Tolkien, Peake, Burroughs and Moorcock, acquired a cult status amongst the counter-culture. For these writers it was a period when, 'a public came to find itself in their work, tying that work to their own historical moment, with each author reaching maximum exposure and circulation through the medium of mass market paperbacks'. Fantasy gave expression to the search for utopian alternatives by working on two distinct but complementary planes. On the level of form, the taste for anti-realist texts among the counter-culture can be seen as 'a kind of literary equivalent to the alteration of consciousness', suggesting new ways of perceiving one's relationship to others, society in general, the natural world, and so on. Similarly, the content of these utopian tales offered the vision of a transformed world of 'human' proportions, an 'organic' society based on the small collective and the needs of the individual. Thus David Glover concludes by remarking that the 'enclosed world' of utopia/fantasy 'provided a touchstone for a critique of existing social structures and the construction of alternatives, social models prefigured in the achievements of literary technique'.

The 'moment' of the counter-culture was brief and by the early 1970s it was largely a spent force. Its demise was registered, albeit obliquely, through the development of popular fantasy which threatened to turn into a parody of itself in the cult of 'sword and sorcery'. My own chapter on *Watership Down* points to a different aspect of this process of political deterioration in the increasing emphasis placed on the traditions of pastoral life. The 'world vision' of the counter-culture had been inspired by 'residual' elements drawn from the past (hence the popularity of Tolkien's writings with their insistence on the need to 'recover' a world which had disappeared with industrialism), but Adams combined these 'archaic' traces with a strong plea for 'traditional' political values and the 'world-vision' at the core of *Watership Down* hinted at something more than a mere revival of pastoralism. In fact, Adams' novel signalled that return to tried and tested conservative values which was to prove such an important component of political rhetoric in the 1970s.

Some Concluding Remarks: A Note on Textual Analysis

This has been a rather lengthy introduction, but it was necessary to examine those key theoretical questions which must inform any cultural reading of popular fiction before embarking on more concrete analysis. The case-studies in this book exist in their own right as self-contained analyses of popular fiction but they are also united by a common interest in the relationship between the internal structures of the text and its wider socio-cultural context. As I noted earlier on, this is not to imply that the authors of the individual chapters all share exactly the same approach or methodology. However, I would argue that one can detect a fair measure of agreement about the kinds of questions which need to be asked and the way we might go about answering them.

Clearly it would be foolish to claim that this book offers a comprehensive introduction to the study of popular fiction. For example, I have chosen studies which concentrate on the meanings which form around the texts, genres or authors, rather than other analyses which might examine the way in which those meanings have been understood by particular groups of readers. In some ways this concentration on the point of production rather than consumption might be seen as the outcome of a certain historical moment in cultural studies, and recent contributions to the field have, understandably, stressed the part played by the process of 'reception' in determining the meaning generated by individual texts. However, whilst accepting the argument that texts can have different meanings for different groups of readers, I am wary of that kind of analysis which, to quote Terry Eagleton, 'merely collapses the work into its various moments of reception'.[25] Instead I would defend the decision to focus on the text as a source of meaning creation. Moreover, I would argue that this concentration on concrete textual analysis allows the student to test his/her own reading of popular fiction against the various approaches on offer here. After all, the function of a book like this should be to encourage others to embark on their own analyses and if it accomplishes this goal, I, for one, shall be well satisfied.

NOTES

1. Quoted in P. Parrinder, *Science Fiction: Its Criticism and Teaching* (London: Methuen, 1980), p. 46.
2. D. Suvin, *Metamorphoses of Science Fiction* (New Haven and London: Yale University Press, 1979), p. 1.
3. See, for example, the recent collection of essays entitled *Popular Television and Film*, edited by T. Bennett *et al.* (London: BFI, 1981).
4. See R. Escarpit, *The Book Revolution* (London: Harrap, 1976).
5. This is a major weakness of Structuralist criticism which tends to confine the notion of 'context' to the literary realm, so that texts are seen as comments on other texts.
6. D. Suvin, 'The Sociology of Science Fiction', *Science Fiction Studies*, 4 (1977), 224. Of course one should not forget that the Leavises did make some attempt to unite literary criticism with a sociological/anthropological approach in the early 1930s. The famous example is Q. D. Leavis' *Fiction and the Reading Public* (1932) which drew on the work of the American cultural anthropologists Robert and Helen Lynd. The latter had examined the fragmentary effects of industrialisation on the cultural life of a small American town (*Middletown: A Study in American Culture*, 1929) and Leavis tried to follow their lead by producing her own 'anthropological' study of the British reading public (see the Introduction to *Fiction and the Reading Public*). Leavis made some interesting comments on the relationship between writers and publishers and authors and readers in a market economy. However, her book was marred by an élitist moral framework which found its expression in unsubstantiated judgements such as the following: 'the training of the reader who spends his leisure in cinemas, looking through magazines and newspapers, listening to jazz music, does not merely fail to help him, it prevents him from normal development' (*Fiction and the Reading Public*, p. 224).
Similarly, Richard Hoggart's reworking of Leavisite criticism in the 1950s (*The Uses of Literacy*, 1957) presented the image of the readers of bestsellers as:

'Souls . . . turned in upon themselves, looking out "with odd dark eyes like windows" upon a world which is largely a phantasmagoria of passing shows and vicarious stimulations' (Penguin edition, p. 246). It was not until the appearance of Raymond Williams' *The Long Revolution* in 1961 that literary criticism was united with social history in a productive manner. Chapter 2 of that book, 'The Analysis of Culture' made a serious attempt to get to grips with the mechanisms that operate in popular narratives and Williams' analysis of the 'magical resolutions' which dominate the fiction of the 1840s is still a good starting point for the cultural reading of popular literature. (Another important text from the same era is *The Popular Arts* by Stuart Hall and Paddy Whannel. Published in 1964 *The Popular Arts* moved away from a wholesale condemnation of 'mass culture' and made an attempt to discriminate *between* popular texts, albeit in a manner which still showed the traces of Leavis' influence.)

7. B. Berelson and P. J. Salter, 'Majority & Minority Americans: An Analysis of Magazine Fiction', *Public Opinion Quarterly*, X (1946), 168–97.

8. F. Jameson, 'Magical Narrative: Romance as Genre', *New Literary History*, No. 7 (1975) 135.

9. V. Propp, *The Morphology of the Folk-Tale* (Bloomington, Indiana: Indiana Research Center in Anthropology, Folklore & Linguistics, 1958); T. Todorov, *Introduction à la Littérature Fantastique* (Paris: Seuil, 1970); U. Eco, *The Role of the Reader: Explorations in the Semiotics of Texts* (Bloomington, Indiana: Indiana University Press, 1979).

10. For a theory which attempts to combine the 'archetypal' and the culturally specific, see J. G. Cawelti, *Adventure, Mystery, and Romance* (Chicago: University of Chicago Press, 1976).

11. C. Lévi-Strauss, *Structural Anthropology*, trans. C. Jacobson and B. G. Schoepf (New York: Basic, 1963), pp. 206–31.

12. F. Jameson, 'Ideology, Narrative Analysis, and Popular Culture', *Theory and Society*, No. 4 (1977), 543.

13. P. Macherey, *A Theory of Literary Production*, trans. G. Wall (London and Boston: Routledge & Kegan Paul, 1978), pp. 159–248.

14. F. Jameson, *The Political Unconscious: Narrative as a Socially Symbolic Act* (London: Methuen, 1981).

15. See for example L. Goldmann, *Towards a Sociology of the Novel*, trans. A. Sheridan (London: Tavistock, 1975).

16. See the interview with Macherey and Etienne Balibar, conducted by James Kavanagh and Thomas Lewis in *Diacritics*, 12 (1982), 50.

17. T. Bennett, 'Marxism and Popular Fiction', *Literature and History*, VII, No. 2 (Autumn, 1981) 151.

18. L. Lowenthal, *Literature, Popular Culture and Society* (Palo Alto, California: Pacific Books, 1961), p. xii.

19. Cawelti, *Adventure, Mystery, and Romance*, p. 1.

20. Parrinder, *Science Fiction*, p. 44–5.

21. T. Adorno, 'Television and the Patterns of Mass Culture' in B. Rosenberg and D. Manning-White (eds), *Mass Culture* (Glencoe, Illinois: Free Press, 1957) pp. 483–4.

22. Cawelti, *Adventure, Mystery, and Romance*, p. 35.

23. See A. Gramsci, *Selections from the Prison Notebooks*, edited by Q. Hoare and G. Nowell-Smith (London: Lawrence & Wishart, 1971), especially pp. 322–4 and 419–25. There is an important discussion of 'common sense' and its application to the analysis of popular fiction in Roger Bromley's article 'Natural Boundaries: the Social Function of Popular Fiction', in *Red Letters*, No. 7, 1978.

24. *Selections from the Prison Notebooks*, p. 324.

25. Quoted in Bennett, 'Marxism and Popular Fiction', p. 156.

1. Science Fiction and the Crisis of the Educated Middle Class

ADRIAN MELLOR

In a pathbreaking review of modern American science fiction, Gérard Klein, the French economist, science fiction writer and critic, has argued that during the 1960s, SF underwent a remarkable transformation. He maintains that a genre which had hitherto been a home for social optimism, coupled with a far-seeing faith in science and technology, became devoted instead to social discontent and cosmic despair. Long-term optimism gave way to short-term pessimism. Faith in the historical role of scientists was overtaken by disillusionment with the scientific outlook and a rejection of the possibility of human historical progress. Klein attributes these changes, not simply to the internal development of an autonomous literary form, nor even to the general external evolution of post-war western societies. Rather, he suggests, science fiction should be seen as the expression of the world vision of one particular social group – that which he characterises as 'the scientifically and technologically oriented middle class' – and the changes in post-war science fiction are to be understood as a reflection of the changing material circumstances of that fraction. The development of SF's increasingly gloomy *weltanschauung* during the 1960s can be explained as the transposition into literary terms of this class's disappointed hopes: its frustrated ambition – promised in the 1930s and 1940s, but never realised – to become the governing class of the western world, and indeed, of the global, human society.[1]

It will be the argument of this chapter that although Klein's approach is substantially correct, his thesis can be revised and extended. In particular, it will be argued that his periodisation of science fiction is over-precise, and that although the transformation which he locates in the 1960s does crystallise at that moment, its roots are much more clearly visible in the previous decade than he allows. Secondly, it will be argued that Klein pays insufficient attention to the fate of his 'scientifically and technologically oriented' class fraction during the period of SF's transformation. Thus what begins in 1950s SF as an index of the crisis of this particular fragment of the middle class, ends a decade later as a literary expression of a much broader crisis permeating a much wider social group. During the 1960s, SF comes to speak for 'the educated middle class' as a whole, and the crisis which is articulated through SF's gloomy prognostications is no longer that of a narrowly defined, scientifically oriented class fraction. Rather, SF becomes one of the vehicles used to express the long-standing pessimism and ambivalence which characterises a much broader section of the educated middle class in capitalist society. This postulated convergence of the material circumstances and social visions of the 'scientific' and 'liberal humanist' fractions of the educated middle class may well provide the framework within which we can begin to understand such well-documented phenomena as, on the one hand, the repeated attempts by some science fiction writers and fans to 'escape from the ghetto' and to 'rejoin the mainstream', while on the other hand, we may better understand the terms upon which some 'respectable' mainstream writers have developed a new interest in science fiction, along with their academic counterparts in western institutions of higher education. Finally, it will be tentatively suggested that developments in post-war science fiction are homologous to those taking place in other contemporary fields of thought: in the social sciences, for example, or in the philosophy of science; and that the understanding of the first process will eventually enable us to understand the second.

This last assertion appears to be curious. Is it not perverse to bracket the vicissitudes of high theory with the mutations of a popular genre? Let us specify more closely what is being suggested. The argument is focused upon the coincident development, both in the social sciences and in science fiction (and in the philosophy of science), of a Highest Common Factor of Embarrassment. During the past twenty years or so, the social sciences (especially sociology) and science fiction have both been transformed; and the pivot of that transformation has been in each instance the development of an ambiguous and embarrassed relationship with the notion of 'science'. Just as sociology has extended its critique of positivism into a suspicion of all claims to scientificity, so science fiction has tried to disencumber itself of any affiliation to science and scientific practice. 'Science fiction', writes Brian Aldiss, chronicler of the genre and a New Wave practitioner, 'is no more written for scientists than ghost stories are written for ghosts.'[2]

One might perhaps attempt to explain each of these developments separately, and internally, in terms either of the logic of the development of the social sciences or of the necessity for popular genres to develop new generic conventions. Alternatively, if one were to seek an external common factor, then changes in the status of science itself might qualify: since Hiroshima 'scientists' are not as popular as they were, nor is 'science' so unambiguously attractive. These things are true. They are real determinants of change, both internal and external; but they are not the only ones. It is also possible to ask whether this changed conception of science is not partially determined by more directly material considerations. Does the flight from science connect with processes that have more to do with power and status than with scholarship? Are the vogues for irrationalism, relativism and pessimism the ideological spasms of a class in crisis? In part, yes. The clearest observation one can make about science fiction and the social sciences is that since the 1960s they have both enjoyed unprecedented growth and each has attempted to abandon 'science'. These phenomena are closely interrelated. The growth both in science fiction and in the social sciences is a direct function of the expansion of higher education, and the growth of 'the educated middle class'. The changes in the content of science fiction and social science are also partially a consequence of that growth. The common flight from science is the expression of the growing pessimism of a class caught in a tragic paradox: its very success in cornering the resources for its own reproduction (the growth of higher education) has led to its own dilution, and a consequent threat to its traditional privileges.

We need to begin by defining more closely the nature of the 'science fiction' with which we are concerned. SF is an unwieldy form and has grown more so in recent years. Amongst historians of the genre we can detect two broad approaches. Firstly, there is what we might call the conventional or 'fannish' account, which treats SF as a distinctively modern and popular genre. It is a chronicle most usually subscribed to by SF writers and active fans – in short, by those who are themselves part of the culture which they are attempting to analyse. With rare exceptions, this approach dominated the secondary literature of science fiction until the late 1960s and 1970s; it is, of course, still represented by much of the critical writing that emerges from within the field. The second account is generally more recent, and derives from the upsurge of academic interest in science fiction which has taken place in the last ten or fifteen years. We could characterise this as the 'scholarly' version, for it owes much to the traditional forms of literary history and, increasingly, to modern frameworks of textual analysis. Both accounts are usually essentialist and prescriptive in their method, each aiming to provide a core definition of science fiction which will admit some texts to the canon and exclude others. Of the two, though, the 'scholarly' definitions provide the broader view of the genre, taking in texts from a greater variety of national literatures and from historical periods other than the most recent. The advantage of the 'fannish' account, on the other hand, is that it allows us to pay some attention to the extra-literary aspect of science fiction. The world of modern SF does not merely comprise a collection of texts, nor is the generic canon established only by licensed critics. Unlike most other literary forms (including the popular genres), the SF canon is authorised as much by lay readers as by professional writers and critics. Elsewhere it is difficult to determine the reactions of a form's readership (beyond the crudely quantitative measures of sales figures and bestseller lists), but this is much less true of science fiction. Modern SF exists not merely as a literary form, but also as an active subculture, comprising both formal and informal regional and national associations, which hold regular Conventions (Cons), and where groups and

individuals issue amateur publications (fanzines). This is an
intensely democratic subculture, where fan critics may gain
intimate access to professional writers, and where the latter
have often risen from the ranks of the former. It is bound
together by its own hallowed traditions and, like many other
subcultures, by a shared argot. Fanzine editors 'pub their ish'
which, as with academic articles, is always 'coming real soon
now'. Fanzines themselves are classified into the 'fannish'
(light and gossipy) and the 'sercon' ('serious and constructive'
– often used pejoratively, or ironically). Overworked fans who
abandon fannish pursuits ('fanac') are said to 'gafiate' (get
away from it all), although those who do so because of outside
pressures rather than indolence are 'forced away from it all'
and therefore 'fafiate'. There is a recognised hierarchy, led by
Trufans and BNFs (Big Name Fans) for whom Fandom Is A
Way Of Life (FIAWOL), although those who prefer to think of
themselves as having a more rounded outlook on life maintain,
to the contrary, that Fandom Is Just A Goddamned Hobby
(FIJAGH). Since 1952, exchange visits for BNFs from both
sides of the Big Pond have been sponsored through the offices of
TAFF, the Transatlantic Fan Fund; and a British BNF with a
long-standing history of service to fandom may well be invited
to join the masonic élite of the Knights of St Fantony.[3] In the
democratic, if incestuous, processes of this subculture, SF
readers are more vocal than those of other popular forms, and
as a consequence, exercise some influence over writers and
publishers. This is not to say that SF fans should necessarily be
regarded as typical of the broader readership of science fiction
(a point which publishers often make very forcibly when
confronted with fannish enthusiasms at Conventions); but the
activity of fans (in their nominations for annual awards, for
example) does have a real effect on both critical discourse and
publishing success. Consequently, any account of science
fiction which emerges from within this subculture must have
more than a passing interest for students of the field.

    Let us attempt to sketch out this conventional history of
science fiction. By the standards of academic literary history it
is, as has been suggested, rather narrow and incomplete. For
our immediate purposes, the subculturally constructed myth is
at least as important as the scholarly substance. We could

choose any of several authorities, but Lester del Rey's recent history presents the argument concisely. One need only refer to his section headings, summarised by his publishers as 'The Five Ages of Science Fiction', which are:

The Age of Wonder	1926–37
The Golden Age	1938–49
The Age of Acceptance	1950–61
The Age of Rebellion	1962–73
The Fifth Age	1974– [4]

Already we can see the limitations of this conventional account. It assumes that the history of science fiction begins with the advent of the American pulp magazines. In this foreshortened perspective, the 'father' of science fiction is Hugo Gernsback (eponymous hero of fandom's annual 'Hugo' awards), and the genre is assumed to have sprung fully-armed from Gernsback's brow when he launched *Amazing Stories* in April 1926.

This is not a view to which del Rey unreservedly subscribes, for he devotes several preliminary chapters to what he sees as the proto-history of the genre, giving credit to all the usually cited precursors, from the Epic of Gilgamesh, through the second-century Greek philosopher, Lucian of Samosata, up to Mary Shelley, Jules Verne and H. G. Wells. However, while recognising that the origins of science fiction are spread over many centuries, and owe much to the incremental efforts of many writers, del Rey still wishes to advance Gernsback's privileged claim to paternity:

> . . . certainly Gernsback was the father of magazine science fiction and was largely responsible for making a viable category of it. He founded the first seven magazines in the United States to use science fiction exclusively. And he spread the faith by contests, slogans, and a readers' league. He began the reader columns that brought readers together. Unquestionably, science fiction as a distinct category of literature begins with Hugo Gernsback.[5]

Unquestionably, of course, it does not. As del Rey has already indicated, and as the researches of I. F. Clarke, Bruce

Franklin and Darko Suvin (amongst many others) have shown,
science fiction ante-dates Gernsback's magazines by a century
or so.[6] What begins with Hugo Gernsback is not a new literary
form, but a subculture. As del Rey himself demonstrates,
Gernsback's importance lay in 'spreading the faith', and in
'bringing readers together'. Only in this limited sense –
irrelevant to the poetics of science fiction, but vital to its
sociology – can Hugo Gernsback be regarded as the genre's
'founding father'.

The remaining elements of del Rey's periodisation enjoy the
same real but limited validity. They assume science fiction to
be almost wholly American, and primarily subcultural. It is the
interwoven stories of pulp-writing and SF fandom, a triumphal
progress of commerce and togetherness: from the ghetto to
respectability; from 2 cents a word to $200,000 for the
paperback rights; from First Fandom letterhacks to an atten-
dance of over 4000 at the Washington 1974 Discon II; Whig
history from the Big Apple.

Thus 'The Golden Age' of the 1940s is defined by the
hegemony of *Astounding Science Fiction* under the editorship of
John W. Campbell, Jr. The post-war 'Age of Acceptance' refers
to the transformation in the status of SF writers from pulp
hobbyists to professional authors between boards: 'Suddenly
writers found they were in the writing *business*!'[7] 'The Age of
Rebellion' does, it is true, have both a literary and a European
referent, for it addresses the rise of a 1960s 'New Wave' of *avant-
garde* writers, largely nurtured by the British magazine *New
Worlds*. In his musings on the late 1970s, however, del Rey
returns to a well-loved topic, for 'The Fifth Age' seems to be
mainly characterised by the fact that publishers were then
prepared to pay more for SF than before – although there were
worrying signs that the bubble might burst.[8]

This disarmingly frank view of the genre is not without
meaning. Even for (some) Europeans, it represents the lived
experience of the subculture. In this century, our experience of
SF has been precisely that of an American, commercial
literature. 'I have been a devotee of science fiction', remarks
Kingsley Amis, 'ever since investigating, at the age of twelve or
so, a bin in the neighbourhood Woolworth's with the label
YANK MAGAZINES: *Interesting Reading.*'[9] It is in these terms

that we can understand why the index to del Rey's history has thirty-six entries for 'Heinlein, Robert A.' (with additional entries for his pseudonyms), but none at all for 'Lem, Stanislaw' or 'Strugatsky, Arkady and Boris Natanovich'. Seen from a commercial and subcultural perspective, science fiction *is* American, and Hugo Gernsback was the 'onlie true begetter'. In this framework, Heinlein is more significant than Lem; the only Europeans who count are the running dogs of a cultural imperialism; and even British SF, for all its local distinction and peculiarities, traces its origin to the American pulps, rather than to a European literary tradition.

We can therefore summarise the argument as one which suggests that modern science fiction is more than just a literary phenomenon: it also comprises a subcultural, social dimension, and our analysis must take this into account. However narrow the view of SF which emerges from within the subculture, we must remember that this is the lived reality for a significant portion of its readership, and that this socially constructed reality has literary consequences. 'Situations defined as real', says W. I. Thomas, 'are real in their consequences.' This is not to deny the possibility of our ever taking a broader view of the genre, or of passing critical judgement on the subculture's own account of itself. That would be to propose an unnecessarily confining cultural relativism. But it is certainly necessary to devote at least a part of the analysis to SF's own lived reality; to accept that for many, if not most of its modern readers, science fiction is a deracinated genre: commercial, popular, American-dominated and contemporary. Given this focus upon the subculturally defined genre, what can we say about its internal, literary development and its contextual, social determinants?

So far as the immanent history of SF is concerned, the most visible change in the modern genre has been the development (culminating in the 1960s, but beginning earlier than that) of a 'soft' or 'New Wave' challenge to the then-existing dominance of 'hardcore' or 'engineers' science fiction. As with the term 'science fiction' itself, neither of these 'hard' or 'soft' variants yields easily to essentialist definition. Generally, 'hard' SF is thought of as being more closely tied to the explicit generic conventions of del Rey's 'Golden Age' writers, and as drawing its science from the 'hard' or 'engineering' sciences. Its exemplars are to be found in the stable of writers through whom John W. Campbell's *Astounding* ruled the field in the 1940s, especially perhaps, with 'the big three': Robert A. Heinlein, Isaac Asimov and A. E. van Vogt.

'New Wave' SF, on the other hand, has generally been thought to show more literary pretension than its stablemate, and to have more frequently dealt in the 'soft' or 'human' sciences, such as sociology and psychology. Between 1964 and 1970, it took institutionalised form in the British magazine *New Worlds*, at that time edited by Michael Moorcock. Accordingly, the New Wave presented a rare example of divergence from the usual absolute US hegemony, and amongst its chief practitioners were the English writers Brian Aldiss, Charles Platt and J. G. Ballard; although several Americans, including John Sladek, Thomas Disch, Samuel Delaney and Harlan Ellison, were also associated with the movement.[10]

The literary ambitions of the New Wave are well displayed by Michael Moorcock's 1969 introduction to *The New SF: An Original Anthology of Modern Speculative Fiction*. The careful recycling of the initials 'SF' was not in itself particularly new, as Robert Heinlein had used the term 'speculative fiction' as early as 1959.[11] A decade later, Moorcock embraces the task of redefinition with the imperialistic fervour of an Alexander. In six pages, he manages to offset the obligatory references to Wells, Gernsback, Asimov and Clarke (amongst other traditionalists), by laying claim to George Macbeth, D. M. Thomas and Christopher Logue (amongst other contemporary poets), to Truffaut, Godard and Fellini (amongst other filmmakers); by inviting comparison between SF's New Wave writers and the works of Samuel Beckett, Ronald Firbank and Thomas Mann; and by extending the term 'SF' to Blaise Cendrars, Bertrand Russell, Angus Wilson, Boris Vian and Jorge Luis Borges (amongst other pillars of 'mainstream' respectability).[12]

It is upon this moment in the history of SF that Gérard Klein focuses his attention. Surprisingly, he makes no explicit reference to the New Wave (perhaps the *nouvelle vague* was less visible from France), and newly developed literary pretensions do not concern him at all. Rather, he seizes upon two other

characteristics of which SF's *avant-garde* writings were em-
blematic, but which extended far beyond the confines of that
youthful coterie, and were as detectable amongst the established generation as amongst the work of the Young Turks.
What agitates Klein about contemporary SF is its deep-rooted
pessimism and its rejection of science. As he himself summarises the argument:

> Around the middle of the 1960's, there was a sudden veering
> in English-language SF: from optimistic, it became as a rule
> quite pessimistic and somber. It used to zoom through vast
> galactic prospects in very far futures, but now increasingly
> dealt with the near – even very near – future, and confined
> itself to the Earth.
>
> . . . The great characteristic of recent SF is a distrust of
> science and technology, and of scientists, especially in the
> exact or 'hard' sciences of physics, chemistry, biology and
> genetics.
>
> . . . in many works of the best authors, the predominant
> feeling is that there is no future – for science, for society, for
> the human race.

In short, argues Klein, we have to ask the question:

> Why is contemporary SF so saturated with rupture, crisis,
> imminent catastrophe, end of the world and humanity,
> rejection of the values of science and even of reason,
> skepticism about social forms and structures? Why does it
> reject historical progress and posit a dissolution of con-
> sciousness and the hostility of nature towards mankind?[13]

Klein attempts to answer this question by locating SF as an
expression of the world vision of a particular social class. In the
humanist Marxist tradition of Georg Lukács and Lucien
Goldmann – and drawing particularly upon the latter – Klein
argues that literary forms have a 'collective subject'; that texts
are not the creation merely of an individual consciousness, but
that literary works have their real origins in (to use Goldmann's
famous phrase) 'a transindividual subject of cultural creation'.

In other words, that they express the consciousness of a social group or class.[14]

In the case of science fiction, Klein maintains that we can deduce the fact of SF's social homogeneity, precisely by virtue of its cultural homogeneity: its internal coherence, its social exclusivity, its rejection by the dominant culture, and the uniformity of its socio-political opinions. Despite some significant (but still nascent) changes in recent years, the world of SF has remained largely white, male and middle-class. During the course of its history, it has been captured for the extremes of neither Right nor Left, but is classically *liberal* in its outlook, evenhandedly opposed to the control of the individual, whether by state or corporation. In this it occupies a median position, being affiliated neither to the ruling nor to the working class. It is part of the 'global middle class', but differentiated from other elements there by an ideological commitment to science and technology. The 'collective subject' of science fiction is, therefore, 'the scientifically and technologically oriented middle class'.

Having thus identified the social group of whose world vision SF is a literary expression, Klein then attempts to show that science fiction itself can be periodised, and that the changes revealed by this literary history reflect similar alterations in the group's outlook and material circumstances. In presenting his analysis he identifies three broad historical periods. Firstly, he suggests, there is that period between the 1930s and the onset of the Cold War when, despite the Depression and the Second World War, the literature of genre SF remains resolutely optimistic. A second period, during the 1950s and early 1960s, he regards as one of transition, in which SF's dominant tone is one of 'confident skepticism'. The third era however, from the mid-1960s onwards, is one in which SF loses all trace of confidence in the future, and succumbs to 'pessimism and imprecation', issuing in a literature dominated by 'the triple malediction: overpopulation, pollution, dehumanization'.

It is worth making the point straight away that Klein's account cannot simply be dismissed as 'economic reductionism'. In both his first and his third periods, SF's world vision runs counter to the prevailing economic climate: optimistic in times of depression; pessimistic in a period of economic buoyancy. Nor is Klein referring to the narrower economic fate of individuals in this process. He fully recognises that, individually, members of 'the scientifically and technologically oriented middle class' were likely to be enjoying a higher standard of living during the 1960s than ever before. What is at stake in this argument is not individual bank balances, but the fate of the collectivity. Klein's argument is that between the 1930s and the 1960s, this fragment of the middle class was confronted by social changes that put absolute limits to its continued increase in power and status. It is the identity of the group that is threatened in these processes, not merely the financial standing of its individual members. Let us therefore consider some elements of Klein's periodisation in more detail, and assess the extent to which it might be justified.

Klein begins by examining the period between the 1930s and the onset of the Cold War. At this time, he argues, the group which provides the social base of science fiction (let us call it 'the SF fraction') lived in the confident expectation of a continual increase in its power and prestige. Despite the Depression and the war (and to some extent, precisely because the prosecution of the war led to an enhancement of the status of technologists), this group anticipated the coming of a rational, technologically oriented 'organisation society', to be built on the ruins of the waning, liberal bourgeois order. The SF fraction could look forward optimistically to this future, serene in its belief that in the imminent era of universal rationalism, when existing social conflicts would finally be resolved by scientific solutions, then scientists and technicians really would inherit the earth. Indeed, their ambitions stretched quite beyond the confines of the West. During this period, American imperialism was seen by middle-class Americans as a progressive, liberating force which was directed primarily against reactionary and militarily aggressive regimes. Just as the SF fraction anticipated that a benevolent US imperialism could, in fact, export a new reign of Reason to those countries as yet denied its benefits, so in science fiction, science and rationality built new empires amongst the stars.

In terms of the internal history of the genre, this period corresponds to science fiction's 'Golden Age'. It is, as Aldiss has observed, a period of synthesis in the magazine fiction. The basic elements had already been provided: on the one hand, Edgar Rice Burroughs' interplanetary fantasies, on the other, Gernsback's didactic ambitions for the form.[15] It is easy today to be blinded to the importance of this latter element. Genre science fiction, of whatever period, is primarily a commercial literature of entertainment and, particularly in its early years, it set out to appeal to adolescent male fantasies of power. But beneath the boy-oh-boy-oh-boy gosh-wowery of space opera's superwars and superweapons, of the mutants with psi-powers, the Bug-Eyed Monsters, the intergalactic cowboys 'n' injuns, there remains none the less a fundamental seriousness. Gernsback's own pious commitment to the educational value of his 'scientification' is well known to students of the genre. His aim was, in his own words, to 'fire young minds with enthusiasm for scientific research and accomplishment'.[16] John W. Campbell, Gernsback's successor as master-editor of the field, was in the 1940s – for all his later quirkiness and misanthropy – no less committed to reason and science. In speaking of the high tide of Campbell's *Astounding*, Aldiss notes the magazine's commitment to scientific and technological optimism. The spaceships which appeared on the journal's covers in those days were symbolic in more than a Freudian sense, he asserts. Primarily, they were symbolic of the mastery of the environment, and Campbell's *Astounding* 'developed into a hymn to this connection'. Equally, Campbell's magazine presented for the first time in science fiction a realistic view of the nature of the scientific pursuit. Where the magazines of Gernsback's era had offered tales of individual inventor-geniuses, *Astounding* revealed instead that science was a collective enterprise: that 'the way to the Moon lay through a door marked R & D'. In short, says Aldiss:

> There were times when *Astounding* smelt so much of the research lab that it should have been printed on filter paper.[17]

This sanguine mood was not to last for ever, although its passing was at first a gradual process rather than a sudden event. The background to 1950s American science fiction is well enough known: Cold War abroad, McCarthy at home. It is the period, argues Klein, in which the SF fraction first begins to glimpse the historical limits to its rise to power, and to sense the resistance to the values which the fraction held as its own. Far from inaugurating a reign of reason, US society in the post-war period spawned new irrationalisms and tensions. Anti-Communist witch hunts at home were accompanied by clear signs of resistance to US imperialism abroad. Most significantly of all, from the viewpoint of the SF fraction, the rise of the American corporation indicated the clear limits which were to be imposed upon the power and prestige of scientists and technicians in the post-war era. Unlike the 'scientifically and technologically oriented middle class', the business corporations were less interested in rationality than in power. In the new scheme of things it was to be the corporations who became the lords of creation, not scientists and technicians. These remained indispensable to the new order, beyond doubt, but from now on they were to be, in Klein's chillingly precise formulation: 'allotted the role of an instrument rather than that of an animator'.[18] The white-coated worker lost precedence to Sloan Wilson's 'man in the grey flannel suit', the rugged individualist colonising the new frontiers of science and technology ceded control to William H. Whyte's 'organisation man'.

If the SF fraction was thus exposed during this period to the limits of its historical development, what of science fiction itself? Here the picture is confused. Klein wishes to argue that the qualitative change in SF's world vision does not really occur until the 1960s. Accordingly, although he readily admits that genuinely pessimistic works of science fiction were published in the 1950s, he maintains that these were relatively isolated in their time. He therefore argues that such novels as Kurt Vonnegut's *Player Piano* (1952), for example, or Pohl and Kornbluth's *The Space Merchants* or Ray Bradbury's *Fahrenheit 451* (both 1953) were untypical of the dominant tone of genre SF, which continued to maintain a qualified optimism. Similarly, he attaches only a limited significance to the prevalence of the 'disaster story' in this era, pointing out that even when biological or nuclear disaster was imagined, this was seen as the cleansing prelude to a rebirth of humanity, rather than its end. From Britain, home of a distinctive variant of the disaster story, we could certainly offer some support for Klein's argument. We need only think of the novels of John Wyndham, for example, whose repeatedly gleeful welcome of the opportunity to start again with a clean slate has been well characterised by Brian Aldiss' designation: 'cosy catastrophes'.[19] In the wake of the disasters caused by comets, triffids and krakens, humanity – at least the fortunate, middle-class few who survive – gets the chance to start all over again, in a world cleansed of strikes, pollution, social conflict, urban blight, industrialism – and other people. Despite the cataclysms on which these tales are predicated, their ultimate message is both tranquil and tranquillising. They are doses of literary Valium for those who feel stranded in the middle of the twentieth century. Unlike J. G. Ballard's later anti-human tales of entropy, there yet remains here some hope, not merely of personal salvation, but of a happier, more ordered future. In the infantile world of the cosy catastrophe, our mothers cuddle us still, and assure us that it will all be all right.

But happy endings notwithstanding, this can hardly be called the literature of 'confident skepticism'. If literary tranquillisers are fashionable, they must be appeasing some powerful anxieties. Indeed, it is difficult, wherever one looks in 1950s science fiction, not to see signs of considerable psychological stress and social anxiety; and these symptoms are precisely expressed in terms of a developing flight from rationality and science. As the motto of the SF film buff of the 1950s had it: 'There Are Some Things Man Is Not Meant To Know'.[20] And although the SF films of the period tend to present the message more crudely and with more paranoia than the magazines, the profound unease about the ultimate ends of science cannot be ignored there either. In a carefully considered review of the magazine fiction of the 1940s and 1950s, drawn largely from the pages of *Astounding*, Tom Shippey takes the view that the SF of the period became a kind of 'thinking machine' 'for the convenience of people largely without academic support or intellectual patronage'.[21] He argues, quite rightly, for the value of a form which, in times of considerable internal and external stress for American society, was enabled to deal frankly with the problems generated by the relationship between science and society. But the very issues for discussion which Shippey identifies from stories of this period should alert us to the extent to which science fiction had departed from its previous sanguine attitude towards both science and society:

> ... the fantastic elements of the stories were a cover, or frame, for discussion of many real issues which were hardly open to serious consideration in any other popular medium: issues such as the nature of science, the conflict of business and government, the limits of loyalty, the power of social norms to affect individual perception.[22]

Shippey's examples tend on the whole to show 1950s SF as being engaged in a rational, albeit profoundly sceptical discussion of both the nature of science and the future of society; but that is not the whole story of the SF subculture at this time, nor even of Campbell's *Astounding*. It is well known to students of SF that during the 1950s the debate on science which ran in the pages and editorials of *Astounding* often assumed bizarre forms. During this period, Campbell was liable to enthusiasms for various forms of pseudo-science or inexplicable gadgetry. L. Ron Hubbard's science of 'Dianetics', forerunner of the later Scientology, was announced in an article in the issue of May 1950; and in the accompanying editorial, Campbell carefully instructed his readers in the logic of the scientific method, before commending dianetics to them as an outcome of that logical process.[23] Hubbard's breathless prose is well displayed in his seminal article, but there seems to be little connection there with either logic or science:

> ... Everybody has a birth. And believe me, birth is quite an experience, very nornic, very aberrative. Causes asthma and eyestrain and somatics galore. Birth is no picnic and the child is sometimes furious, sometimes apathetic but definitely recording, definitely a human being with a good idea of what's happening when he isn't anaten. And when the norn rises he knows analytically all about it. (And he can dramatize it, if he's a doctor or she can dramatize it if she's a mother. Wow, lots of dope here. Hot dope.)[24]

In later years the readers of *Astounding* were treated to Campbell's further fancies for psionics, including his instructions, published in an editorial of June 1956, on how to build a Hieronymous machine, which worked on mental energy alone, along with his later espousal of the Dean Drive: the brainchild of a real estate broker, and a machine which Campbell believed was a potential 'space drive'.[25]

It is easy to mock; and it is only fair to point out that Campbell's enthusiasms always took the form of attempting to defend the openness of the scientific method against what he saw as the closed minds and bureaucratic stuffiness of the scientific, military and governmental establishments. To that extent, one must suppose that some kind of rationality still persists here: that we retain the forms of the scientific pursuit if not its substance; but taken as a whole, the world of 1950s science fiction is less than fully committed to reason and progress. As I. F. Clarke sums up the decade:

> . . . during the 1950's, in keeping with the movement of contemporary literature, the tale of the future finally abandoned the old faith in the power of intellect and in the progressive improvement of civilised life.[26]

Clarke's focus is rather different from that we have adopted here. He is more concerned with English and European science fiction, and with its more 'literary' examples. His implicit assumption appears to be that 'the tale of the future' simply acts as a mirror to its broad historical context, and he has little difficulty in demonstrating that the actual horrors of both world wars were translated by many contemporary writers into an increasingly gloomy and pessimistic view of the future of the human race. Those distinctions in outlook which he notes are based on national, rather than class, differences; and he draws attention to the fact that whereas the British dystopia attempts to confront political oppression, its American counterpart is more concerned with the terrors of a mechanised society.[27] In this connection we should remind ourselves that the mainstream American literary culture has, of course, always borne an ambivalent attitude towards technology. As Leo Marx has argued at length, a recurrent theme in American thought and literature is a yearning towards a precisely defined pastoralism: a longing for 'the middle landscape', that place where the

shepherd dwells which suffers neither from the pressures of
urban life nor from the risks and uncertainties of the wilderness.
From Jefferson, through Thoreau, Melville and Twain we see a
reiterated desire to have the best of both worlds: to enjoy the
material benefits of manufacture without suffering the atten-
dant miseries of industrial life. The impossible aim is to resolve
the contradiction between the threat of the machine and the
dream of the garden.[28]

It is here, perhaps, that we might sharpen Klein's analysis.
In this shared ambivalence towards science and technology we
can see the early beginnings of a convergence between the
outlook of SF and that of the broader 'educated middle class'.
Klein recognises that by the 1960s the SF fraction has lost its
distinctive identity, and that science fiction speaks to a broader
section of the population than hitherto. But he sees the death of
the 'scientifically and technologically oriented middle class' as
a process of proletarianisation: 'It is in a way returned to the
anonymous mass of workers, and can no longer avail itself of
any qualitative privilege, especially intellectual privilege'.[29]
Now this may well turn out to have been true of a later period,
in the 1970s and 1980s, when the developing economic crisis
extended to the middle, as well as the working classes; but in
the 1950s and 1960s it surely seems more plausible to assume
that the SF fraction loses its identity within a wider grouping of
the middle class. What we are seeing at this earlier moment is
the ideological convergence of two fractions within the middle
class itself. In the 1950s and 1960s, SF (and the class which
constitutes its collective subject) both return home.

One might well ask why this should be the case. Why should
SF's desertion of science, technology and social optimism
reconcile it to the mainstream culture of the middle class? One
can perhaps begin to understand this process through Pierre
Bourdieu's distinctions between the 'dominant' and 'dominated' fractions of the dominant class, and between 'material'
and 'symbolic' or 'cultural' capital. Bourdieu denies that,
under capitalism, the ruling class is to be regarded as a
homogeneous entity. There is a distinction to be made between
that dominant fraction which is concerned with the sphere of
production and which reproduces itself through material
capital and, on the other hand, the dominated fraction which

exercises symbolic power, and therefore reproduces itself through the use of cultural capital. It is this second group, 'the dominated fraction of the dominant class', which has been referred to here as 'the educated middle class', with which we are primarily concerned. As Bourdieu shows, the relationship between the two fractions is not harmonious. Although the function of the dominated fraction is ultimately to produce the ideological legitimations of the structure of capitalist social relations, it does so in an ambivalent fashion, for it also has its own sectional interests to defend. Against the power and importance of economic production, the dominated fraction must defend the legitimacy and value of cultural capital. Against the philistine (but materially effective) values of Industry, must be ranged the civilised (but materially problematic) values of Culture. As Bourdieu himself puts it:

> The dominated fraction always tends to place cultural capital, to which it owes its position, at the summit of the hierarchy of the principles of hierarchization.[30]

Accordingly, this group always exists in tension. Its material interests and position in society always depend on its being able to resolve an unresolvable contradiction. Its very existence depends on the continuation of the existing structure of capitalist society, but the basis of that society in material production fundamentally challenges the values upon which the group's claim to social privilege rests. This dominated fraction therefore assumes the form of capitalism's 'loyal opposition': engaged in perpetual struggle with the dominant fraction in which the costs of ultimate victory are likely to be as great as those of ultimate defeat.

One cannot help but be reminded here of Lucien Goldmann's analysis of the *noblesse de robe* in seventeenth-century France. The main thrust of Goldmann's argument suggests that that fraction too was caught in the double-bind of an unresolvable contradiction. It derived its position and prestige in French society directly from the power of the monarchy, for which institution it acted as a kind of civil service; but during the course of the century, royal patronage was transferred elsewhere, to other social groups. Accordingly, argues Goldmann, the *noblesse de robe* found itself in the uncomfortable position of being at the same time both dependent upon and opposed to royal absolutism. It is to this tension in the life situation of the *noblesse de robe* that Goldmann traces the homologous theological and literary tensions exhibited by the Catholic heresy of Jansenism, the *Pensées* of Pascal and the theatre of Racine. The unresolvable contradictions in the fate of the *noblesse de robe* issued, suggests Goldmann, in a distinctive world vision: a 'tragic vision' in which unresolvable contradiction and its consequent stasis were raised to the level of universal principles.[31]

We might therefore borrow more from Goldmann than simply his general method. for it appears that the actual substance of his analysis of seventeenth-century French literature may well have a bearing on our discussion of modern science fiction. Is it not the case that those features of contemporary SF which Klein delineates – its pessimism, loss of social hope, abandonment of science and rationality, its historical passivity – do not these all constitute an index of the rebirth of a 'tragic' world vision? If we accept that this is the case, then it becomes possible to explain the mechanisms by which the SF fraction finally rejoins the fate of the broader 'educated middle class', and by which science fiction finally achieves a wider readership and the kudos of 'mainstream' respectability.

In short, our thesis must be that science fiction remained culturally marginalised for just as long as it continued to embrace science and technology, and to view the future with optimism. To the extent that it abandoned this world view, embracing instead the values of pessimism and tragic despair, so it was in turn embraced by the 'dominated fraction' of the dominant class. For the 'tragic vision' whose origins can clearly be discerned in SF from the 1950s onwards, is itself expressive of core values of the educated middle class. Mainstream culture's new interest in SF, the vast growth of college science fiction courses in the United States, the advance of certain SF texts to the status of cult objects within the (middle-class) hippie counter-culture; all this becomes explicable as a meeting of ideological minds. It is not the educated middle class that has changed, it is science fiction. The retreat into pessimism and cosmic despair is viewed by the dominated fraction of capitalism's dominant class as a maturation, a welcome end to the isolation enforced upon a subculture by virtue of its faith in the future.

In these terms, those SF dystopias of the 1950s which Klein considers to have been atypical take on a new significance as visible indices of the processes at work. For it is precisely these works of science fiction which gained an audience beyond the usual readership of 1950s SF, and which, even up to this day, have been accorded some measure of acceptance by the dominant culture. Amongst the earliest products of the SF ghetto to achieve academic respectability was the work of Ray Bradbury, and it is significant that *Fahrenheit 451* presents a dystopian vision of a future whose chief characteristic is the systematic attempt to extinguish literary culture. Bradbury's novel displays a fear and disdain for modernity, coupled with a romantic nostalgia for the threatened values of a literary culture, whose civilising mission is defended with a passion that might well have issued from F. R. Leavis himself (though in a form of which Leavis could hardly have approved).

We could make similar arguments for such novels as Kurt Vonnegut's *Player Piano* or Pohl and Kornbluth's *The Space Merchants*. Today, these seem uncannily prescient visions of the ultimate alienations to be inflicted upon us by American late capitalism. In the year following publication of his collaborative satire on Madison Avenue, Frederik Pohl published a short story in *Galaxy* in which he summarised the case against 1950s American capitalist society: the vulgarity of its mass culture, its obsessional consumerism, the built-in obsolescence of its consumer goods, and the scapegoating and social intolerance of its ruling ideology – all delineated with a passion that would have done credit to Theodor Adorno, but with a directness that Adorno rarely achieved:

> Have you got a freezer? *It stinks!* If it isn't a Feckle Freezer, *it stinks!* If it's a last year's Feckle Freezer, *it stinks!* Only this year's Feckle Freezer is any good at all! You know who owns an Ajax Freezer? Fairies own Ajax Freezers! You know who owns a Triplecold Freezer? Commies own Triplecold Freezers! Every freezer but a brand-new Feckle Freezer *stinks!*[32]

Similarly, Vonnegut's *Player Piano* (for all the backward glances to Sinclair Lewis's *Babbit*, which have been noted in Peter J. Reed's perceptive 1972 account[33]) none the less appears today, a decade after Reed's analysis, and thirty years after its original publication, as an uncomfortably lucid extrapolation from 1950s American society. In the world of *Player Piano*, goods are designed by computers, built by robots and sold to morons. In an economy in which the rapid spread of new technology has devastated the labour force, a new and rigid meritocracy has developed. Only PhDs can hope for gainful and meaningful employment. The remainder have an ample choice between life in the Army (but no access to real guns, unless on active service abroad), or a boring existence of make-work in the Reconstruction and Reclamation Corps (the Reeks and Wrecks). Our hero, Paul Proteus, belongs to the managerial caste, but joins forces with a motley collection of doomed romantics in order to begin an equally doomed revolution. After an orgy of machine-breaking (including the automated bakery and sewage-disposal plant), the old Adam reasserts itself amongst the revolutionaries, and in a trice, latter-day Luddites are reconverted to gadgeteers and inventors:

'Filled the cup almost to the top that time; and she's nice and cold now, too,' called the man by the machine's spout.
'But the light behind the Orange-O sign didn't light up,' said a woman. 'Supposed to.'
'We'll fix that, won't we, Bud?' said another voice from behind the machine. 'You people get me about three feet of that red wire hanging out of the shoeshine machine, and somebody let me borrow their penknife a second.'[34]

Much of the creative tension in Vonnegut's novel derives from the ambiguity of this ending. It is not so much the strength of corporate capitalism that defeats the revolutionaries, as that of an indomitable (and indomitably perverse) 'human nature'. Vonnegut's ambivalent attitude to this old Adam (half-incredulous and despairing at the persistence of human stupidity, half-admiring at its sheer persistence) reveals in this early work a trace of the whimsicality that mars his later novels.

For all its concern with alienated labour, and the deeper alienation that comes from having no labour at all, Vonnegut's critique of American society is essentially limited. In the last analysis, his is a tale which posits an unchanging human condition. Whatever the disgust aimed at socially created institutions, there is ultimately nothing to be done about the human creature itself. One can rage about this, or celebrate it; but eventually it is all one: eternal and unalterable. In this sense, Vonnegut's novel is a true precursor of those later works of science fiction (similar in tone if less explicit than Ballard's work) in which a genuine pessimism obtains. We are invited finally to step beyond Prometheus: not merely to despair, but to embrace despair, to abandon the struggle.

We therefore might well extend to the educated middle class as a whole, Klein's characterisation of the SF fraction during the 1960s: an era in which the group 'lives endlessly the hour of its death'. At this later moment in his analysis Klein gives passing recognition to the convergence we have identified as occurring in the 1950s; although without attempting to delineate the nature of the mainstream 'tragic vision'.

> Of course, in this process it is not only the social group that is the bearer of SF which finds itself threatened by servitude, but all the social groups pertaining to the American – or even the global – middle class. This explains the convergence of the specific pessimism in recent SF, expressing a localised tragedy, and of the anxieties latent in a vast audience.[35]

If this is the case, however, we should be able to extend our analysis beyond science fiction and its 'localised tragedy', and even beyond the literary culture as a whole, to discover in quite different fields of contemporary thought and culture other expressions of these 'anxieties latent in a vast audience'. One of the fields we might briefly explore is that of the social sciences. The growth of these disciplines over the last twenty years is registered even within the sociology of science fiction fans. In an extremely valuable analysis of the major surveys of SF fans and magazine readers which have been conducted since 1948, Albert Berger draws attention to one of the more significant changes registered in the statistical data:

In 1958, 66.1% of *Astounding* readers had majored in either the physical or biological sciences. By 1973, only 48.6% of the Toronto convention-goers had done so. Between 1958 and 1973, the social sciences, including education, library science and communications, had grown from 19.8% to 30.5%, and in the fifteen years separating the two surveys, studies in the liberal arts, including law and journalism, had grown from 12.8% to 24.5%.[36]

Here is massive evidence of the swing away from the 'hard' sciences within SF's active readership. (Although we must, of course, make the usual reservations about the self-selected nature of these samples; and we cannot offer any causal generalisation about effects on the literature itself. It is impossible to state with certainty that changes in the audience initiate changes in the literature, or vice versa. We can only note the coincident nature of the phenomena.)

A movement away from the 'hard' sciences does not necessarily reflect a rejection of science in its broader aspects, however. Darko Suvin, one of the most perceptive (and scholarly) of SF's 'scholarly' critics, has attempted to define science fiction precisely in terms of this broader conception of science. In Suvin's essentialist terms, science fiction is to be equally distinguished from 'mainstream' realism, myth, fairy story, fantasy, or even Gernsbackian technological didacticism. He characterises the form as being 'the literature of cognitive estrangement'. In so far as SF is an 'estranged' literature (the term is borrowed from Brecht and the Russian Formalists) then it is to that extent differentiated from literary 'realism'. SF presents us with a 'novum', 'an exclusive interest in a strange newness', which acts as an equivalent to the 'alienation-effect' of Brechtian theatre. It is a non-naturalistic device that produces in its audience an 'astonished gaze'. Rather than drawing us into the world of the story through the narrative conventions of realism, an estranged literature makes us aware of the narrative as a constructed artefact. It induces critical evaluation of the ideas it presents, rather than their unconsidered acceptance.

It is, though, the other term of this equation that we are primarily concerned with here: the notion of 'cognition'. If SF's estranged 'novum' is what differentiates the form from mainstream realism, then it is its concern with cognition that distinguishes it from all kinds of fantasy, and even from the popularisation of scientific and technological 'facts'. By invoking the notion of cognition, Suvin wishes to suggest that SF is a literature of 'science' in the broad sense: in the sense of the German *Wissenschaft*, for instance. Here science is released from its Anglo-Saxon ties to the 'hard' sciences, and becomes synonymous instead with a broader notion of 'the scientific method' or even with 'rationality' itself. Suvin argues forcibly that although SF is thereby to be differentiated from myth and fantasy, in which rational explanations are not required, equally the 'science' in science fiction is not to be conceived – contrary to the tradition that runs from Verne to Gernsback – in the narrow sense of merely popularising the content of contemporary bodies of scientific knowledge: 'The novum is postulated on and validated by the post-Cartesian and post-Baconian scientific *method*'.[37]

If these are to be the strict criteria upon which we establish the canon of contemporary science fiction, then it is likely to be a fairly slender body of work; but we could say much the same for other forms of intellectual enterprise which also claim some relation to science. We could point, for instance, to the consequences of that process during the past twenty years, in which the dominant trends in sociological thought have defined themselves as a variety of negations of positivism. Almost without exception, these welcome critiques of crudely atheoretical and empiricist modes have resulted in most unwelcome forms of relativism and conventionalism. From ethnomethodology, through a variety of neo-Marxist perspectives, the grounds upon which any generalised statement may be made about the external social reality have steadily narrowed. Deprived of a positive external focus for its operations, sociology has turned its gaze inwards. The nature of its own existence as an intellectual practice has now become its first, and often its last, concern.

We could offer similar arguments about those developments in the philosophy of science which have most clearly affected the social sciences. Despite its author's own careful qualifications, the publication in 1962 of Thomas Kuhn's *The Structure of*

Scientific Revolutions was widely perceived as legitimating a view of the process of science in which the succeeding 'paradigms' of a discipline were 'incommensurable'. That is, that scientific knowledge was historically-relative, and that comparisons could not usefully be made between differing theoretical perspectives. In these terms, the notion of scientific 'truth' becomes reduced to nothing more than that which a particular community of scientists currently upholds, and developments in science have less to do with the pursuit of objective knowledge than with the social processes of the scientific community. Imre Lakatos may well have been less than fair to Kuhn himself, in describing the latter's view of scientific advance as 'irrational, a matter for mob psychology', but he certainly captured the views of many of Kuhn's most enthusiastic supporters.[38]

More recently, we have seen a similar vogue for the views of Paul Feyerabend, whose declared aim as a philosopher of science is to 'defend society against science' and to dethrone science from its position as the unquestioned *doxa* of contemporary society. In the terms of Feyerabend's 'anarchistic epistemology', science is seen as an ideology, just like any other; no more and no less defensible. And he argues that we should escape from the totalitarian tyranny which science now exercises over us, by teaching in our schools the alternative accounts of myth, magic and religion, alongside the unprivileged assertions of science:

> Of course, scientists will not play any predominant role in the society I envisage. They will be more than balanced by magicians, or priests, or astrologers.[39]

We can observe similar trends at work if we turn our attention to fields of literary and cultural studies, although the process there is more recent, and its irrational termini are only now becoming apparent. In the post-structuralist abandonment of semiology's 'dream of scientificity', we have moved far along the paths of relativism and despair. Again, what began as a welcome sophistication of textual analysis is now increasingly beginning to look like a fashionable obscurantism. As the 'relative autonomy' of the text slides into absolute autonomy, so the text is gently disengaged from its social and historical context, only to disappear into the black hole of language. Language itself has lost its referential function. Reduced to nothing more than a system of arbitrary differences, language no longer permits us access to a shared, external reality. Where only talk is real, and all reality is constructed in discourse, we must turn our heads aside from the sensible world. What offends us is constructed in and through language and must be mended there. At the precise moment when social reality is more offensive than for many decades past, we have lost not only the imperative, but also the means by which we might intervene in it.

This is not to say that no gains have been made at all in this long era of Kuhn, Feyerabend, Althusser, Lacan and Derrida. It is important to know that science has a social dimension, and that scientists can hold their views for irrational reasons; that literary texts and ideologies are not merely reducible to the economic infrastructure; and that in analysing these we must take account of determinants other than those of social class. Nor is it to suggest that social optimism is necessarily progressive, and pessimism reactionary. In science fiction, the optimists of the 1930s and 1940s were generally (but not always) to the right of the 1960s pessimists. On the issue of the Vietnam war, for instance, SF's rising generation of New Wave pessimists was noticeably less hawkish than the stars of the establishment.[40] And in the social and cultural sciences, the new perspectives have generally aligned themselves with left and even far-left positions; whilst the approaches that have been overtaken by these new critiques: functionalism in sociology, Popperian philosophy of science, Leavisite approaches to literary and cultural studies – all these could fairly be characterised as conservative or élitist.

In their collective evolution, however, these new perspectives have issued in ways of seeing the world which, by and large, militate against our acting in it. Despite their self-proclaimed radicalism, they ultimately bear the hallmarks of a middle-class ideology: they have the stamp of a group which, because it is in its life divorced from the sphere of production, is reduced in its thought to appropriating the world in purely passive ways. The characteristic mode of these new perspectives is one of contemplation: in their relativism and in their obsessional epistemological ambivalence, in their rejection of historical modes of analysis, and – at their termini – in their embrace of intellectual nihilism and irrationalism, they opt for non-involvement, for social abstention, for an inner emigration from an unbearable present and a problematic future. In the social and cultural sciences, just as in science fiction, there have developed both pessimism and a rejection of the values of science – both of which we can identify as elements of the world vision of a class caught in historical tensions which it cannot resolve without abandoning its own corporate identity.

But to reveal the class-conditioned nature of these developments is not to assert that they are inevitable. The cultural field is one of ideological struggle. Both in the human sciences and in science fiction it is possible to posit the expression of alternative world views which are equally critical of existing social reality, but which also might enable the active pursuit of social change. In the academic disciplines, irrationalism and passive contemplation may be struggled against; in science fiction, the Sorcery can be put to the Sword.

NOTES

1. G. Klein, 'Discontent in American Science Fiction', *Science Fiction Studies*, IV, No 1, Part 1 (March 1977), 3–13.

2. B. Aldiss, *Billion Year Spree: The History of Science Fiction* (London: Weidenfeld & Nicolson, 1973; Corgi edition, 1975, p. 1).

3. A brief selection of fan cant appears in the glossary to L. del Rey, *The World of Science Fiction, 1926–1976: The History of a Subculture* (New York: Garland Publishing, 1980), Chapter 31. An altogether more massive collection of fannish lore and slang is to be found in an invaluable and much sought-after amateur publication: R. H. Eney (ed.), *Fancyclopedia II* (Virginia, USA, 1959), 205 pp., including 'Additions and Corrections', 1960. There is also a full-length study of these amateur publications themselves: F. Wertham, *The World of Fanzines: A Special Form of Communication* (Southern Illinois University Press, 1973).

4. del Rey, *World of Science Fiction*.

5. Ibid., p. 35.

6. See, for example, I. F. Clarke, *The Pattern of Expectation: 1644–2001* (London: Cape, 1979); H. Bruce Franklin, *Future Perfect: American Science Fiction of the Nineteenth Century* (Oxford University Press, 1966, revised edition,

1978); D. Suvin, *Metamorphoses of Science Fiction: On the Poetics and History of a Literary Genre* (Yale University Press, 1979).

7. del Rey, *World of Science Fiction*, p. 222.

8. Anyone who continues to doubt the argument for the material base of culture need only read a selection from the memoirs of science fiction writers. In his introduction to one such collection, Brian Aldiss makes the point concisely: 'There is a certain emphasis on finance in our memoirs, and with reason; for the smaller the payment, the larger it looms'. B. Aldiss and H. Harrison (eds), *Hell's Cartographer's: Some personal histories of Science Fiction writers* (London: Weidenfeld & Nicolson, 1975), p. 3.

9. Kingsley Amis, *New Maps of Hell* (London: Gollancz, 1961; New English Library, Four Square, 1963, p. 7).

10. See P. Nicholls (ed.), *The Encyclopedia of Science Fiction* (London: Granada, 1981), pp. 46, 273, 425, 556. Nicholls' *Encyclopedia* is now undoubtedly the best English-language, single-volume work of reference on science fiction.

11. R. A. Heinlein, 'Science fiction: its nature, faults and virtues' in B. Davenport (ed.), *The Science Fiction Novel: Imagination and Social Criticism* (Chicago: Advent, 1959; 3rd edition, 1969, p. 15).

12. L. Jones (ed.), *The New SF: An original anthology of modern speculative fiction* (London: Hutchinson, 1969; Arrow, 1970, pp. 7–13).

13. Klein, 'Discontent in American Science Fiction', p. 3.

14. L. Goldmann, *The Hidden God: A Study of Tragic Vision in the Pensées of Pascal and the Tragedies of Racine* (Routledge & Kegan Paul, 1964), especially Chapter V.

15. Aldiss, *Billion Year Spree*, pp. 240–1.

16. H. Gernsback, *Ralph 124C41+: A Romance of the Year 2660* (New York: Frederick Fell), Preface to the 1950 edition, p. 10. Cited in A. Berger, 'The Magic That Works', *Journal of Popular Culture*, V, No 4 (Spring 1972), 874.

17. Aldiss, *Billion Year Spree*, pp. 264–6.

18. Klein, 'Discontent in American Science Fiction', p. 6.

19. Aldiss, *Billion Year Spree*, p. 335.

20. J. Baxter, *Science Fiction in the Cinema: 1895–1970* (London: Tantivy Press, 1970), p. 138.

21. T. A. Shippey, 'The cold war in science fiction, 1940–1960' in P. Parrinder (ed.), *Science Fiction: A Critical Guide* (London: Longman, 1979), p. 108.

22. Ibid., p. 107.

23. J. W. Campbell, Jr, 'Concerning Dianetics', *Astounding Science Fiction*, VII, No 10 (June 1951). (British edition – which appeared later than the American issue – pp. 2–3.)

24. L. Ron Hubbard, 'Dianetics: The Evolution of a Science' in ibid., p. 36.

25. See Berger, 'The Magic That Works', pp. 912–17; Nicholls, *Encyclopedia*, p. 480.

26. Clarke, *Pattern of Expectation*, pp. 278–9.

27. Ibid., p. 275.

28. L. Marx, *The Machine in the Garden: Technology and the Pastoral Ideal in America* (Oxford University Press, 1964).

29. Klein, 'Discontent in American Science Fiction', p. 8.

30. P. Bourdieu, 'Symbolic power' in D. Gleeson (ed.), *Identity and Structure: Issues in the Sociology of Education* (London: Nafferton Books, 1977), p. 115. Useful reviews of Bourdieu's oeuvre are provided by N. Garnham and R. Williams, 'Pierre Bourdieu and the sociology of culture', *Media, Culture and Society*, 2, No 3 (July 1980); and by P. DiMaggio, 'Review Essay: On Pierre Bourdieu', *American Journal of Sociology*, 84, No 6 (1979).

31. Goldmann, *The Hidden God*, especially Part Two.

32. F. Pohl, 'The Tunnel under the World', *Galaxy* (1954), collected in B. Aldiss (ed.), *The Penguin Science Fiction Omnibus* (Harmondsworth: Penguin, 1973), p. 344.

33. P. J. Reed, *Kurt Vonnegut, Jr.* (New York: Warner Paperback Library, 1972), Chapter I.

34. K. Vonnegut, Jr., *Player Piano* (1952) (London: Panther, 1969), p. 283.

35. Klein, 'Discontent in American Science Fiction', p. 8.

36. A. Berger, 'Science Fiction Fans in Socio-Economic Perspective: Factors in the Social Consciousness of a Genre', *Science Fiction Studies*, IV, No 13, Part 3 (November 1977), 237.

37. Suvin, *Metamorphoses*, Chapter 4, p. 65; see also Chapter 1.

38. I. Lakatos and A. Musgrave (eds), *Criticism and The Growth of Knowledge* (Cambridge University Press, 1970), p. 178. See also T. Kuhn, *The Structure of Scientific Revolutions* (University of Chicago Press, 1962).

39. P. Feyerabend, 'How to Defend Society Against Science', *Radical Philosophy*, No 11 (Summer 1975), 8. See also P. Feyerabend, *Against Method* (London: New Left Books, 1975).

40. See R. Lupoff, 'Science Fiction Hawks and Doves', *Ramparts*, X, No 8 (February 1972), 25–30. In commenting upon Lupoff's findings – that the writers of 'hard SF' were both reactionary and socially optimistic, whilst 'New Wave' radicals were anti-utopian pessimists – Parrinder has made the pointed observation that:

... it is a very odd situation in which the tradition of utopian optimism in western thought has come to seem the natural inheritance of right-wing hardware specialists, behaviourists, and futurologists. The utopian impulse, and the awareness of how temporary and man-made conditions frustrate that impulse, are the main links between science fiction and classical left-wing thought.

P. Parrinder, 'The black wave: Science and social consciousness in modern science fiction', *Radical Science Journal*, No 5 (1977), 44.

2. Contemporary Futures: The Analysis of Science Fiction

MARTIN JORDIN

The principal aim of this chapter is to explore some of the mechanics of analysing science fiction novels so as to reveal their social and historical character. I have chosen to discuss Pohl and Kornbluth's *Wolfbane*,[1] but my main concern is less the inherent interest of this novel than illustrating a possible step-by-step procedure for moving from the words on the page to the complexities of their socio-cultural context. Readers approaching the analysis of SF texts for the first time will, I hope, find it useful to reapply such a procedure for themselves until they are confident of adopting a more flexible approach without sacrificing completeness. For this reason I have spelt out some of the more laborious detail which is often only implicit in critical analyses. Moreover, since any critical method is only ever the crystallisation of theory, whether or not conscious and explicit, I have tried throughout to suggest the theoretical rationale behind the procedures and their broader theoretical implications.

As I have implied, the choice of *Wolfbane* is fairly arbitrary. Its main claim on our attention is its very ordinariness as a text most readers would probably accept as unambiguously SF. Outside the genre, however, 'ordinary' might not seem quite the right description. The malnourished remnants of humanity survive precariously on a frozen Earth long since torn from its orbit by a group of alien, semi-robotic Pyramids and which now circles a weak and periodically rekindled artificial sun in the company of the aliens' home planet. Our hero, Glenn Tropile, is outlawed as an individualist 'Wolf' from the ritualised and contemplative society of the Citizens or 'Sheep'. Fleeing execution, he discovers a rival community of Wolves which has retained both a technological culture and the will to resist the aliens. Tropile agrees to join an expedition against the Pyramid on top of Mount Everest. Unfortunately, he inadvertently brings his existence to the notice of the Pyramids by falling into a meditative trance and, like many of the constantly meditating Sheep, is whisked off to the alien planet to become an unconscious component in a giant, organic computer.

Tropile accidentally awakens in a nutrient vat, neurologically linked with seven other humans whom he revives to form a group entity with a collective consciousness and enormously enlarged mental powers. This new being, the Snowflake, proceeds to stage a rebellion, surreptitiously teleporting to the planet fully conscious Wolves and Sheep from Earth. The Snowflake stimulates them to a uniform aggressiveness by manipulating their food supply and drives them forth to do battle with the Pyramids. Using information obtained from the archives of the organic alien species which made and was destroyed by the Pyramids, the rebels are victorious, though the Snowflake is destroyed in the process. Tropile himself survives, however, and retains enough knowledge to enable the humans to return to Earth. The experience of a collective consciousness, superhuman powers and a glimpse of advanced alien civilisations elsewhere in the universe, nonetheless leave him dissatisfied both with his own isolation and with a human society which is rapidly relapsing into the old cultural patterns of Wolves and Sheep. He chooses to return to the alien planet, partly to tend the artificial sun but also in pursuit of his vision of an enlarged potential for the human race. The novel ends with his wife, once a timid and conservative Sheep, deciding to link her fate with her husband's, as a signal that others will follow and his vision be realised.

It hardly needs saying that the social relations of mid-century America are not immediately in evidence here. What SF demonstrates with particular force is a fundamental truth of even the most realist text: that literary works do not offer a simple reflection or picture of the real world but construct a fictional world with its own horizons of possibility and impossibility in which, potentially, anything can happen. But if the logic of this fictional world is not a reproduction of reality's logic, and if we assume it is not wholly arbitrary (in which case it would be meaningless), according to what principles or system is this fictional world defined and its story constructed?

Since anything can be said, everything which *is* said in fiction constitutes a potentially significant choice, a selection of meaning which has potential significance in the context of the real world. But whether an element is in fact significant, and what its meaning actually is, cannot be decided in advance of a textual analysis. The meaning of any element in a fictional work is partly determined by the ideological or semantic content the term brings with it from outside, from its currency in the real world. But meaning is never fixed once and for all; each element is defined and redefined by the systematic relations it is given with the other elements of the fiction. A recognition of this is particularly important in SF where we commonly have to explain elements with no immediate referent in reality, like the organic computers, group minds and aliens of *Wolfbane*. But it is equally important for the more mundane elements. *Wolfbane* defines the opposition of Wolves and Sheep, for instance, as a contrast between a pack and a flock, signifying forms of collective behaviour, but specifically *not* as a relationship of predator to prey.

A useful starting point for criticism is to identify the structural relationships within which elements are simultaneously *opposed*, defining the specific meaning of each term by their difference one from another, and *combined*, in order to generate a new common meaning at a level of generality beyond the concrete and unique particularity of the fictional world. Each element is, of course, defined within a multiplicity of relationships and each generality can itself become one element in higher order relationships which again define it and produce still broader generalities. What is revealed is a loosely converging hierarchy of significances constituting the text's ideological structure and thus having some as yet undefined relation to the historical context in which the text was produced. The hierarchy extends from the variety and detail of the world shown by the text to a limited number of general ideological propositions at the summit which the text 'says' without necessarily ever stating them explicitly. The objective, however, is not to reduce the text to these general propositions, nor to seize subjectively on one or other of them as *the* theme which, like the Hegelian Idea, can then be revealed in every corner of the text, magically generating the complexity of its fictional world. We need instead to understand the text as the process of actively constructing and accumulating meanings, as the total, complex structure extending from the fictional base to the ideological peaks, as not a pre-given, organic unity of meaning but a web of contradictions between meanings.

Wolfbane offers two major structural relationships – between the Sheep and the Wolves, and between the definition of humanity thus produced and the non-human existence of the Pyramids. The society of the Citizens with which the novel opens, however, defines the basic ground-rules for the *whole* of this new fictional world (only later are the Citizens contextualised within it as Sheep by contrast with the Wolves). The significant differences between the norms of the novel's and the reader's worlds are foregrounded by the mild incredulity of the hero, who is fairly normal in our terms but an outsider in his own society. The differences are, firstly, that this is a subsistence economy dominated by the shortage of food; and secondly that its culture is meditative, passive, conformist. The novel makes it clear that the two are more than accidentally connected, though it defines their connection less as an economic-cultural one than as the biological determination of the social:

Engineering is possible under one condition of the equation:

$$\frac{\text{Total Available Calories}}{\text{Population}} = \text{Artistic-Technological Style.}$$

When the ratio Calories to-Population is large . . . then the Artistic-Technological Style is *big*. People carve Mount Rushmore; they build great foundries . . . At the other extreme where C:P is too small, life does not exist at all. (p. 23)

Tropile's discovery of the Wolves' society and its contrast with that of the Sheep allows the terms of the novel to be further defined. Apart from the universal principle that the biological determines the social, the two societies are virtual polar opposites. The limited food surplus of the Wolves results in an aggressive society of competitive individualists with a rationalist and technological ethos that serves to redefine the meditative culture of the Sheep as irrationalist, mystical, anti-scientific. Moreover, their relative freedom from food shortages allows the Wolves to concern themselves with the longer range question of survival: regaining control of the world from the Pyramids. 'And then we go back to our own solar system, and an end to the five-year cycle of frost and hunger. And then the Wolves can rule a world worth ruling' (pp. 50–1). If both societies are dominated by more or less pressing material necessities, the Wolves' society introduces the new questions of power and control in relation both to the Pyramids and to the Sheep, the latter being secretly though paternalistically manipulated by the Wolfish 10 per cent of the human race.

Almost all the ideological themes of the book are already present in this contrast of the two societies: the biological, the social, rationality, power. If we now move on to the second major structural relation, between the human world and the Pyramids, we can see how these provide the terms of reference which allow the meaning of this non-existent reality to be defined, while the terms themselves are further specified in the process.

The existence of an alien in an SF novel necessarily introduces an anthropological dimension, an implied or explicit contrast of the non-human with the human. As alien invaders, the Pyramids are opposed to the humans in terms of power, oppressing and exploiting them with a vast, impersonal indifference to anything but 'a need for certain complex mechanisms which grew on this planet' (p. 40). Yet as the embodiment of Power, the aliens reproduce at a higher level the Wolf–Sheep relation which characterises humanity, albeit more benignly. Moreover, the invaders are not simply aliens, they are Pyramids, *things*. They stand in opposition to the humans as machines to organic beings, as artificial intelligences, mechanical in both structure and thought: 'The Pyramids . . . . were not engineers. They employed a crude metaphysic based on dissection and shoving. They had no elegant field theories. All they knew was that everything came apart and that if you pushed a thing it would move. If your biggest push would not move a thing, you took it apart and pushed the parts, and then it would move' (p. 24). But again, as the epitome of mechanical rationalism the Pyramids are also equated with the humans. Like their power, their technical knowledge is immeasurably superior to Man's, but qualitatively just as crude and utilitarian and in this respect, too, they stand towards the humans as the Wolves stand to the Sheep.

This double relationship in which the Pyramids are materially opposed to the humans while in broader ideological terms they represent humanity writ large is also expressed by a constant and deliberate confusion of the biological and the mechanical. Humans are 'intricate mechanisms [which] grew, ripened and were dug up at the moment of usefulness, whereupon they were quick-frozen and wired into circuits' (p. 39). Conversely, what finally defeats the Pyramids is the destruction of their metabolic complex, leaving them vainly waiting until the end of time 'for food to adsorb so they could go about their business of making more food to adsorb, so they could . . .' (p. 152). If the Pyramids are quasi-biological computers, humans have been reduced to little more than pre-programmed organisms, to animals like wolves and sheep. The existence of both is ultimately trapped within the same stimulus-response mechanisms of biological survival so that the description of a Pyramid comes to apply equally well to the best of *Wolfbane*'s materially and culturally impoverished humanity: 'Its philosophy was, Unscrew it and push. Its motive was survival' (p. 39).

Such a representation of human nature is only provisional, however. Developed in the first part of the novel dealing with the Pyramid's conquest of the Earth, it is qualified in the second half which depicts the human conquest of the alien's planet. It is worth reminding ourselves here that the novel is not just this 'vertical' hierarchy of meanings we are attempting to reconstruct. The relationships which produce and define these meanings are those of the 'horizontal' development of a narrative plot, the story of a world. And the text emerges from the interplay involved in the posing and gradual resolution of a specific, fictional problem which is progressively interpreted

and generalised by the broader ideological meanings it gener-
ates.

The problem in this instance is how Tropile can escape the
horrific domination of Man by the Pyramids; generalised as the
search for a human existence liberated from mechanical
servitude, for a genuine community where men are relatively
free from permanent subordination both to the natural constraints of mere physical subsistence and the social constraints
of power. Hence the societies of the Sheep and Wolves are not
just an ideological contrast. Tropile's movement from one to
the other marks the first step towards a solution of his problem
and the broader problem of the novel as a whole. Not only are
the Wolves trying to fight the Pyramids, they offer a less
repressive, more egalitarian and more rational society than the
Sheep, further removed from the immediate problems of sheer
survival. A competitive individualist himself, Tropile is considerably more at home in the Wolves' society but he still
remains something of an outsider. What now sets him apart is
his reluctance to concur in the general condemnation of the
Sheep's meditation as a mere religious narcotic: 'How could
anything that felt as good as Oneness be bad?' (p. 54). This
desire for Oneness and Community which the Wolves' society
still does not satisfy leads to his involuntarily taking the
second step towards a solution. Surreptitiously meditating on
'connectivity', he is 'harvested' by the Pyramids eventually to
become part of the group mind he calls the Snowflake.

Like the Pyramids, the Snowflake is a sign without a referent
whose meaning is defined within the terms of reference already
established, redefining those terms in the process. It represents
a definite advance over the Wolves as the model of a new kind of
social organisation apparently escaping the laws of human
nature as it has so far been characterised. Biologically, the
relative food surplus of the Wolves has become the absolute
sufficiency of the nutrient vat in which the eight, surgically-
linked humans float, freed from bodily necessities to the extent
that even breathing is redundant. Socially, the humans are a
genuine collective, transcending all divisions of age, sex or
nationality in a shared unity of memory and thought that is
necessarily also mutual acceptance of the good and bad in each
individual. The Sheep/Wolf distinction likewise becomes

redundant. The members of the Snowflake were originally either, like Tropile, Wolves in Sheep's clothing; or cynics who saw no significant difference between the two; or mentally retarded and unable to perceive the distinction.

However, if the Snowflake is also a considerably more effective opponent for the Pyramids than the Wolves, it remains physically confined to its vat and has to recruit several hundred humans from Earth to mount the rebellion. The abundance of food with which the Snowflake supplies the humans soon makes Sheep and Wolf physically and culturally indistinguishable, uniting them in a common aggressiveness. But the stimulus-response relationship of the biological and the social is still clearly at work. The humans are united, but only as a pack of wolves, still animals in their mindless, glandular aggression. As their leader reflects, 'Cul-chah and aesthetics petered out the first week on unlimited calories, and then went manners . . . Yes, we've got to give them something to do before they get *fat* and begin killing one another' (p. 102). Mutual dependence for survival is all that holds the social pack together; and on its own, material abundance produces not social harmony but its opposite. The missing factor, a rational purpose to bind the humans together, is possessed only by the Snowflake which, by suddenly cutting off the supplies, aims at using the humans as 'mice' to wreck the Pyramids' environment in their migratory search for food.

The Snowflake and the humans thus become opposed in terms of reason and power: as a community of minds dominating and manipulating a mindless community of bodies. For the first time in the novel, rational purpose, Mind, takes over and directs the physical body instead of representing merely a mechanical response to biological necessity. But this relationship and the community of the Snowflake are only a further step towards the solution sought by the novel and its hero, not the solution itself. For just as the Sheep are transformed into Wolves, so the Snowflake gradually becomes indistinguishable from the Pyramids. Its exponentially expanded mental powers serve only to make mechanical calculations, its need for information leads it to accumulate massive technological extensions, it loses the ability to make a significant differentiation between complex machines and living organisms and

coldly manipulates and oppresses the humans. All of which
Tropile finally recognises. ' "What are we doing? . . . We've
ripped our friends out of the Earth and turned them loose to be
vermin for our convenience . . . We were a machine!" he cried.
"We were as much a machine as the Pyramids. There was no
soul in us, no pity" ' (p. 129). And ultimately, it is the same
principle of mere survival that is shown to motivate the
Snowflake's existence. Having dissolved back into its component personalities, the Snowflake reforms itself only to resist
the attack mounted on it by the Pyramids.

The group mind is not the final solution sought by the novel,
but it is enough (with its human allies) to settle the problem of
the Pyramids. At this point, the fictional problem and the
ideological problem of the novel (destroying the invaders;
discovering a new basis for human social organisation), which
previously had paralleled and informed one another, part
company. Or rather the latter, which had hitherto existed in
the text only as generalisation or metaphor, now becomes
(somewhat surprisingly) the 'real' problem which the fictional
hero directly confronts. Tropile is again an outsider: the group
mind has gone, humanity has redivided into Sheep and
Wolves, where is Oneness to be found?

The novel's progressive definition of the problem as a
relation of Power, Reason, the Biological and the Social now
provides the terms of the solution. In the first place, this will be
a community of minds. A genuine social *community*, that is, not
the quasi-social pack divided by a competitive drive for power
and advantage which is the best that existing human nature
can offer. And in order to transcend the limitations of this
human nature, the principle of the new social unity must be
Reason. Not the abnegation of consciousness in meditation, nor
a cold, mechanical logic that is the mere reflex of bodily
survival – both of which reduce humanity to the 'Tropological',
stimulus-response existence of animals or machines. But a
Reason that transcends biological existence in giving it a
meaning and a purpose – the quest for Oneness with the
universe through rational knowledge of it, the disinterested
drive for pure knowledge, for the 'elegant field theories' (p. 24)
which, having no immediate survival value, have been forgotten by the humans and were always beyond the grasp of the

Pyramids. This solution is represented in the novel by the universal community of alien species, the harmonious, symbiotic partnership of intelligent beings everywhere in their search for pure knowledge transcending the immediate material world:

> there's a tri-symbiotic race in the Magellanic Cloud beloved by all that part of the Galaxy. You see, they have learned a fact about – call it God. We wanted to visit them. And the Coalsack Nebula isn't a dust cloud at all; it's a hole in space. There are races in the Universe whose entire cultural history is the building of a slow understanding of the nature of that hole. (pp. 158–9)

But as it stands, this is yet another partial solution which, like the Snowflake, turns its back on most of the human race:

> How could anyone ask him to stay in the mire when the stars challenged overhead? He walked slowly down the street, alone in the night, an apprentice godling renouncing mortality. There was nothing here for him, and therefore why this sense of loss? . . . Flesh said (or was it his soul – whatever that was?): 'But you will be *alone*.' (pp. 159–60)

For the solution must also be a fully *human* community even while transcending existing human nature, a social union of both Mind *and* Body. The missing part of the solution is the family, as the harmonious unity of biological and social union. Having followed Tropile's path from Sheep to Wolf, his wife Gala finally decides also to accompany him back to the alien planet. The full solution has three elements: the Community of Minds and the Family of Man linked (as the above quotations indicate) in a broadly Christian humanism where the rational soul of Man transcends the Body/Mind dualism of human nature.

We began by asking according to what logic the fictional narrative was organised. We must now answer that it is determined by not one but *two* relatively independent logics. As we have seen, the world of *Wolfbane* constructs or obeys the *ideal* logic of a generalised ideological argument about human nature and society. But it is also a relatively coherent world of *quasi-real* relationships constructed by analogy with the real world. It is a world which is *like* (in ways we have yet to determine) the real world.

Novels are made out of language, a language whose signs already possess an ideological content. While, as we've seen, these meanings are redefined, 'over-determined', by the second-order ideological structure unique to a given text, they are not thereby abolished but on the contrary remain the precondition of its existence and intelligibility. Every text is thus a series of constant allusions to conventional understandings of the real world. How far this necessary allusion constrains the fiction depends both on the degree of internal coherence or systematicity the fictional world offers by analogy with the real and on the precise nature or terms of the analogy. While fantasy texts, for example, can never wholly escape the analogical *connection* between the fictional and the real, they are relatively less constrained by the relationship than realist texts. The latter, without ever wholly effacing the analogical *difference* between the two realms, seek to structure the fictional world as an extension of both the empirical contents and the relations of the existing world as conventionally understood. SF, for its part, typically abstracts from this empirical content of the existing reality to create radically new worlds, while aiming to systematise the latter in accordance with the laws conventionally understood to govern the existence of the real. Borrowing a term from the Russian Formalists, one can say that SF has traditionally been regarded as a genre which 'motivates' the fantastic in terms of a current rationalist or scientific world-view.

In both the style and content of its opening chapters, *Wolfbane* presents itself as a dystopian satire on mid-century America. But it is a specifically SF satire. The satiric fictional world is not merely a metaphorical equivalent for the contemporary world, it is also a metonymic extension of it, the product of historical extrapolation into the future. (The 'survival' of identity bracelets and parkas from the Korean War establishes this relation from the very first.) And this extrapolation is *motivated* in terms of a current scientific framework of explanation. The future world is the product of an historical process obeying universal material laws; namely, that social and cultural developments are, in the last analysis, determined by the struggle for the material necessities of life. That this struggle is not itself conceived of as socio-economic in character but rather as a biological relation of the organism to its physical environment, may not appear very scientific to everyone. Nonetheless, this biologism does represent an attempt to explain sociological phenomena on the basis of known scientific principles, an attempt which has been and still is widely adhered to and which 'explains' not only the fictional world of *Wolfbane* but the contemporary real world as well:

> When the ratio Calories-to-Population is large – say five thousand or more . . . people carve Mount Rushmore . . . Japan, locked in its Shogunate prison, picked scanty food from mountainsides and beauty out of arrangements of lichen and paper. The small, inexpensive sub-sub-arts are characteristic of the 1,000–1,500 calorie range. (p. 23)

The relationships between the societies of the Sheep and Wolves are not designed merely to support general arguments about social division, rationality, human nature, etc., but simultaneously to dramatise what are felt to be the decisive historical characteristics of society in the mid-twentieth century. The world of *Wolfbane*/America is described as a modern 'Mass Society'. At its base is a relatively pauperised mass of unthinking individuals, rigidly conformist and anti-individualist, and obsessed by problems of consumption from which they are distracted only by mindless escapist rituals. Above this mass, and benevolently supervising and protecting it, there exists a competitive technocratic élite with a marginally better standard of life, intent on regaining its legitimate position as the more rational and far-sighted director of human destiny. Dominating both, is the massive, impersonal weight of a sort of totalitarian corporatism – inhuman, mechanical and lacking any purpose beyond ensuring its continued existence and growth; but also intelligent, active, possessed of the ultimate in technology and capable of intervening in human affairs with apparent omniscience and omnipotence.

Moreover, the extrapolative relation between the fictional

world and its twentieth-century 'past' dramatises a real historical connection perceived to exist between the America of the 1950s and its own earlier history. The world of *Wolfbane*/ contemporary America is the product of a *decline*, consisting of a relative impoverishment, the disappearance of human purpose and vision, the loss of the independent and leading role of the technological Wolves and intensified social division and conflict. The root cause of this decline has been the emergence of the monstrous corporatism represented by the Pyramids.

We now have an initial clarification of the relation between the text of *Wolfbane* and the real historical context out of which it emerges. This relationship, however, does not consist of a simple fictional reflection of reality, the dramatising of some objective historical analysis. What *Wolfbane* involves is at best a partial and approximate knowledge of the social and historical realities, for that knowledge is not only a *reflection* but also a materially determined *part* of those realities. It is therefore in its historically determined limitations, in the very 'partiality' of its reflection of reality that *Wolfbane* reveals its actual, historical conditions of existence. One internal indication of this 'standpoint' which determines the novel's experience and understanding of reality is provided by the Wolfish character of its hero. The narrative viewpoint of the novel is closest to that of its technological middle-class élite, even if the two do not coincide precisely.

To take our understanding of this relation between text and history further, it is useful here to draw on the arguments of a justly praised article by Klein, 'Discontent in American Science Fiction'.[2] Klein applies to the analysis of SF since the 1930s a critical method derived from the work of Lucien Goldmann, the first of its two main theses being that 'the real subject of a literary work (or group of works) is the situation of the social group which the author belongs to' (p. 4). The article argues that the social base of SF has been the scientifically and technologically oriented stratum of the petty bourgeoisie; a group including not only a core of professionals occupationally concerned with the production, application and dissemination of formalised knowledge, but also those having a general cultural involvement with questions of science. Although Klein's delimitation of this social base is thus rather vague and to some extent almost tautological, it is nonetheless at least descriptively adequate for our present purpose.[3]

The first thirty years of American SF since the late 1930s corresponded to the emergence, consolidation and expansion of American 'Mass Society'. The fortunes of SF's social base were intimately entangled with the consequent radical reorganisations of production and their effects: constantly accelerating technological revolution; the systematic intensification of a 'rational' division of labour in every sphere; and the increased 'rational' co-ordination of social life in general, as a limited number of immense monopoly corporations progressively brought ever larger sectors of production, distribution and consumption under their direct control and established ever more intimate connections both between themselves and with the institutions of the American socio-political apparatus. In the first phase of this development, which Klein dates as ending with the start of the Cold War, the scientists and technologists saw their numbers and their importance enormously increased. The penetration of the forms of capitalist rationality into every corner of social life (to say nothing of the apparently benevolent exporting of its values and methods abroad) enabled this group to perceive American society as the apotheosis of Reason in human history and development – an almost Saint-Simonist vision of the ultimately rational society in which all social problems were questions of Technique and Reason and in which the scientists and engineers would therefore play the decisive social role.

In the Cold War period, however (the period of *Wolfbane*) such confidence was severely challenged. The rationality introduced by the monopolies now appeared in its true light as a by-product of their drive for power and profit rather than their dynamic and goal. The independence of science as the embodiment of a Reason standing above society, and consequently the relative independence of scientists and technologists as a cohesive social group, were seriously reduced. For this social group faced not only the witch-hunts of McCarthyism but also its own increasing integration into the designs of the monopoly corporations and the growing extension to scientific and intellectual work itself of the same, externally imposed and mechanical division of labour which dominated the other spheres of social labour. The scientifically and technologically oriented middle class was thus forced to recognise that it was not, in fact, the animating or leading force of social development, but rather an instrument manipulated from elsewhere; that far from being a caste of social engineers, it was joining the ranks of the engineered and controlled. Nonetheless, in so far as it still survived as a coherent social group, the belief in an independent social role for itself remained. The corporate society now appeared as a perversion of Reason by crude materialism. And this social group viewed itself as the repository and guardian of its values, attributing to itself a key ideological role as a kind of humanist conscience or ethical arbiter on the social uses and abuses of knowledge. In the third phase, however, beginning with the expansion of the 1960s, the continued existence of this stratum as a distinct social group was virtually dissolved, leaving few vestiges of its faith in the possibility of detaching any humanitarian values or power of resistance from a science so wholly subservient to the interests of monopoly capital.

Being principally concerned with SF since the 1960s, Klein's article only relates developments in the 1940s and 1950s to a general shift in SF from 'optimism and faith in scientific progress' to 'confident scepticism'. But we can see that even this very general account provides an historical underpinning to the quite specific features of *Wolfbane*'s analogical dramatisation of reality as well as to the general 'scientism' of its basic motivational principle. It is this historical experience of the scientific and technical petty bourgeoisie which accounts for the coupling of a hostility to corporatism with a rather contemptuous attitude to the routinised world of the Sheep; for the identification of the Wolfish technological élite, in its decline, with both the mechanical, self-serving nature of the Pyramids and the blinkered and powerless existence of the Sheep, and so on. But this historical experience not only defines what aspects of reality are selected as constituting a problem, but also the terms of the novel's solution to it. The key values which distinguish a liberated human nature from mechanical servitude to material interests are those of a disinterested, pure science; it is the power of a liberated Reason which enables the Snowflake to destroy the Pyramids and which is the principle on which its ideal community rests; and it is the vision of a fresh start, that is also a return to the ideals of the independent and universal community of science, which is upheld in the novel's closing section.

However, if *Wolfbane*'s relation to history is not a question of simple, objective reflection, neither is it a simple dramatising of a particular, unified and internally consistent class perception of that history. This history, and the ideological experience of it, is in fact profoundly contradictory, and it is above all the effects of these real *contradictions* which are systematically manifested by *Wolfbane* in its own, specifically literary contradictions.

We have said that the fictional world of *Wolfbane*, its organisation and development, is doubly-determined. Since it is organised to generate a series of ideological propositions and arguments, the fictional world necessarily receives a relatively adequate explanation or interpretation from them. And organised as a fictional analogue to dramatise a number of observed phenomena and relations from the real world of mid-century America, the world of *Wolfbane* is similarly unimpeachable. But the fictional world of this, as of every novel, immediately appears as at least potentially contradictory in so far as it is obliged to support both orders simultaneously. In so far, that is, as the ideological interpretations attempt, through the mediation of a fictional analogue, to give a structure, meaning and interpretation to these partial and contingent perceptions of mid-century American realities; and, conversely, in so far as these perceived realities are offered, through the same mediating fiction, as adequate demonstrations, tests or proofs of the validity and accuracy of the ideological explanations.

What a reading of *Wolfbane* confronts us with is the story of a unique and apparently independent fantasy world, self-contained in its *de facto* unity as a discourse where nothing can be added or subtracted, with its beginning, middle and end, its specific fictional problems and their solutions. But the formal unity and independence are more apparent than real. This apparently unitary fictional narrative is in reality only the resultant of two conflicting forces; both site and product of an ideological struggle to give coherent formulation to ideological experience, and to evaluate and redefine pre-formulated ideological positions against that experience. As a literary text, *Wolfbane* represents an active process of ideological construction and reconstruction, the contradictory dynamic of which critical analysis must reveal. So far, its narrative has certainly appeared to support both a dramatisation of real problems, and an ideological argument supplying humanist solutions, with reasonable harmony and coherence. But between problem and solution there lies the major structural contradiction of the novel.

In saying that *Wolfbane* dramatises the problems of contemporary American society by extrapolative analogy, we have ignored one discrepancy. While the Pyramids are metaphors for the corporate state or the monopolies, they are *not* extrapolations in the sense that the Wolves and Sheep are. (An equivalent extrapolation of contemporary corporatism, for example, would be something like a supertechnological, totalitarian world-state or national government by a single corporation.) We noted earlier that the book falls into two halves, corresponding to the alien conquest of the Earth (the problem) and the human conquest of the alien world (the solution). The whole of this second world, in fact – the world of group minds, Pyramids and the green and tentacled aliens who created them – is of a quite different order of motivation from the extrapolated human society. Disguised by the uniformly fantastic character of the novel's world, there are in fact *two* significantly different forms of SF at work, bearing quite different analogical connections to reality. On the one hand, SF as dystopian social satire; on the other, SF as the heroic fantasy of Space Opera, in which our hero rescues the human race from an alien menace and which is closer to the Gothic in its confrontation of the supernormal forces of Darkness and Light.

Despite the different forms in which it is manifested, the logic of the dystopia is roughly the *real* logic of our own world transposed to a new context – both are in accord with the presumed scientific law that social phenomena are determined by Man's struggle to wrest a living from Nature. The logic of the struggle between the Pyramids and the Snowflake, however, is essentially an *Ideal* logic, the conventional logic of Good versus Evil, human versus alien. It is true that the *forms* in which these archetypes are embodied are scientifically motivated and thus constrain the development of the heroic fantasy – little or nothing in the existence of alien beings, artificial intelligences, neurosurgical linking of brains or any of the superscience hardware contradicts in principle the framework of contemporary science. But the essential logic and dynamic of the heroic fantasy itself is derived from elsewhere.

What are we to make of this generic discontinuity?[4] The crucial point is that problem and solution are of different orders. The real problem (the nature and effects of corporatism) is defined by the relation of the dystopia to the contemporary real world. The Ideal solution (the destruction of the Pyramids/corporatism by a Snowflake/?) is defined by the relation of the space opera to the abstract logic of the text's ideological argument. There is no common logic whereby the terms of the real problem lead necessarily to the concrete nature of the solution. The space opera is, in fact, doubly displaced from the real world, revealing the same analogical dislocation from the norms of the dystopia as the latter reveals between itself and the norms of twentieth-century reality. Between fictional dystopia and reality there is both a metonymic connection and the distance of metaphor. Earlier, we noted that the world of the Pyramids is similarly both part of the *dystopian world*, a 'real' extension of it, while also standing above or outside *it* as a metaphor for the mechanically-determined existence of the Sheep and Wolves. The dystopia defines a problem that is real for us; the space opera defines a solution that is real for the inhabitants of the dystopia; but the space opera does not provide a solution that is real for us, only metaphorical, symbolic.

Although this contradiction is literary or generic in form it is fundamentally ideological in nature. We can refer here to the second thesis of Klein's article: 'literary works . . , are attempts to resolve through the use of the imagination and in the aesthetic mode, a problem which is not soluble in reality' (p. 9). In realist texts, these imaginary or 'magical' resolutions are relatively easily identified as infringements of verisimilitude – improbable coincidences, convenient legacies out of the blue to rescue the hero from difficulties, etc. In a fantastic literature like SF, however, they are less evident (and can thus be more sustained) since the whole text is 'magical' to begin with.

Nonetheless, the infringement of verisimilitude by fantastic elements in realism is no more than the breaching of its particular norms of motivation by the need to sustain the Ideal logic of the text's ideological argument. The mechanism at work in *Wolfbane* is not qualitatively different. The norms of extrapolative motivation, resulting in a fantastic, dystopian equivalent of the real world, are interrupted by the need to sustain an optimistic, humanist interpretation of that world, and are consequently overlaid by the 'meta-fantasy' of space opera.[5]

What is the real contradiction to which this magical resolution is the response? On the one hand, the problem to be solved is the historical existence and effects of corporatism. That a solution must exist, is not only an ideological imperative for the survival of SF's social base, it is also implied by the latter's perception of its history. The society of Reason without corporatism can exist in the future since it apparently has already existed in the past (specifically, in the 1940s). Consequently, *Wolfbane* harks back to the lost glories of science and the human race before the Pyramids; while the Pyramids themselves, as non-extrapolated metaphors for corporatism, are not an integral part of the human societies of the Sheep and Wolves but a mysterious, alien, external interruption to their normal development, removable by equally external and mysterious means.

On the other hand, however, this social group perceives no force in the real world capable of destroying corporatism. In this period of McCarthyism and Cold War, where resistance to corporatism is branded Communism, all solutions seem merely to reproduce the problem; while totalitarianism and corporatism themselves appear to be the norm of historical development in industrial societies everywhere. In this light, the problem seems to be universal and inescapable, a problem of human nature which corporatism merely epitomises and accentuates. It is precisely as such a problem of human nature, the entrapment of humanity in the necessities of material survival, that *Wolfbane* defines its dystopian world. While abstractly the alternative to corporatism can be envisaged and must be possible, the actual process of changing an unchangeable human nature to get to that alternative can only be a magical one.

What is rather surprising, is that this is what *Wolfbane* itself admits in rejecting the ideal community of the Snowflake as an unreal solution and by returning, in the final section, to the original dystopia and its problems of human nature. One might have expected the novel to end with the destruction of the apparently omnipotent Pyramids, with the newly acquired social unity of the Wolves and Sheep and with the Snowflake as the perfect community of Reason, since it is in this magical overcoming of impossible obstacles that the entire dramatic force of the novel rests. The ultimate solutions offered are anti-climatic, dramatised as they are in Glenn Tropile's new-found marital harmony (which until then is hardly an issue for the novel) and in his hurriedly introduced prize of membership in a hitherto unmentioned interstellar community of scholars.

This limp conclusion has the effect of exposing the Pyramids as something of a diversion ideologically, in so far as their destruction leaves intact the essential problem of human nature. But the importance of the conclusion is that it suggests instead that though the previous solutions were magical, magical solutions do actually exist in the real world. It attempts to *motivate* the magicality, to translate the empty magic of space opera back into the more down-to-earth, 'rational' forms of magic which, in their very familiarity, appear compatible with the materialist logic common to the dystopian and real worlds. This 'rational magic' is that of a Rationalist Idealism expressed through the images and terminology of that most 'rational' of religions, Christianity. Rather than resolving the real social problems resurrected in its final section, the novel abandons them for a pre-Lapsian vision of an Adam and Eve starting the human race afresh from new first principles. Although the content of the vision is rationalist and humanist (Man's collective pursuit of pure knowledge), what is affirmed as the solution is essentially a religious transcendence, the mysterious power of a vision, of faith, of the human soul to transcend even the biological constraints of human existence which have provided the ground-rule and the stumbling-block of the novel's world.

Let us briefly review the understanding we have arrived at of the socio-historical character of popular literary texts. The specifically literary contradictions of *Wolfbane* express, and in their own way attempt to resolve, the historically determined, ideological contradictions of its social base. Now this position, while not in itself incorrect, nonetheless seems to me capable of supporting a severely one-sided understanding of literature that still falls short of a fully historical account. The limitations arise if (as Klein does) one simply takes as given the pre-existing unity of a social group reflected in the relative unity of its world-view and the relative unity of a literary genre. Such a position constitutes a strict *sociology* of literature in that it tends to reduce the social nature and existence of literature to an external and mechanical relation between a Society 'over here' and a Literature 'over there', in which, like colliding billiard balls, ideology passively reflects the action of social relations and literature passively reflects that of ideology.

These limitations derive from the fact that literature is being treated exclusively from the standpoint of its socio-historical conditions of *production*, but not as itself an active agent in the historical *reproduction* and transformation of those conditions in the first place. The apparently 'given' unity of a social group is in fact only the provisional product, seized at a given moment in time, of the continuing process of constructing and reconstructing a social unity out of a variety of contradictory social relations. Similarly, the apparent coherence of a world-view becomes much more heterogeneous and contradictory when viewed historically. Rather than a world-view being an inherent property or possession of a social group, it is one of the constantly changing manifestations of a process of ideological struggle to build a rebuild a\ particular ideological unity; whereby, at least in part, that contradictory unity of social relations is itself constructed and transformed. And literature, in its turn, is one of the mechanisms through which that temporary unity-in-contradiction of ideology is defined and redefined – not only within individual texts, but also in the historical construction and reconstruction of generic unities out of the contradictory variety of these texts.

It is for this reason that we have stressed the way *Wolfbane* *constructs*, rather than reflects, an ideological position, in seeking to give perceptions of historical reality ideological consistency and coherence; while simultaneously *reconstructing* the terms and logic of the ideological argument in the attempt to reconcile it with that historical experience. This second aspect is particularly difficult to recognise if one treats SF as the mere expression of the world-view of its social base. The texts of a given period then appear only as so many contingent literary variants of a single world-view, formally linked by reference to their common ideological core, but with no concrete historical connections between one and the next.

Moreover, studied in terms of what they have in common rather than their differences, reduced to their unity rather than explored in their contradictions, what emerges as their common world-view is at first sight rather odd. Klein, for instance, identifies the values of SF's social base as 'egalitarian, rationalist and democratic' (p. 9). But these are the dominant values of American society as a whole, the ideology of the dominant class and not specifically of a technological petty bourgeoisie. A rather better definition of the common 'world-view' of SF, one we can recognise in *Wolfbane*, would be to say that it articulates the contradiction between Rationalism and Humanism; exploring the belief that the rational ordering of society necessarily leads to the liberation of the individual from superstition and servitude and to the general fulfilment of Man's potential. But again, these are the twin banners under which capitalism has always advanced since it emerged from the destruction of feudalism. While of particular relevance to a scientifically-oriented middle class, they represent much more the dominance of ruling-class ideology over the whole of society. The point is that if the Rationalist-Humanist couple is what all SF texts have in common ideologically, each individual text is much more than this; a testing, defining and reconstructing of this ideology in the process of interpreting the changing content of specific historical experience.

As our earlier historical account suggests, SF was able to emerge as a relatively new and coherent genre in the America of the late 1930s in so far as it offered a non-antagonistic renewal of this Rationalist-Humanist ideology, on the basis of the historical experience of the professional functionaries of scientific and technical knowledge. For this group, the 'rational' mass society genuinely appeared to represent the liberation of humanity through Reason. By the late 1950s, however, the contradiction has become more acute. What *Wolfbane* argues is not that Reason necessarily leads to human liberation, but that Reason itself must first be liberated; that the pre-condition of successfully pursuing the rule of Reason is the creation of a new egalitarian and humanitarian social order – a reversal of the previous order of priority in SF. What is ultimately involved in all this is the nature of ideological struggle. It is not that the petty bourgeoisie has a world-view of its own which it opposes externally to that of the bourgeoisie. Rather, it is that resistance to the dominant ideology is expressed within the hegemonic terms of those dominant ideas themselves. The world-view of the petty bourgeoisie is not a formulated ideological 'object', but its struggle to redefine the dominant ideology in line with its own material experience and interests.

This is one reason why it is so important that analysis should begin from individual literary texts and their internal ideological conflicts, rather than from generalisations about a period or genre. Given that it is the dominant ideology which popular literary texts have in common, it can seem natural to argue, as Cawelti does, that their *function* is to perpetuate that consensus; or even to take the further step of implicitly or openly denigrating texts for succumbing to capitalist co-option, perpetuating illusions or generally being 'incorrect'. When we look at the ideological conflict within each text, however, it becomes clear that it is also potentially subversive of that consensus. *Wolfbane*, for example, turns the Rationalist-Humanist ideology against itself in a humanist critique of the 'rational' society. Measured against some abstract standard of scientific correctness, or Truth, of course, the critique is limited by remaining within the dominant ideological terms of reference of that society. But since both the critique and its shortcomings are historically determined, the goal is rather to analyse them as material interventions in their historical context.[6]

It is true that *Wolfbane*'s solutions to the problems of American society do not start, for example, from the revolutionary movement of the working class. But not only was this necessarily invisible as a solution for the social base of SF in the period, it was not *materially* in evidence as a solution except as a distant organisational goal. Conversely, what the novel's final section offers as potential starting points for the transformation of monopoly capitalism do not, in historical retrospect, seem wholly unrealistic or unjustified as historically real sites of humanist and democratic resistance to its forms and effects – the liberal intelligentsia, a humanist renewal of broadly religious impulses and movements, a democratic and communal socialising of familial relations.

The approach to literature from the standpoint of reproduction thus stresses the hegemonic character of texts, this internal relation of resistance to the dominance of an ideology which defines the precise character of that very dominance. Such an approach avoids attributing a false inevitability to literary history. For the extents to which the potentially critical or consensual aspects are historically mobilised, the real ideological effects or significance of a text, that is, do not reflect an unchanging social function but are the outcome of a continuing struggle or balance of forces in the appropriation of literary texts. We have been talking of literature as an ideological form, but it is, of course, a specific *kind* of ideological form with a relatively independent existence and history. It is above all in the construction of specifically literary orders and relations between texts, as both effect and condition of reproducing ideological unities, that the historical appropriation of literature is conducted – in the construction of selective traditions, hierarchical canons, generic orders, etc.

This process of genre is, I believe, the proper object of a genuinely materialist history of literature, the literary process in its real, material complexity as the social production, appropriation and reproduction of literary texts. Constructed by writers, readers and critics, but also by publishers, booksellers, librarians, the network of relations established between literary texts are of many contradictory and overlapping orders – women's literature, the thriller, popular literature, satire, SF etc. Such orders are formal but with necessary material effects. By bringing the ideological contradictions within and between texts into a particular formal unity, they contribute to the ideological formation and transformation of the social relations between readers, which are in turn one form of the existence of class struggles. Conversely, the ideological effects of such class struggles are continually manifested in the development and transformation of literature's generic unities.[7]

74   Popular Fiction and Social Change

Critics will naturally accept that literature does not exist independently of society. The converse, however, is less well explored, though equally true. Society does not exist independently of literature, and genre is one of the modes through which social relations exist, their literary mode of existence. Adapting Marx, one might even legitimately say that the generic relations between literary texts are simply the determinate social relations between men that assume, in their eyes, the fantastic fetished form of relations between things.

NOTES

1. F. Pohl and C. Kornbluth, *Wolfbane* (Harmondsworth: Penguin, 1979). All quotations are from this edition. The work first appeared as a two-part serial in the October 1957 edition of the magazine *Galaxy* and as a novel in 1959 (New York: Ballantine).

2. G. Klein, 'Discontent in American Science Fiction', *Science-Fiction Studies*, IV, 1 (March 1977) 3–13. While the historical account which follows is close to Klein's, I have enlarged on and modified it in some respects.

3. Its descriptive adequacy is very broadly confirmed by empirical readership surveys such as that offered by A. Berger, 'Science Fiction Fans in Socio-Economic Perspective: Factors in the Social Consciousness of a Genre', *Science Fiction Studies*, IV, 3 (November 1977) 232–46. The tautology involved in defining the social base of SF as a group with a cultural interest in science can be avoided only if the social base is analysed historically as both precondition *and* effect of generic developments – a point I shall return to.

4. The marked division of the novel into two halves is almost certainly attributable to its original serial publication, but this is not enough to account for the parallel generic differences between the parts. In *New Maps of Hell* (New York: Arno, 1975) p. 125, Kingsley Amis notes the coexistence of satire and space opera in the collaborative work of Pohl and Kornbluth, attributing the former to Pohl and the latter to his partner. Again, however, this is insufficient as an explanation. While it may say something about the mechanism by which each element finds its way into the text, it says nothing about where each element ultimately derives from, and more importantly, nothing about the conditions, nature and effects of their textual combination.

5. This general principle of the contradiction in literary texts between the demands of motivation and those of an ideological argument, offers the possibility of distinguishing 'popular' and 'élite' texts without reifying the differences between them. At one extreme, formula texts are dominated by the need to preserve the Ideal logic of their ideological positions at the expense of contradictions and their magical resolution on the level of motivation. At the other, the texts of the élite literary canon try to preserve motivation, verisimilitude etc., at all costs, with consequent contradictory complexity at the ideological level – these ideological contradictions usually

being taken as the mark of their richness, cognitive value and adequacy, etc. Where the more formulaic texts correspond to the question 'What happens next?' and to the closing down of meaning around the reproduction of received terms of reference, the more élite texts produce the question 'What is the significance of this?' and demand that the reader generate new ideological discourses to synthesise or transcend the contradictions.

As SF reveals particularly clearly, however, extending as it does over the whole range from formula writing to masterworks of the élite literary canon, these differences are not absolutes but questions of the *relative dominance* of motivation or of ideological theses. Not only genres, but all individual texts are intermediate to varying degrees, having elements of both the popular and the élite in complex, fluctuating relations which only critical analysis will reveal. On the one hand, there is no reason why essentially the same critical method cannot be used for both popular and élite texts. On the other, the categorisation of a given text, the way it is read, and the nature of its ideological effects form part of a socio-historical process of literary appropriation, rather than simply reflecting the text's fixed, internal essence.

6. The consensualism and functionalism of J. Cawelti's *Adventure, Mystery, and Romance* (University of Chicago Press, 1976) are natural developments of the sociology of literature with its external relations between literature and society. The not-unrelated tendency to treat popular literary texts abstractly as ideological illusion rather than as material interventions in a history, might be illustrated in SF criticism by P. Fitting's 'The Modern Anglo-American SF Novel: Utopian Longing and Capitalist Cooptation', *Science Fiction Studies*, VI, 1 (March 1979) 59–75. The nature and popularity of such approaches to popular fiction, and their effects in perpetuating dismissive and reductionist attitudes towards it, are well discussed by T. Bennett, 'Marxism and Popular Fiction', *Literature and History*, 7, 2 (Autumn 1981) 138–65.

7. There is no room here to situate *Wolfbane* properly in such complex historical processes. But one can recognise these processes at work within SF in the uninterrupted transformation of the genre since the 1940s. From being dominated and defined by texts strictly motivated in terms of the physical and applied sciences, the unity of the genre was first recast into two broad camps with the flourishing of texts motivated simply in terms of a common-sense materialism and then fragmented into a competing multiplicity of generic variants with the wholesale abandonment of materialist motivations by New Wave writers of the 1960s.

This struggle to redefine the genre's unity (and its standards, classics and traditions thereby) is both cause and effect of struggles over the ideological hegemony of 'Scientism' and between the different intersecting readerships of SF. The generic and ideological discontinuities of *Wolfbane* mark its place as a contributory moment in this history. An adequate account of this history from SF critics, however, is unlikely to appear until they overcome the present split between empiricist readership surveys on the one hand, and interminable arguments over formal definitions of the genre on the other. And this in turn means abandoning the traditional question 'What is SF?' and asking instead 'What has SF been historically, and why?'

3. Thrillers

JERRY PALMER

Gabe was a great reporter, but he could be a royal pain in the ass. He lived in a world of plots and conspiracies, and because the real world had in recent years often approximated Gabe's most terrible fantasies he had become a celebrated journalist.

Patrick Anderson, *The President's Mistress*

Tragedy, Aristotle tells us, 'does not produce any chance pleasure, but the pleasure proper to it';[1] tragedy – especially Greek tragedy – is far from our subject, but Aristotle's principle is universal: any formula, or genre, conforms to this description by producing a form of pleasure which is specific to it. The form of pleasure evoked by thrillers is, by common consent, suspense, but suspense is a term which is capable of many definitions: at its broadest, aesthetic suspense consists of reading a story in order 'to find out what happens'. As Colin MacCabe argues, 'every narration is always a suspense story', in the sense that it is in the resolution of narrative – the ending – that the sense, the identity, the closure, of the narrative can be experienced.[2] Whatever the truth of this assertion, there is clearly a discernible difference – even if one is that subordinate to the principle MacCabe elaborates – between suspense in (say) George Eliot's *Middlemarch* or Tolstoy's *War and Peace*, on the one hand, and in a Mickey Spillane or a James Bond novel on the other. According to conventional literary critical wisdom, this is because thrillers are 'sensationalist', and all the usual desiderata of the Great Tradition are sacrificed to the appetite for excitement: character development, moral complexity, linguistic tautness. That the traditional distinction is evaluative rather than descriptive need not retain our attention here, for our purpose is solely to single out the type of suspense that is specific to the thriller. It may be formulated thus, in a single dogmatic assertion:

Thriller suspense consists of experiencing everything from the point of view of the hero.

The commonest narrative form of the thriller, starting with Poe and the Sherlock Holmes stories, consists of the elucidation of a mystery: 'Whodunit?' Clearly, within this structure it is impossible for any of the events in the story to be seen through the eyes of, from the point-of-view of, the villain: it is essential to the structure of the story that the villain's identity should be hidden from the reader, and therefore by definition we cannot see things from his/her perspective. It is easy to test this proposition with the limit case of Agatha Christie's *The Murder of Roger Ackroyd*, which is narrated in the first person and where at the end the narrator is revealed to be the murderer; in a sense, therefore, we see everything through the villain's eyes, but only on condition that his villainy, that is his identity, is masked: for instance, as Poirot tracks him down he should feel some measure of apprehension but this is never indicated to the reader, and cannot be, since it would give the game away. That is to say, in so far as events are seen from the position that the villain occupies this is achieved by denying the most important aspects of his character.[3] And this is merely an extension of the principle that structures the concealment of the villain in all the tradition of writing of which Agatha Christie is perhaps the most famous exponent: the principle of the least likely person, according to which the villain is always the person who apparently had least motive and least opportunity. For this, as Raymond Chandler pointed out,[4] involves falsifying their character by making a significant part of their motivation and behaviour unavailable to the audience in just the same way as in the case of *Roger Ackroyd*.

One of the significantly original aspects of Ian Fleming's James Bond novels was his coverage of the villain's point of view: in every novel some of the story is narrated through the villain's eyes, and the reader therefore has access to information not at Bond's disposal; for instance, in *From Russia With Love*, the reader knows that the Soviet Secret Service are setting a trap for Bond whereas Bond and M think that the situation is normal.[5] By making the villain visible to the reader in this way, Fleming is able to present him/her as a fully individualised portrait, thus avoiding the problems Chandler perceived in the classic detective story; but by the same token, he has to avoid allowing the readers to empathise too much with the villain, and he achieves this in two ways: firstly, by making the villains caricaturally repulsive; secondly, by careful manipulation of the point of view. In this passage from *Casino Royale* the villain successfully ambushes Bond:

> Le Chiffre was concentrating half on the road ahead and half on the onrushing glare of Bond's headlights in the driving-mirror. He seemed undisturbed when not more than a mile separated the hare from the hounds and he even brought the car down from eighty to sixty miles an hour. Now, as he swept round a bend he slowed down still further. A few hundred yards ahead a Michelin post showed where a small parochial road crossed with the highway. '*Attention*', he said sharply to the man beside him. The man's hand tightened on the lever. A hundred yards from the cross-roads he slowed to thirty. In the mirror Bond's great headlights were lighting up the bend.
> Le Chiffre seemed to make up his mind.
> '*Allez*'.
> The man beside him pulled the lever sharply upwards. The boot at the back of the car yawned open like a whale's mouth. There was a tinkling clatter on the road and then a rhythmic jangling as if the car was towing lengths of chain behind it.
> '*Coupez*'.
> The man depressed the lever sharply and the jangling stopped with a final clatter.
> Le Chiffre glanced again in the mirror. Bond's car was just entering the bend. Le Chiffre made a racing change and threw the Citroën left-handed down the narrow side-road, at the same time dowsing his lights.
> He stopped the car with a jerk and all three men got swiftly

out and doubled back under cover of a low hedge to the cross-roads, now fiercely illuminated by the lights of the Bentley. Each of them carried a revolver and the thin man also had what looked like a large black egg in his right hand.

The Bentley screamed down towards them like an express train.

CHAPTER 16

THE CRAWLING OF THE SKIN

As Bond hurtled round the bend, caressing the great car against the camber with an easy sway of body and hands, he was working out his plan of action when the distance between the two cars had narrowed still further. He imagined that the enemy driver would try to dodge off into a side-road if he got the chance. So when he got round the bend and saw no lights ahead, it was a normal reflex to ease up on the accelerator and, when he saw the Michelin post, to prepare to brake.

He was only doing about sixty as he approached the black patch across the right-hand crown of the road which he assumed to be the shadow cast by a wayside tree. Even so, there was no time to save himself. There was suddenly a small carpet of glinting steel spikes right under his off-side wing. Then he was on top of it.[6]

In the first half we see events from Le Chiffre's point of view, but at the transition from one chapter to the next, at the moment that Le Chiffre's plan bears fruit, the narrative reverts to Bond's point of view: this is essential, for, from Le Chiffre's point of view the ambush is a triumph, whereas from Bond's it is a disaster, and although by this time the reader is no doubt sufficiently on Bond's side to resist any temptation to evaluate the event in Le Chiffre's terms, to experience it through his eyes would introduce a considerable element of ambiguity. I know of no thriller novel in which any important incident is experienced from the villain's point of view, but in the film *Coma*[7] one moment of a decisive confrontation with the heroine is experienced from the villain's point of view: an armed killer is pursuing the heroine, alone, at night, through a deserted part of the hospital where she works; she hides in the freezer storage room of the anatomy laboratory, in which frozen corpses awaiting dissection are hung like suits on rails along which they can move; she pushes a line of corpses along the rails and as they reach the end where the villain is standing, they fall on top of him. During this sequence one shot is taken from the villain's point of view: we see the line of corpses, encased in transparent polythene, trundling towards the camera just as the villain would see them advancing on him. It is a genuinely horrifying moment and it somewhat reduces the exhilaration induced by the heroine's ingenious outwitting of her would-be killer. Nevertheless, it is only a brief moment in a scene otherwise shot either neutrally or from the heroine's point of view: any further elaboration of the villain's point of view would risk compromising our sympathy for the heroine.

Moreover, in the passage from *Casino Royale* the first section is only apparently written from Le Chiffre's point of view. We are told that he 'was concentrating' but that he 'seemed undisturbed', later that he 'seemed to make up his mind'. In using the phrase 'was concentrating' Fleming is using the conventional omniscient voice of realist narrative, but by saying 'seemed . . .' he is drawing back from Le Chiffre: at this point we do not see things as Le Chiffre sees them, although 'was concentrating' is equivalent to Le Chiffre's perspective. Similarly with the details of Le Chiffre's gadget: we are told of 'the lever', and a 'tinkling clatter' and a 'rhythmic jangling as if the car was towing lengths of chain', but this information is not sufficient to tell us what is happening, and is not the information which Le Chiffre himself possesses. This suppression of information, clearly, is done in the interests of suspense: we know enough to know Bond is threatened but not enough to know exactly how, and we want to know the outcome of the situation. That is to say: in the interests of suspense information deriving from the villain's point-of-view is suppressed in order that we shall adopt the hero's point of view.

By various means, therefore, the thriller narrative compels

us to adopt the perspective of the hero: by entirely hiding the identity of anyone who could furnish an alternative perspective, by making the villains caricaturally repulsive, by manipulating the point of view in the narrative. In all thrillers, the end result is the same: we side whole-heartedly, exclusively with the hero. Or, more exactly, in so far as we enjoy the story, we adopt the hero's perspective; if we fail to do so, we fail to derive pleasure from the story.

To adopt the hero's perspective entails a particular evaluation of him: a positive evaluation. What qualities are there in the hero which evoke, or help evoke, this evaluation? This question may be answered in the form of a second dogmatic proposition:

> the hero is distinguished from the other characters by his professionalism and his success.

In the world of the thriller there are three forms of action: amateurism, professionalism and bureaucracy. Of the three forms, the hero always and exclusively adopts the second, professionalism. The amateur is most commonly to be found in the thriller either in the form of the average citizen or the onlooker, who is helpless because caught up in a rush of events with which he/she has no connection, or in the form of a woman who has an attachment to the hero (or who will have). In this passage from Donald Hamilton's *The Removers*[8] Matt Helm (hero and narrator) reflects on his attempts to persuade his ex-wife to distract the villain's attention by going to bed with him:

> I mean, she was obviously going to be raped anyway. It had been inevitable since early that morning when she'd let them take the shotgun from her. I'd assumed she'd known it – hell, all she had to do was *look* at the guy – and was planning on it, figuring how best to make use of the fact that she was female, for the common good. . . . I guess the fact is that I'd been counting on her as I'd have counted on a good female agent in the same spot – or any woman with courage or good sense, for that matter . . . But it was fast becoming obvious that the thought hadn't crossed her mind, or that if it had,

she'd dismissed it as something too horrible to be seriously considered. A provocative glance or two, maybe, even a smile, perhaps, but if anybody seriously expected her to go into that room with this vile man and entertain him . . . Well! How disgusting could you get, anyway? I wasn't going to get any help from her, that was abundantly clear.

The contrast Helm draws between his ex-wife and a 'good female agent' is clear: his ex-wife is an amateur, for whom the act of deliberately prostituting herself is beyond her self-control; we shall see a clear contrast with this in the final section of this essay, à propos *The Day of the Jackal*.

The figure of the bureaucrat is to be found either in the role of the villain or in the role of incompetent people who are, in some sense, on the same side as the hero. Most – though not all – of Fleming's villains are bureaucrats.

'The Corsican section', he said softly, 'will put forward recommendations for the replacement of No. 12. But that can wait until after completion of Plan Omega. On this matter, there are certain details to be discussed. Sub-Operator G, recruited by the German section, has made an error, a serious error which radically affects our timetable. This man, whose membership of the Red Lightning Tong in Macao should have made him expert in conspiracy, was instructed to make his headquarters at a certain clinic in the south of England, an admirable refuge for his purposes . . . Unfortunately this foolish man took it upon himself to become embroiled in a hotheaded fashion with some fellow patient, at the clinic, . . . This will involve an irritating but fortunately not a serious delay in Plan Omega. Fresh instructions have been issued . . . The date of his flight will be communicated to Sub-Operator G and he will by that time be recovered and will post The Letter according to plan. The Special Executive . . . will readjust their flight schedules to Area Zeta in accordance with the new operational schedule'.[9]

The tone of voice is specifically that of the bureaucrat, as is the terminology. Elsewhere, the villains also evolve master-plans: Goldfinger (model for Blofeld in the previous passage) with his meticulously planned invasion of Fort Knox, SMERSH's finely planned attack on Bond in *From Russia, With Love*, complete down to the detail that Bond is to be killed with a single bullet fired from a gun disguised as a copy of *War and Peace* at the exact moment his train enters the Simplon Tunnel. These plans take account of all possible contingencies, in theory, but in practice Bond's interference is always the one loophole that no allowance was made for, and it is the fact that the plans are so inflexible that allows Bond the space to manoeuvre: Goldfinger is so certain that the visible evidence of his plan's success is irrefutable that he never suspects a trap; it is the delay the plan imposes on Red Grant's shooting of Bond that gives Bond time to counter his attack in *From Russia, With Love*.

Where it is incompetent helpers who are bureaucrats, the situation is essentially no different: the contrast between the incompetent bureaucrats and the competent professional hero is structured in the same way as the contrast between the incompetent villainous bureaucrat and the competent professional hero: it is a question of inflexibility versus flexibility. In several of the Sherlock Holmes stories we meet Inspector Lestrade of Scotland Yard, who is always, in the end, discomfited by Holmes' brilliance. In *The Norwood Builder*[10] a young man is, apparently, very obviously guilty of murder: he is unexpectedly made the heir to a rich old man, goes to the old man's house, and during the same night the remains of a body are discovered in a pile of burning wood at the back of the house, there are signs of a violent struggle, the old man is missing and the young man's stick is discovered, bloodstained, in the house. Holmes proves that no crime was committed, that the old man had faked the whole thing in order to disappear fraudulently, to avenge himself on the young man's family, because he is struck by the unexpectedness of the inheritance and finds out, as a result, that the old man virulently hated the young man's family. As he explains to Watson '. . . we have in this case one singular incident coming close to the heels of another singular incident. The police are making the mistake of concentrating their attention upon the second because it happens to be the one which is actually criminal' (p. 595). In short, the police, because bureaucrats, are incapable of seeing beyond the end of their own procedures, whereas Holmes, with his experience and mental flexibility, finds it easy to conceive of another inferential chain.

Similarly in Carter Brown's Al Wheeler novels: the hero is an unorthodox 'trouble shooter' policeman whose methods always get him into trouble with his boss, and whose results always avert the threatened trouble. In *The Body*, Wheeler provokes the villain, Rodinoff, into shooting someone else in his presence, but with no other witnesses, and then shoots him. The solution is to say the least of dubious legality, and he tells the Sheriff that Rodinoff committed suicide in his presence; his boss is unimpressed, since the story will sound thin in court and anyway he has had a tail on Rodinoff for days and would soon have apprehended him by more regular means. He then notices that Wheeler is wounded (there was a brief exchange of shots that ended in Rodinoff's death) and the true story emerges:

> It was my turn to stare. 'Then what made you suspect Rodinoff?' 'I didn't suspect Rodinoff', he said coldly.
> 'Then why put a twenty-four-a-day tail on him?'
> 'Dammit!' he roared. 'I didn't! That was fiction. I couldn't stand listening to you any more. I have my pride, though what use it is to me I'm not sure! You think I liked standing there listening to you telling me how I'd fallen down on my job! I had to say something!'
> He grinned at me suddenly. 'I should resign and give you my job, Wheeler. But I won't, of course!' he added hastily. 'You had every moral right to kill Rodinoff, even if you had no legal rights. The story of the suicide will stick'.[11]

Similar incidents occur in almost all the Al Wheeler novels. Beneath them lurks the distinction between bureaucratic action and professional action.

Amateurism consists in the incapacity for appropriate action in the circumstances defined by the thriller. Bureaucracy consists in the incapacity for flexible response. Both categories exclude the possibility of acting upon experience: the amateur has no relevant experience because of the total novelty of the situation, and the rigidity of the bureaucrat's planning and procedures prevents the assimilation of experience into the plan once it is launched; or his mental ossification precludes flexibility of thought. Professionalism consists of the capacity for planning, in a flexible manner, for learning from experience, for improving fast on the basis of experience. In *From Russia, With Love* the delay SMERSH's master plan imposes on Grant gives Bond the space to improvise. He lights a cigarette and manages to slip the case into his breast pocket; the bullet only bruises him. He shams death and contrives to fall close to a knife concealed among his luggage.

The knife represents the existence of programming amongst Bond's activities. When he leaves on this mission the gadgets branch of the Secret Service gives him a specially constructed briefcase:

> In each of the innocent sides there was a flat throwing knife, built by Wilkinsons, the sword makers, and the tops of their handles were concealed cleverly by the stitching at the corners . . . More important was the thick tube of Palmolive shaving cream in the otherwise guileless spongebag. The whole top of this unscrewed to reveal the silencer for the Beretta, packed in cotton wool. In case hard cash was needed, the lid of the attaché case contained fifty gold sovereigns. These could be poured out by slipping sideways one ridge of welting.
>
> The complicated bag of tricks amused Bond, but he also had to admit that, despite its eight pound weight, the bag was a convenient way of carrying the tools of his trade, which would otherwise have to be concealed about his body. (Chapter 13)

Despite the ironical 'bag of tricks', he is glad enough of it when it comes to the point. A contingency has been foreseen, although not in any detail, and Bond benefits from this planning. However, this professionalism does not distinguish the hero from the villain, for it is often the case that the villain too is fully professional.

At the end of Spillane's *The By-Pass Control* Tiger Mann hunts down a Soviet spy in the middle of a tract of deserted sand-dunes:

I stopped long enough to study the topography, trying to choose the exact spot he would have picked for the ambush.

There was one, a peculiarly shaped dune that seemed to have a dish-shaped back that covered all fields of fire and could hide a man completely from anyone making an assault . . .

I started up the incline.

Above me the low flying gull wheeled suddenly and made a startled ninety degree turn toward the water, flapping in to land beside the sandpipers.

It was enough. The gull had seen him first.

That dune was a clever trap. It was the spot I'd look for. There was only one other left.

The waiting was over. I ran.

He was half buried in a hollow he had dug for himself, secure in the knowledge that he controlled the action . . .

He had it too, that feeling for the *thing*. He knew I was there as I came over the rise . . . .[12]

Moreover, as has often been pointed out, it is difficult to distinguish between the hero and the villain on the grounds of any set of personal characteristics.[13] However, there are two clear narrative characteristics that do ground this distinction. The first is that the hero never starts the action of a thriller: he always reacts to prior aggression; the second is that the hero always wins.

If it were not for evil enterprise and ingenious murders, Sherlock Holmes would find it difficult to make a living; chemical analysis might serve, but there was not much of a market for surrealist violinists at the time. The same applies to James Bond: minus his government salary he would have to rely on professional golf and gambling, which his instincts as a gentleman might find sullying; or perhaps he could be a gigolo. In any event, the point is clear: were it not for evil disruptions of the status quo, thriller heroes would have no function, and there would be no story. At the beginning of *The Return of Bulldog Drummond* our hero is fast asleep, in the mid-afternoon, lazily enjoying life on a friend's country estate, without even a thought of interesting knavery; nonetheless, it occurs, to his surprise: 'Great Scot! chaps, think of the bare possibility of

having stumbled on something!'[14] And in *Wisteria Lodge* Holmes
ruminates on redundancy: 'My dear Watson, you know how
bored I have been since we locked up Colonel Carruthers. My
mind is like a racing engine, tearing itself to pieces because it is
not connected up with the work for which it is built. Life is
commonplace, the papers are sterile; audacity and romance
seem to have passed for ever from the criminal world' (p. 892).

Thus the thriller hero is distinguished from the thriller villain
by the fact that it is always the villain who makes the first move,
usually in the form of murder, although it may be some slighter
activity which initiates the plot, leading to something bigger –
for instance, Drax cheating at cards in Fleming's *Moonraker*.[15]

The second, equally important element in the narrative
distinction between hero and villain is the hero's success: in the
thriller it is always the hero who wins in the final confrontation,
who successfully completes his mission. It is true that there are
many thrillers, among the best by common consent, where this
appears problematic. To take only an extreme example: *The Spy
who Came in From The Cold*.[16] At the end Sean Lemass effectively
commits suicide, and clearly therefore in a sense he has lost.
What has happened is that he has triumphantly succeeded in
completing his mission only to find that his mission was part of
a larger plan whose nature he was not aware of and which has
the unfortunate by-product of betraying the woman he has
fallen in love with; professional success, personal loss: this
disjunction marks many thrillers – *The Maltese Falcon*, *The Long
Goodbye*, etc.[17] But it is essential in all these cases that the hero
is, in a technical, professional sense, the winner: whatever his
mission is, he completes it. In the absence of such success we
are in the presence of a form of writing which is not a thriller.

Thus the hero is typified by three characteristics: he is a
professional, not an amateur or a bureaucrat; he wins; and he
always reacts to prior aggression. His professionalism does not
distinguish him from the villain, necessarily, although it
commonly does in the classic English detective story – but the
obvious exception here is Moriarty in the Holmes stories. The
other two features do distinguish him from the other characters. That is to say: not only do they distinguish him from the
villain, but also from everyone else, and most essentially from
those people who are on his side, his back-up team.

Consider the position of Dr Watson in the Holmes stories. The conventional explanation of his role is that he enables a first person narrative without giving away essential evidence which the narrator would have to possess if he were the detective;[18] while this is true, it omits the essential: this first person narrative is also an admiring narrative, for again and again it becomes clear that Watson feels intensely the inequality that separates him from Holmes. This inequality, crucially, is also felt by the reader: in Chapter 1 of *The Hound of the Baskervilles* Holmes invites Watson to attempt some deductions from a walking stick; Watson's pitiful efforts contrast spectacularly with Holmes' success.[19] Watson, in short, has the prime function of inadequacy in order to provide a contrast with Holmes. In just the same way, figures like James Bond or Mickey Spillane's Mike Hammer and Tiger Mann have back-up teams who are gunned down, burnt up, exploded or eaten alive by barracuda with quite monotonous regularity, whereas Bond and Mike Hammer/Tiger Mann live to triumph and perhaps to rescue their less adequate helpers.

The hero, in fact, must not only be capable of winning in the sense of defeating his enemy, but must be exclusively capable of winning, by being visibly better than all his friends. In this sense, heroism is a competitive process; in the final analysis the hero is distinguished from the other characters by distinguishing himself through superior professional competence.

In what cause does the hero exert his competence? We know that he reacts to prior aggression on the part of the villain, but that is scarcely a feature peculiar to thrillers; and since the type of hero we have described is also, clearly, not peculiar to the thriller – the Western hero, for instance, could be described in similar terms, despite the absence of bureaucrats in the Western genre – so far there is little in what has been said about the nature of the hero which applies exclusively to the thriller. However, a more precise analysis of what the hero undertakes to do (as opposed to an analysis of how he undertakes it) will provide the *differentia specifica*; it too can be formulated in the form of a dogmatic proposition:

the hero undertakes to solve a heinous, mysterious crime which is a major threat to the social order.

Not every crime can serve as the subject matter of a thriller: tax evasion, shoplifting, hit-and-run are all crimes, but are not suitable material for the thriller hero. The crime that he investigates must be more grandiose; specifically, it must be evil as well as criminal; in legal terms it must involve intentional violence against the person and not just an attack upon property; in the legal terminology current in Britain until the end of the eighteenth century, the crime in question must be 'heinous'.[20] The crime in question is therefore a major threat to the social order either because it consists of a conspiracy to subvert it entirely, as in the monstrous conspiracies outlined in Ian Fleming's and Mickey Spillane's novels; or because – as in the case of the murders that are the usual subject matter of the classic detective stories – personal security from the potential malevolence of those closest to oneself is a central desideratum of the daily social order.

This crime, moreover, must be mysterious, in the specific sense that the identity of the criminal, or at least the modality of his actions, is hidden from both the reader and the hero. If the threat to the order of normality is not mysterious, we are not in the presence of a thriller: in both Westerns and horror stories, for instance, the hero (if there is one) faces a major threat to the social order; but in neither is it mysterious in the specific sense here: in neither case does the assailant deliberately hide his/its identity. In the thriller the story starts when there is a mysterious disruption of, or irruption into, the order of the normal; the story ends when the mystery is solved, the identity of the assailant is revealed and the threat posed by his/her continuing non-identification is averted.

Because the hero is investigating a mystery, the world that he moves in is opaque; incidents occur which are largely incomprehensible:

> I kissed her easily, feeling her mouth tremble beneath mine, the restraint inside her. I'll call you earlier next time', I said.
> She winked and went up the steps. When the inside door closed I started back to the cab and had one second to spot the car coming down the street. It was like a whistle going off in my head, a sudden premonition of what was going to

happen and I threw myself to the side and hit the pavement
behind a pair of ash cans as the first staccato thunder from a
tommy gun rolled out of the window.[21]

In this passage, the curious sentence structure – the uncon-
nectedness of the two clauses joined by 'and' in the fourth
sentence – is an index of the unpredictability of the event in
question: how did these gunmen know where he was? Why are
they trying to kill him now? The mystery is thus the driving
force of the thriller plot. It is what impels the story into motion,
by providing the starting point; it is also the motor of the plot in
the sense that all the incidents in it are caused either by the
mystery itself or by its investigation. At the end of *Day of the
Guns* we learn that the woman the hero was kissing in the
passage quoted above is in fact the villain, and the incident
described here was therefore an ambush she organised.

In summary therefore, the structure of the thriller can be
formulated in three dogmatic propositions:

(1) Thriller suspense consists of experiencing everything
    from the point of view of the hero.
(2) The hero is distinguished from the other characters by
    his professionalism and his success.
(3) The hero undertakes to solve a heinous, mysterious
    crime which is a major threat to the social order.

In these propositions (elaborated as above) we have the core of
the thriller genre. This does not mean that these are the only
features of thrillers; but they are the most important, dominant
ones, universal in time (Sherlock Holmes → James Bond) and
in all texts that can fall under the heading 'thriller'. That does
not imply, of course, that all texts characterised by suspense –
our starting point and our finishing point – conform to the
description outlined here. We have already seen that different
varieties of suspense are possible; this chapter will close with
the analysis of an enormously successful, and enormously
suspenseful, novel which systematically contradicts the
analysis of the preceding pages and yet which is clearly closely
related to the thriller genre as outlined here: *The Day of the
Jackal*.[22] In essence, therefore, what is being asserted here about
the *Jackal* is that it is *not* a thriller: despite its undoubted

capacity to create suspense, despite its subject matter, it establishes a different pattern; yet, at the same time, because of the similarities that we shall see, it is clearly related to the traditional thriller. It thus suggests the birth of a new genre, arising out of certain features of the old, but operating certain displacements at the same time.

The central feature of the *Jackal* is the disruption of the relationship between the hero and the conspiracy. Instead of the single professional hero who acts to avert a conspiracy started by somebody else, in order to preserve the status quo, we have a professional hero who starts a conspiracy, a ruthless, unjustified conspiracy, against the established order. He confronts neither a faceless irruption – as in Spillane or Chandler – nor bureaucratic evil – as in Fleming – but a bureaucratic second hero: Inspector Lebel. Here lies the *Jackal*'s novelty and the key to its enormous success. In other words, in the terms laid out here, the *Jackal* has neither a hero nor a conspiracy. It displaces both with a conflict between two men of equal stature, albeit that one is characterised by professionalism and the other by bureaucracy (in my sense of the words).

The world in which the Jackal himself moves is entirely dominated by professionalism. Amateurs who impinge on it are victims: Colette de la Chalonière, murdered as soon as she has an inkling of her lover's identity; Jules Bernard, the homosexual who suffers the same fate. The Jackal's own professionalism is beyond doubt: the meticulous planning, the fallback identities, combined with a flair for improvisation – completely repainting his car, taking refuge with Colette, the brilliantly extemporised homosexual identity – all recall the mixture typical of the thriller hero. The people with whom he is involved are characterised by the same capacity for abstraction from preconceptions and adaptability to changed conditions:

> When faced with his own concept of France and the honour of the French army Rodin was as bigoted as the rest, but when faced with a purely practical problem he could bring to bear a pragmatic and logical concentration that was more effective than all the volatile enthusiasm and senseless violence in the world. (p. 31)

The Belgian armourer who supplies his custom-built rifle is no different:

> M. Goossens' eyes gleamed with pleasure.
> 'A one-off', he purred delightedly. 'A gun that will be tailor-made for one man and one job under one set of circumstances, never to be repeated. You have come to the right man. I sense a challenge, my dear monsieur. I am glad that you came.'
> The Englishman permitted himself a smile at the Belgian's professional enthusiasm. 'So am I, monsieur.' (p. 74)

A less demanding circumstance, no doubt, but essentially the same reaction: the combination of commitment, experience and flexibility. Perhaps the best example is Jacqueline Dumas, the OAS girl who is placed inside the Elysée Palace as a mistress to de Gaulle's aide Raoul de St Clair. To become the elderly courtier's mistress is an act of self-mutilation which she is prepared to undertake to avenge her brother and her lover, both dead in Algeria:

> Would she be prepared to undertake a special job for the Organization? Of course. Perhaps dangerous, certainly distasteful. No matter . . . She knew enough about men to be able to judge the basic types of appetites. Her new lover was accustomed to easy conquests, experienced women. She played shy, attentive but chaste, reserved on the outside with just a hint now and again that her superb body was one day not to be completely wasted. The bait worked . . . Once inside her flat, [she] glanced at her watch. She had three hours to get ready, and although she intended to be meticulous in her preparations, two hours would suffice . . . She thought of the coming night and her belly tightened with revulsion. She would, she vowed, she would go through with it, no matter what kind of loving he wanted. (pp. 102–3)

This professionalism is essentially the same as in the thriller: commitment and experience combined to produce flexibility and expertise. But it has a degree of coldness that is absent there. The Jackal kills with absolute detachment, with no sense of emotion at all; Jacqueline's self-prostitution is equally detached. No doubt this is because if it had the emotional qualities of violence and sex normal in the thriller, one would be led to empathise unequivocally with one side or the other. For the same reason we see very little indeed of the subjectivities of the people involved: everything is presented in terms of externally observed processes, meticulously recorded but scarcely ever seen from within.

The world of his opponents is a world of bureaucratic procedure. Lebel is presented very precisely as the type of policeman who would never be the hero of a thriller:

> . . . he had never lost sight of the fact that in police work ninety-nine percent of the effort is routine, unspectacular inquiry, checking and double-checking until the parts become a whole, the whole becomes a net, and the net finally encloses the criminal with a case that will not just make headlines but will stand up in court. (pp. 193–4)

If there is anything outstanding about him, it is determination, but a determination exercised exclusively in a bureaucratic framework: certainly it is he who is responsible for tracking down the Jackal, but only in the sense that he organises the efforts of others, to the point that the essential information does not come from his efforts, but from the research done by the Special Branch in London. Even in the final confrontation, where Lebel himself shoots the Jackal, it is first and foremost bureaucracy that triumphs. All the planning of Lebel and his colleagues failed to stop the Jackal getting to his destination, the flat overlooking de Gaulle's final ceremony, but in order to get there he had to pose as an elderly cripple and the CRS man who let him pass remembered him. When he mentions a crutch and a greatcoat, on this blazing summer's day, Lebel realises who it is and follows. The Jackal is in principle more than a match in personal confrontation for an elderly inspector and a young CRS man, but his planning has let him down. He has assumed that the only weapon he would need once he had reached his destination would be the one-off rifle, which is a bolt-action gun that only takes a single cartridge at a time. He shoots the young CRS man, but does not have time to reload before Lebel grabs the machine gun and shoots him.

No doubt there is an element of improvisation on Lebel's part here: the pull of the traditional notion of heroism is so strong that a personal confrontation of the traditional type is alone adequate to give the book a climax, even when it is to the detriment of plausibility. The type of man that Lebel is portrayed as, in order to give the contrast that alone makes the moral structure of the novel acceptable (as we shall see), would be no match at all for the Jackal in hand-to-hand combat, and the Jackal has more than enough time to disarm Lebel and kill him by hand.

Suspense depends on the unequivocal acceptance of the moral perspective of the person who is understaking the series of actions described, as we have seen. Characteristically, in the thriller, this involves a single perspective, the hero's. The suspense of the *Jackal* is double, for we empathise alternately with each of the protagonists (even though the second one is effectively an entire bureaucracy). This is possible only because each of the moral perspectives involved is ambivalent. The Jackal's perspective is acceptable because of his professionalism and because our sympathies for his intended victim are blunted by the foreknowledge (spelt out explicitly on page 62) that he survives. It is unacceptable to the extent that his motives are dubious, because exclusively mercenary, and that this preference for things against people carries over into the detachment with which he kills. Lebel's perspective is acceptable to the extent that he is averting an unjustified murder, dubious to the extent that it represents a bureaucracy tracking down an individual. The balance between the two perspectives is helped by the equal ruthlessness displayed by the French security services: the abduction and torture of Kowalski are an intrinsic part of the moral balance of the work.

The balance between the two perspectives extends beyond the characters centrally involved. In the section devoted to the Special Branch's contribution to the manhunt, this judgement is passed:

> Assistant Commissioner Dixon, whose job among other things was to keep tabs on all the weird and crazy of Britain

who might think of trying to assassinate a visiting politician, not to mention the scores of embittered and cranky foreigners domiciled in the country, . . . (p. 224)

Underlying this judgement is instinctive sympathy for the status quo, for the supposed stability of civilised society that is one of the foundations of the thriller, and a similar perspective underlies the expressions of professional sympathy that all the British policemen express at Lebel's predicament. On the other hand, this description of Rodin's views derives from a different set of values:

> Like most combat officers who had seen their men die and occasionally buried the hideously mutilated bodies of those unlucky enough to be taken alive, Rodin worshipped soldiers as the true salt of the earth, the men who sacrificed themselves in blood so that the bourgeoisie could live at home in comfort. To learn from the civilians of his native land after eight years of combat in the forests of Indo-China that most of them cared not a fig for the soldiery . . . (p. 27)

This is traditional heroism: contempt for the stability of civil society, admiration for the dangerous and the exceptional. In fact, Rodin and his men are precisely the 'weird and the crazy' of the previous judgement, or at any rate their French equivalent. In the thriller these two sets of values are thoroughly imbricated, to form the dominant procedure of the genre. Here they are separated and opposed. The dual moral perspective is incarnated in the narrative structure: from the beginning we see the plot and the counter-plot. Inevitably, the focus in the early chapters is mostly on the Jackal, but already in Chapters 3 and 4 Colonel Rolland has started the abduction of Kowalski; in Part Two the balance is restored, and maintained thereafter.

The focus here is on the Jackal because it is the OAS initiative and the Jackal's planning that provide the initial impetus to the story; as pointed out above, in the thriller the hero reacts to prior aggression; here, one of the heroes is the prior aggressor. If the *Jackal* was the only text to manifest this pattern, then it would be jejeune to place too much weight upon it; but where the hero's role as prime aggressor is concerned there are many other texts which show the same rupture with the traditional thriller: Richard Stark's Parker series, Don Pendleton's Executioner series, Joseph Hedges' Revenger series, for instance.[23] In these the hero either is simply engaged in a criminal enterprise, with no justification beyond wanting more money, or is engaged on an act of private, personal vengeance. In both cases his opponents are principally Mafiosi and other criminals who are presented as morally the hero's inferior; often they are criminal bureaucrats, killing in cold blood, contrasted with the hero who is a professional who only kills when forced to. In either set of circumstances it is impossible to see the hero as the incarnation or defender of the social order, for he is acting entirely in his own interests, and in this respect there is a substantial measure of conformity between these texts and the *Jackal*. One could call this new narrative form the 'post-thriller' or the 'Enforcer Story'.[24]

This is particularly significant if we try to interpret thrillers and subsequent forms of popular writing as ideology. Thrillers can be said to be answering one of the conundrums posed by many Anglo-Saxon philosophers: if all individuals are inherently self-seeking and competitive, how is it possible that the social order exists? It is true that the thriller portrays admirable people – the hero – as, precisely, competitive: in so far as we admire the hero, enjoy suspense through sympathy with him, approve of his actions, etc., what we are doing is enjoying a portrayal of a self-seeking, competitive life, the portrayal of actions whose internal sense is given entirely by the aggrandisement of self that is their ultimate goal; this is especially clear in the Bond series, especially the films, which conventionally close with Bond enjoying his reward, female and horizontal.

If all people were like Bond, how could there be a social order? What is the justification for acts like these? The philosophers answered these questions in various ways: for Hobbes, the solution was absolute monarchy, to prevent natural selfishness destroying the social fabric; for Adam Smith, man's selfishness was the essential precondition for the social order, since by following his own interests each man created price equilibrium and thus furthered everyone else's interests as well as his own.[25] In the thriller the justification of the hero's actions is that the social order is constantly threatened, from within, by disruptive evil: the criminal mystery that the hero deals with. The hero is the person, the only person, who is capable of countering this threat and therefore all his actions are justified by their results. In every thriller he saves the social order and thus simultaneously asserts his competitive individuality and his sociability; the thriller does not assert that everyone can be like this, but that those who are are admirable and eminently social, because justified.

But in post-thriller writings, as analysed above, this justification is missing, for there is no prior aggression, or if there is, it is a purely personal prior aggression evoking a purely personal response – we could call it the 'vigilante syndrome', also to be found in films such as *Death Wish*. I have insisted that the roots of the thriller are to be found in ideology. One implication of this emphasis must be that the change manifest in the emergence of a new narrative form out of the interstices of a well-established genre is similarly to be explained in ideological terms: what type of ideological change is indicated in this writing?

I do not think that I am capable of anything beyond the most tentative of answers, drawing upon some suggestions made by Habermas, in *Legitimation Crisis*. The administrations of advanced capitalist societies, he suggests, are obliged by their foundations in constitutions to provide legitimation for their actions; but at the same time the pressures created by a class-based society and the conflicts that derive from this basis inevitably make such legitimation increasingly difficult. Therefore, he suggests, we confront a 'legitimation crisis', in which it is no longer possible for administrators to provide an explanation for their actions which will satisfy all sections of society.

> . . . a legitimation crisis can be avoided in the long run only if the latent class structures of advanced capitalist societies are transformed or if the pressure for legitimation to which the administrative system is subject can be removed. The latter, in turn, could be achieved by transposing the integration of inner nature *in toto* to another mode of socialisation, that is, by uncoupling it from norms that need justification.[26]

98 *Popular Fiction and Social Change*

NOTES

The pages of this article devoted to *The Day of the Jackal* have already appeared in my book *Thrillers* (Edward Arnold, 1978) of which this article is a précis.

1. Aristotle, *Poetics*, ed. Lucas (Oxford University Press, 1968), Chapter 14.

2. Colin MacCabe, 'Theory and Film', in F. Barker *et al.* (eds), *Literature, Sociology and the Sociology of Literature* (Essex University, 1976), p. 66.

3. Agatha Christie, *The Murder of Roger Ackroyd* (London: Collins, 1926).

4. Raymond Chandler, 'The Simple Art of Murder' in *Raymond Chandler Speaking* (London: Hamish Hamilton, 1962), pp. 96–8.

5. Ian Fleming, *From Russia, With Love*, 2nd edn (London: Pan, 1959); in the film version they realise there is a trap, but without knowing the details.

6. Ian Fleming, *Casino Royale*, 2nd edn (London: Pan, 1955), pp. 107–9.

7. Based on R. Cook, *Coma*, 2nd edn (London: Pan, 1978).

8. Donald Hamilton, *The Removers* (London: Hodder Fawcett, 1966), p. 153.

9. Ian Fleming, *Thunderball*, 2nd edn (London: Pan, 1963), pp. 58–9.

10. A. Conan Doyle, *The Norwood Builder*, in *Sherlock Holmes. The Complete Short Stories* (London: Murray, 1928), pp. 583–610.

11. Carter Brown, *The Body* (London: NEL, 1963), p. 125.

12. Mickey Spillane, *The By-Pass Control*, 3rd edn (London: Corgi, 1968), pp. 210–11.

13. See J. Palmer, *Thrillers* (London: Edward Arnold, 1978), pp. 16–23.

14. Sapper, *The Return of Bulldog Drummond* (London: Hodder and Stoughton, 1932), Chapter 1.

15. Ian Fleming, *Moonraker* (London: Cape, 1955), Chapters 1–7.

16. John le Carré, *The Spy Who Came In From The Cold* (London: Gollancz, 1963).

17. Dashiell Hammett, *The Maltese Falcon*, 2nd edn (London: Cassell, 1930); Raymond Chandler, *The Long Goodbye* (London: Hamish Hamilton, 1953).

18. See for example J. G. Cawelti, *Adventure, Mystery, and Romance* (University of Chicago, 1976), p. 83.

19. A. Conan Doyle, *The Hound of the Baskervilles* (London: Newnes, 1902).

20. This is of considerable sociological significance; see my *Thrillers*, Part IV, §.2 for further analysis.

21. Mickey Spillane, *Day of the Guns*, 3rd edn (London: Corgi, 1966), pp. 137–8.

22. Frederick Forsyth, *The Day of the Jackal* (London: Hutchinson, 1971).

23. The Parker series is published in London by Coronet Books/Hodder Fawcett; the Executioner and Revenger Series are both published in London by Sphere Books.

24. I have borrowed this latter term from J. G. Cawelti. See my *Thrillers*, pp. 211f.

25. See my *Thrillers*, pt. IV, §.1.

26. J. Habermas, *Legitimation Crisis* (London: Heinemann Educational, 1976), pp. 93–4.

4. True to Me Always: An Analysis of Women's Magazine Fiction

BRIDGET FOWLER

This chapter explores the plot structures and images of society contained in the fiction of low-priced magazines for women. It is suggested that the writers' world-view vacillates between heroic individualism and fatalism. There is no evidence of any sustained radical critique of society, despite the choice of the 1930s as the period from which the magazines were sampled. In the absence of any close correspondence with models from the élite novel, attention is drawn to the problem of how the popular writer aims the stories to be read. For this reason, one story is analysed in depth, indicating the devices used to signal the preferred meaning of character, plot action, etc. The particular function of domestic stories is to provide 'pastoral' advice on how life can and should be lived.

The idea is to give the bored factory girl or worn-out mother of five a dream-life in which she pictures herself – not actually as a duchess (that convention has gone out) but as, say, the wife of a bank-manager. Not only is a five-to-six pound a week standard of life set up as the ideal, it is tacitly assumed that this is how working-class people really *do* live. The major facts are simply not faced. It is admitted, for instance, that people sometimes lose their jobs; but then the dark clouds roll away and they get better jobs instead. No mention of unemployment as something permanent and inevitable, no mention of the dole, no mention of trade unionism. No suggestion anywhere that there can be any-

thing wrong with the system *as a system*; there are only
individual misfortunes, which are generally due to somebody's wickedness and can in any case be put right in the last
chapter. Always the dark clouds roll away, the kind employer raises Alfred's wages, and there are jobs for everyone
except the drunks . . . .

(George Orwell, 'Boys' Weeklies')

It is often argued that popular literature is so dominated by
the need for commercial success and the fantasy desires of its
audience that it does not merit the serious internal analysis that
works of art receive.[1] Yet these external pressures do not shape
popular literature in an entirely random manner: certain
structural patterns can be uncovered, although these are not all
obvious from a superficial reading. Here the pioneering work of
the Russian Formalist, Vladimir Propp,[2] has much to offer. His
study of fairy-tales in 1928 is still the most fertile starting point
for popular literature, because it illuminates the underlying
rules governing the construction of these stories, or rather of
those stories that survived as part of the intellectual capital of
the community storyteller. Propp's work has justly been
subjected to radical criticism, principally by Lévi-Strauss, but
such criticism has also been fired by admiration for his
scholarship and insight. Propp's innovation lay in drawing
attention to the predictable rhythms of a uniform plot and in
diagnosing in this the source of an appeal quite unfathomable
to the basic assumptions of Romantic theories of art. No later
study of popular culture can afford to ignore him. His method
lay in sweeping aside all variations in character and setting in
order to display the unity in the structure of plots. His work
revealed that, whether in elaborated or skeletal form, there
were always certain key elements, or relationships between
elements, on which stories were dependent. Central among
these were the idea of an initial period of tranquillity, the entry
of evil in the figure of a villain or, alternatively, the perception
of an unsatisfied desire which the hero must fulfil, the solitary
heroic quest to find the villain and/or to annul this lack, the
return, the transfiguration of the hero into a grand personage,
the restoration of a happy state. Altogether thirty-one structural elements or functions were elaborated, although of course

any one story might not possess the completeness of the ideal type and the actual telling of the story permits more flexibility than the building-block structure would imply.

Propp's treatment of the fairy-story as a totality rather than as a number of fragmented elements meant that his paramount interest was in abstracting the actions of the stories rather than other aspects of their content. Actions, or functions, had certain fixed numbers of transformations (e.g. magical helpers might be replaced by religious references) but Propp made a firm distinction between functions, which were structural, and accounts of motivation, character descriptions, settings, and so on, which, as we have seen, he viewed as variable. This is the reason for his view that the type of characters used (e.g. rich, poor, etc.) or their motivation (gullible, avaricious, etc.) are seen as 'multiform, picturesque and colourful [providing] the folktale with its brilliance, charm and beauty'.

But the attempt to avoid systematic analysis of the content is a perilous mistake.³ Stories are patterned as much by their content as by their plot. No analysis can afford to miss the significance of a noble hero (say, a king) marrying a common heroine (say, a shepherdess). It is in this respect as much as in considering plot that we need to find out what are the areas of creative freedom and what are the areas of convention, or uniformity. But despite his striking depiction of favourite Russian fairy-tale characters, such as the witch Baba Jaga in her bizarre house revolving on chickens' legs, Propp abstains from any deeper questioning of content categories.

It is partly for this reason that the recent revival of interest in the genre of melodrama is worth exploring. Melodrama emerged in the eighteenth century in opposition to the tragic art of the aristocracy. Like the fairy-story studied by Propp and like tragedy from which it was born, melodrama revolves round a strong plot, stark moral contrasts and the minimum of individual psychological complexity. Unlike these earlier forms, which discussed the nature of social order or the state, the arena of melodrama is firmly fixed within the family and local community. Its heroes and heroines are ordinary citizens, not rulers preoccupied with problems of descent or legitimacy. Struggles over family property, the successful preservation of personal reputation or the integrity of the community become its motive force.

Women's magazine stories, on which I want to concentrate, contain all the elements of the melodramatic mode. It is conventional to be quickly dismissive of 'mere melodrama'. I shall argue that this is a mistake, for two reasons. First, such literature is a key source for the articulation and reinforcement of certain moral norms. As such it has a strategic role, especially amongst an urban working-class audience without formal religious interests and without other links to dominant bourgeois culture, such as through the medium of books. The domestic story of women's magazines, like the classical novel, creates a world 'forsaken by God' (Lukács) and foreign even to secular asceticism. Nevertheless, it has taken over one of the central functions of religion in its unambiguous moral passages, its provision of standards or expectations for life, its revelation of desire, resembling the confidence of the confessional, and its fostering of a spirit of interior quasi-Puritan self-scrutiny. If we were to characterise the place of domestic stories in the ideological division of labour it would be by the distinctive combination of such a pastoral element with key ideas about romantic love, private consumption and status groups.[4]

The second reason why melodrama merits more than casual dismissal is that any analysis of melodramatic form shows that it is susceptible of different types of development. It can be used for expressing ideas critical of the social order or it can be used as an equivalent to bread and circuses, providing fantasy compensation, consolation and diversion for its readers. Thus Annie S. Swan, OBE, much revered writer of women's fiction, writes in 1934: '. . . one of the functions of the imagination is to carry us as far as possible from the realm of reality. Without it, life indeed would be drab, often unendurable'.[5] But, despite Swan's assumptions, the conventions which emerge in popular literature are not indicative of iron laws about popular taste. There is no fixed need for a certain amount of fantasy gratification. Much more accurately, literature is shaped by the balance or, indeed, clash of certain *social forces*. In this respect eighteenth-century and early nineteenth-century French popular literature is particularly absorbing because it shows contrasting paradigms as to what a popular story should consist of.[6] Thus, prior to the 1789 Revolution, stories frequently figured exemplary heroes and heroines conducting a moral crusade against corrupt aristocrats. The symbol of unlegitimised power was the aristocrat's rape of the heroine. Far from being blithely optimistic, the stories often related a tragic end for the hero, unable to free himself from the trap of economic necessity or political intrigue. In contrast, French Restoration drama was also melodramatic but the form had become trivialised. Happy endings replaced tragic ones, *deus ex machina* figures appeared to solve plot contradictions and suffering was now attributed naively to the evil of individuals, so that whether these were lumpen proletariat or aristocratic made no difference to the story. Thomas Elsaesser has commented on this shift:

> Since the overtly conformist character of such [later] drama is quite evident, what is interesting is certainly not the plot structure, but whether the conventions allow the author to dramatise in his episodes actual contradictions in society and genuine clashes of interests in the characters . . . All this is to say that there seems a radical ambiguity attached to the melodrama . . . Depending on whether the emphasis fell on the odyssey of suffering or the happy ending, and on where and in what context the rupture (moral conversion of the villain . . .) occurred, . . . melodrama would appear to function either subversively or as escapism — categories which are always relative to the given historical and social context.[7]

In the following account we shall show that 1930s popular stories can be seen, like the most conservative of French Restoration dramas, as legitimating the social order and thus indirectly providing social control. Especially significant are identities between these two periods in the role of luck, the centrality of the happy ending, the individualising of evil and the solution of problems by moralising or by magic. That this is not simply the necessary outcome of the new capitalist domination of the book trade is shown by the enormous commercial success in the 1840s of Reynolds' cheap

serialised stories, which sold even larger numbers than
Dickens' works, and yet contained an uncompromising, if
somewhat anachronistic, attack on the aristocracy as a parasitic class.

But despite the 'radical ambiguity' inherent in melodrama it
is not at all clear precisely to which social currents and
contradictions popular literature responds nor what elements
of class or party articulation bear on its content. Thus the
character of stories offered by authors to magazines, the process
by which gate-keepers such as fiction editors choose what
seems right for their publication, the pressures exerted by the
magazine's existence as a corporate commercial enterprise: all
remains uncharted.

Furthermore, we need to specify more clearly what is meant
by the 'social control' consequences of such popular fiction as
women's magazine stories. This requires a fuller analysis of the
structure of the stories and the images of society they incorpo-
rate. We shall begin to provide this below. Secondly, it requires
some preliminary ground-clearing about the mechanics of
control or influence. One question which immediately needs
answering concerns the origin of the attitudes implicit in the
magazine stories.

The absence of didacticism in this fiction and the prevalent
tone of 'relaxing domestic entertainment' makes it probable
that the stories reveal not just the attitudes of the author but
that these are at any rate *partially shared* by the readership. As
one reader said to me, 'You like to read something nice, even if
real life isn't like that'. Those for whom these particular images
of society have lost all plausibility are very unlikely to have
continued in the 1930s to read the stories week by week, just as
those in the Women's Movement now are unlikely to submit to
the implicit criticism of their thought represented by the sexism
of modern stories. Having said this, it is equally wrong to make
any simplistic equation of the mental universe found in the
stories with that of the readers. It is very likely that the practical
action of the readers emerges also from *other* cultural values –
such as those of dissent and militancy – which are totally absent
from the magazine universe, while the adherence to some story
values may well be more at the level of the ideal or fantasy than
concrete reality. It is in this sense that the story-world is at

once known and familiar territory and a region of tranquil escape.

It is not enough merely to map this territory and thus to uncover the cultural belief-systems relating to class, sex-roles, country and city life, and so on, which are embodied in these stories. Understanding them properly means linking these ideas to particular interests. Ultimately, too, we must elucidate the position of these magazines in the power structure by showing the elective affinities between their stories and more general class world-views. The Durkheimian or Freudian assumption that such ideas are moulded entirely by unconscious collective currents emanating from the whole society is an unrealistic abdication from analysis.

The alternative is not to argue that a direct Machiavellian interest in social control explains the character of this fiction. Although when stripped of the invitations to escape and live out fantasies the stories display the ambitions, hopes and world-images of a heroic or progressive bourgeoisie, it is also obvious that such literary values do not resemble *mechanically* the social thought and the tensions of the inter-war ruling class or even, more loosely, the 'middle classes'. Popular literature is a form in which conventions, literary traditions, are more immediately apparent than in 'high' art. Archaic elements litter its pages, both in style and the images of society it employs. It is these which make the fantasy potential of the stories so powerful. All of these factors serve to *reinforce* culturally the normality of the status quo situation. At its most conscious, such social control is exerted by editorial selection on the basis of practical rules of thumb about the genre and 'what the audience wants' which filter out any ideologically or stylistically alien product. Part of the success of the dominant class lies in the creation of the tacit assumptions that this selection process is routine and has been cut off from the area perceived as ideology and propaganda. It is consequently not seen as a form of class cultural control but as *axiomatically* following from the nature of the genre. At rare historical moments the homology between the genre and dominant or middle-class world views may be unmasked. This may even acquire the character of a political campaign with considerable popular acceptance, for example in the Allende Government ban on Mickey Mouse, but the conditions under which this may happen are fragile and not entirely clear.

Methodology

I have chosen for analysis stories published in popular twopenny magazines and sampled them at four-weekly intervals for the period mid-1929 to mid-1930. The sample was increased by adding magazines of a similar type from later in the 1930s if publication was not started until then. One magazine, *People's Friend*, was sampled twice to see if any consistent differences occurred in the stories relating to the order in which they appeared in each issue. In addition, some serialised stories were also studied since these contain scope for fuller characterisation and richer details of setting and speech than are available to the short-story writer.

The magazines were chiefly bought by working-class readers, although the evidence for this is impressionistic, gathered second-hand from accounts in George Orwell's 'Boys' Weeklies', Richard Hoggart's *The Uses of Literacy*, Robert Roberts' *The Classic Slum*, and Annie S. Swan's *My Life*.[8] A survey carried out in 1946 included three of these magazines and largely confirms these impressions. Since the other magazines sampled are homogeneous in editorial tone, format and price to those studied in this survey[9] it seems reasonable to conclude that their readership was the same. The profound stratification of culture into 'high' or 'low' according to the rules about social honour formed by different status groups, makes it unlikely that the cheaply produced and luridly illustrated magazines popular in the back-streets' newsagents would have had much of a sale in the middle-class suburbs. There is one women's magazine in this price range, *Home Chat*, which was reported in the 1946 sample to have equal numbers of readers in each of the three income groups (AB, C and DE). Interestingly enough, this has not just an entirely different and more sober format but also a different genre of story from the others sampled. This wider appeal made it to some extent a predecessor of *Woman* which was, in 1937, to break through from a class to a mass readership, following the innovation of cheap colour technology. *Answers* and *Tit-bits* also aimed at a different market from

Magazine	Date sampled	Publisher	Number of stories sampled	Range of authors appearing within each sample: their sex, as indicated by Christian names	
I Women's					
Women's Way	July 1929–May 1930	D. C. Thomson	12 + serial	9	9 female
Weekly Welcome	June 1929–May 1930	D. C. Thomson	13 + serial	7	4 female / 3 sex unknown
Red Letter	Jan. 1930–Dec. 1930	D. C. Thomson	13	8	3 female / 2 male / 3 sex unknown
Family Star	Aug. 1934–June 1935	D. C. Thomson	12		Authors' names unpublished
Home Chat	July 1929–June 1930	Amalgamated Press	15 + serial	16	12 female / 2 male / 2 sex unknown
The Oracle	July 1933–June 1934	Amalgamated Press	13		Authors' names unpublished
My Weekly	July 1929–June 1930	John Leng & Co	13	11	10 female / 1 sex unknown
People's Friend	July 1929–July 1930	John Leng & Co	14 (28 in total) + serial	23	12 female / 2 male / 9 sex unknown
Lucky Star	Sept. 1935–Aug. 1936	Newnes & Pearson	13		Authors' names unpublished
Silver Star	Oct. 1937–Sept. 1938	C. Arthur Pearson	12		Authors' names unpublished

Magazine	Date sampled	Publisher	Number of stories sampled	Range of authors appearing within each sample: their sex, as indicated by Christian names	
Family Herald	June 1929–May 1930	J. T. Elvidge	12	9	3 female 1 male 5 sex unknown

Total of women's popular stories sampled: 160 (including 4 serials)

II General

Answers	July 1929–July 1930	Amalgamated Press	14 + serial	11	2 female 6 male 3 sex unknown
Tit-bits	July 1929–July 1930	Newnes & Pearson	14 + serial	14	2 female 9 male 3 sex unknown

Total of popular stories sampled: 190 (including 6 serials)

III Middle-class Control

Women's Journal	July 1929–July 1930	Amalgamated Press	13	13	9 female 4 male
The Lady	July 1929–July 1930	The Lady Ltd	12 + serial	11	8 female 1 male 2 sex unknown

Total of middle-class magazine stories sampled: 26 (including serial)

Total of all stories sampled: 216

that of the women's magazines, whose traditionally narrow range (fiction, home, cooking, fashion features, letters, and 'personal problems') was a product of the drastic pruning of the more general and, specifically, of the more overtly *political* content of women's magazines in the early nineteenth century.[10] Both these billed themselves as 'family entertainment', included articles by well-known politicians, businessmen and journalists aimed at stimulating public debate, and seem likely to have had in the 1930s both a wider circulation amongst the middle class and a greater readership amongst men than had, say, *My Weekly* or *The Oracle*.[11]

As an attempt to disentangle what is distinctive in the literature read in the 1930s by working-class women, two magazines with a middle- and/or upper-class circulation were studied, *The Lady* and *Woman's Journal*.[12] The most profound contrast here was in style, the latter magazines having all the ornaments of high culture, notably the use of figures of speech, complex vocabulary and syntax and literary allusions. On occasion there is a strong element of conspicuous literary consumption about such language, rather than communicative effect. In their stories' content there are also divergencies with the working-class magazines: a far greater range of subjects appears, particularly in *The Lady*, where the traditional romantic love plot has a much smaller place. The treatment of character lacks the straightforward dualism of the working-class women's magazines: bigamy figures here, for example, but without the melodramatic moral panic it provokes in the main sample. *Woman's Journal*, like *Home Chat* in the main sample, specialises in stories featuring divorce as unnecessary and recounting the revival of romantic love and sexual attraction within marriage. In this magazine there are some hints of Freudian theory in the writing, alien of course to the black-and-white ethical world-view of the cheaper magazines. But, despite this, there endures an extraordinary harmony between the apparent needs of the unconscious and the bourgeois virtues of family, work and responsibility.

The General Themes: Plots

If we are to categorise this fiction as a whole, we need to assess what the stories are 'about'. How closely do they resemble Propp's model of the fairy-story? Put another way, how are elements of reality selected, manipulated, incorporated with fantasy by the author? How is class handled and what assumptions about, say, sex-roles underlie the character portrayal and moral meaning of these fictional stories? A problem exists, clearly, as to how precisely these stories are *interpreted*. When we say, as sociologists, that a story really deals with the problem of social order, or conflict, is this how the readers perceive it? As an example: if the readers experience class in prestige or personal terms, without integrating individuals into wider structural relationships, it presumably does not add anything to the readers' interpretation of the story for the sociologist to state that its effect is to deny the existence of social conflict. In other words, we must be careful not to attribute to readers the general statements about the handling of class, sex-roles, and so on, in the stories which sociologists might note. We do not yet know what assessment of the stories is made by the readers nor how far the general world-view of the authors becomes part of the mental apparatus of the readers.

We need initially to go into more detail to characterise the 'domestic story' introduced earlier. A preliminary, perhaps even obvious observation is that the genre is constituted by three features: a serious tone, psychological realism and an emphasis on moral education. These elements immediately remove *Home Chat* from the canon, a magazine that on other counts I have already noticed as being peripheral to the major sample. *Home Chat* tends to adopt a more light-hearted style of writing and to be preoccupied more by the surface of things, such as minute issues of manners or mechanisms by which romantic lovers can avow their passion, rather than by the deeper social and personal issues handled in the other magazines. It is probably wrong to see the wider readership as itself influencing in any direct way the divergent style since later mass magazines such as *Woman* and *Woman's Own* have continued the domestic story genre. I would guess this realistic situating of stories has a stronger attraction for women, at any rate for working-class readers, permitting as it does some means of identification deriving from the everyday life with which they must struggle. In all these 'realistic' stories, it might be said that certain experiences are being hinted at, a certain recognition of everyday difficulties is made and that from identification with this follows the readers' desire to complete the story, to see how such issues are resolved. Romantic love is frequently the mainspring of these stories because it bears the promise that individuals can, together, transcend structural contradictions. Just as fundamental differences in life-chances may be neutralised in the stories by the more powerful electric attraction of the romantic tie, so also any discrepancies between life as it is and life as it was expected to be can pale into insignificance once matrimonial love exists to compensate for them. Implicitly, unhappiness, dissatisfaction and deviance can be read from these stories as simply the consequence of insufficient love: 'the good relationship' is the solvent of all or any troubles felt by the disconnected individual.

The domestic story is not a tragic genre. Only five of the stories sampled fit this category, and these often resemble an older strand of Gothic novel. For example, in one of these, the hero marries a beautiful woman he has been warned against only to discover she is mad and incurably ill. By contrast, the model domestic story bathes its world in a sunny light of optimism, conclusions are invariably happy and, more importantly, all 'ends' are tied up, all villains killed off. Most noticeably, there is no possibility of outcomes having 'costs', or of the continued rankling of any event occurring earlier. Thus an illegitimate baby, say, may die at birth, signifying the moral wrong the heroine must expiate, but such terrible suffering is invariably over by the time the conclusion is reached. In brief, there is no struggle of 'right' against 'right', the values of an old order against those of a new, nor, as we shall see, is there any sustained critique of contemporary British society.

The quintessential women's magazine story, like the classical novel, has a plot structured around the pursuit of romantic love. Ninety-three of the stories sampled fit this description. Amongst these, there is a generic type of love-story which fits very closely the functions in the fairy-story dissected by Propp. Reproduced over and over again is the account of a peaceful initial period marred either by the breaking of social rules *or* a sense of lack, misunderstandings or physical separations keeping hero and heroine apart, tests to be undergone before obstacles are finally surmounted, followed by the happy marriage. They differ from Propp's stories in that the commitment of the hero to a set of ethical rules occurs more often than a physical fight as a test of courage, and the heroines more often have an active role in combating forces of evil.

Western popular culture has nurtured the ideal of 'perfect competition' in romantic love. Paradoxically, while many of these plots (25 stories) do revolve around such a transcending of the market boundaries of good looks, wealth and social class, nevertheless stories with a quite different structure also proliferate. The sociologist might interpret all these stories as dealing with the relationship between the cultural ideal of open romantic love and the reality of deeply stratified society. But again it is difficult to know whether this is in all cases the *readers'* interpretation of events or even whether the author wants this general 'meaning' to be extracted from the relationship of individuals in the story. There are in fact as many stories in which the apparent inequalities between hero and heroine magically disappear by the end as there are stories of the chorus girl married to duke variety. For example, stories often continue the device used by writers of the East End in the 1880s, such as Gissing, in which 'cryptoproletarian' characters are used.[13] The heroine, in love with a doctor, may emerge ultimately to be not truly working class but a foundling taken from a slum and brought up by working-class parents; a hero may be cut off by his father and family and forced to live a working-class mode of existence; or an unexpected inheritance may alter the total dependence of the lower-class heroine on the upper-class hero. Thus, in social origin the hero and heroine may ultimately turn out to be alike although the bulk of the story has concerned the proving of their fitness to marry each other. It is tempting to align these stories with the earlier fairy-story in which once the princess had brought herself to kiss the beast or marry the frog, he became a prince. The analogy makes the class insult even more apparent.

Alternatively, stories may contrast reality with illusion and equate the discovery of reality with happiness. Thus a heroine who is the 'good girl next door', homologous in class to the hero, may be counterposed to the vampish sophisticated charm of the rich upper-class woman. In this case the hero may be temporarily entrapped in the world of the evil seductress until accessible for reconversion to the correct moral sense of the heroine. It is noticeable here that the contradictions between the culturally ideal and reality are masked. Thus because the upper-class woman is invariably portrayed as dangerous, there is no sense of loss souring the victory of the homely girl over her higher-ranking rival. Real difficulties in the choice of action are therefore minimised.

The plot complication provoked by class differences by no means exhausts the full range of romantic themes. Hero and heroine may be beset by quite different obstacles or become estranged from each other by gulfs in attitudes or behaviour. In one story the heroine, an industrial militant, initially confronts with hostility the boss she is ultimately to marry, in another the happy-go-lucky girl member of a gang becomes converted to the straight and narrow (and also to the detective hero) through her repugnance to child-kidnapping tactics. In other stories heroes are assumed to be too insensitive, too frivolous or too dependent to merit the heroine's love but finally manage to prove their worth. Misunderstandings play a crucial role in accounting for estrangements between hero and heroine: explanation and reform are thus the two principal mechanisms by which plot complications can be resolved.

Finally, there is a type of romantic plot which focuses particularly on sacrifice and its rewards. The heroine is presented with a dilemma in which duty opposes itself to the little hard-earned pleasures of everyday life: for example, the sudden request to mind a child restricts the freedom of action 'natural' to an unmarried woman, or a distant relative needs help with harvesting just at the time a holiday is planned. The heroine distinguishes herself from other women by her capacity to give up her own interests. In so doing she is shown as creating for herself an opportunity for romantic love which the other women lack. Thus duty and desire are shown as mutually reinforcing each other.

The archetypal ending of the women's magazine story is the union of romantic love with marriage, but some stories revolve round different themes. The pursuit of happiness *within* marriage is often the subject (42 stories) and, necessarily, these become the arena for recognition of everyday problems which must be removed before the plot is resolved. Adultery, the maltreatment of children, the consequences for family life of chronic poverty, unemployment or alcoholism, the problematic relationship between wage labour ('career') or domestic labour for women, the nature of obligations to the wider family; all appear as subjects. The interesting element here is not so much the predictable bourgeois morality embedded in the ending but the degree of realism employed in the depiction of the problem and the method by which the problem is surmounted, given the underlying commitment to romantic monogamous marriage. In particular, it can be suggested that the difficulty of harmonising the claims of 'reality' with the romantic marriage imperative gives rise to a curious subgenre of the domestic story, the bigamy plot. Bigamy, I would argue, reflects in these stories not its frequency in reality nor even its role as ominous spectre to the innocent spouse, but rather springs from the literary need to find some way of preserving intact such a romantic imperative with a desire to depict honestly the potential horrors of the marital state. So a 'good' partner locked in an unhappy marriage can be released for his true destiny in a happy, romantic marriage by the discovery that his earlier wedding was illicit. Bigamy plots thus permit the ending of marriage without the legitimation of divorce, for in this fiction, despite the date, divorce was never seen as a way out. Bigamy altogether appears in ten stories and as a subplot in five others. It thus figures in quite a sizeable proportion of marriage plots. As a dramatic device it is ideal, for it can account for why a highly approved character can find himself in an unhappy marriage. Either it is the result of the guile of the offending partner or it is the consequence of a good partner's false belief that the bad partner has died. Even where the intention to commit bigamy is absent, however, there is no lessening of the horror surrounding its discovery. The ritual damage inherent in the infraction of social structures seems to outweigh any ethical concern with motives. In the stories bigamy is viewed as so shameful that horrific sacrifices on the part of the good are required before social order can once again be restored. Thus bigamously conceived offspring invariably die; the heroine must submit herself to the worst conditions of wage labour; total isolation of approved characters and *anomie* prevail.

The form of the bigamy plot permits an unhappy marriage to be transformed into a happy one. Other plots have strong structural similarities: pre-marital and extra-marital affairs always being shown as destructive of social order and always dividing those involved into an aggressor and a weak victim, the latter being led astray by the untamed passions of the predator. There is no recognition that pregnancy followed by marriage might be a well-established pattern. This reinforces points made earlier as to the dependency of the story-writers on dominant or official values rather than on accommodative working-class morality.

Finally, there is the question of divorce or separation. These are never seen as an acceptable alternative to marriage in the story world, despite their occasional advocacy in the adjacent correspondence columns. Nevertheless, some plots depend on this theme. In *My Weekly* and *Weekly Welcome* these either revolve around obstacles temporarily separating husband and wife, just as hero and heroine had been separated in the romantic love story, or there is a semi-comic episode held by either partner to indicate a suspected decline in romantic love within the marriage but in fact demonstrating the reverse. Only in the more marginal *Home Chat* is there any consideration of divorce as a subject for serious contemplation by approved characters. And in these stories they emerge as being mistaken about their interests. An accident or a benevolent outsider reveals their potential loss from divorce and convinces them of the foolishness of their plans.

Despite this rejection, there is some recognition in the magazine plots of changes within British society, particularly in those cases where the arena of the plot is defined by *sexual politics* or disputes over sex roles. Here the question of how women should act is faced in a context in which some other social changes may also be acknowledged. These include such areas as the rationalisation of work (not seen of course as to any one group's advantage), the precarious economic base of the landed gentry, the decline of tradition and the greater salience of friendship over blood-ties.

One area, which becomes the subject of a number of stories,

is the contradiction between the relative liberation of women
outside marriage and their position within it. This contradiction, or disparity, gives the story its tension and suspense, and
is located most frequently in a clash between generations,
although it may receive its dynamic force from dissatisfactions
felt by husband and wife or from remedial work for family
problems taken by an outsider. For example a new daughter-
in-law alienates her traditional mother-in-law by her efficient
partnership in farm management with her husband. With the
birth of the first baby the daughter-in-law sheds her non-family
interests. Or again a young wife's nostalgic longing for the
freedom of her work before marriage and children is alluded to
in one story where husband and wife temporarily swap roles.
After this imaginary experiment both recognise with new eyes
the greater satisfactions inherent in the conventional segre-
gated roles and embrace whole-heartedly an order of things
which had before seemed unjust. In all these cases orthodox
sexual roles are questioned and alternatives explored but the
traditional order within the family is reconsecrated. The
mechanism by which this conclusion is reached is the revelation of a hidden hand ensuring the harmony between conventional morality and personal desire.

Images of Society

Up to now the stories have been treated as totalities. This
section, at the risk of fragmentation, aims to consider certain
elements of the stories taken collectively. We shall inevitably
need to go beyond content analysis to search out the implicit
meanings or world-views which can illuminate the manifest
content. It is appropriate to ask, first, how inequality is handled
in this fiction as a whole. Implicitly many of these stories can be
seen as providing 'theodicies' of good and bad fortune. In doing
so they tend to vacillate between ethical and magical explanations of social inequality and in particular alternate between a
naïve individualistic theory of social rewards and a fate-
determined good luck.

From the many possible readings of inequality only the
following interpretations and explanations appear in the
stories. We assume therefore that these ideas have a key

significance in the writers' perception of social inequality. They are:

(1) the significance of a work ethic viewed both as recipe for success and as a moral imperative;
(2) the frequency of social mobility, both up and down;
(3) the portrayal of wealth as permitting the gratification of desire, not as engendering status group or class formation;
(4) allied to this, the perception of snobbery as the crucial ethical problem in an unequal society.

The importance of work emerges with overwhelming clarity throughout the magazine stories. Work is considered intrinsically valuable and not merely instrumentally tied to other values, such as wealth. The ethic is universalistic. Hence a life of conspicuous leisure, even if highly civilised, is viewed as unjustifiable parasitism.

Descriptions of heroes typically include some reference to commitment to work, as though this were a necessary affidavit of fitness for the heroic role. If a hero is in any sense socially marginal, for example through adolescent rebellion, it is by exhibiting great dedication to work that he establishes himself firmly in the readers' affections and becomes worthy of the heroine's love. Moreover, disillusionment with the work ethic when it fails to create prosperity is severely criticised. Here, as elsewhere in the stories, any incipient response of disenchantment with the material position of the working-class is carefully suffocated.

Despite structural unemployment when these stories were written, their authors' strong moral concern with work implies that any portrayal of the unemployed worker will carry connotations of disapproval. Thus although both valued and disapproved characters are episodically unemployed, *no* valued characters remain unemployed at the *end* of the stories. Furthermore, their eagerness to find work and their dedication to labour in other spheres, such as housework, is consistently emphasised, as though in compensation.

In the delineation of valued characters, unemployment is always seen as arbitrary, the product of fate, beyond human control. Contradictory to this, but nevertheless pervasive, is the assumption that in the long run it is only the morally inadequate who consistently fail to get jobs. 'Spoilt, weak and selfish' is how one long-term unemployed man is labelled and this typifies the fictional treatment of the endemically unemployed as a whole. Thus unemployment is a sign of moral danger, a 'deviant' role – like illness – that may be occupied only for a certain length of time and only as long as a genuine desire to return to work remains undiminished.[14]

Yet somewhat surprisingly, despite the Smilesian ideology of effort above, the stories portray success as being due to good luck as often as it is to more institutionalised ladders of achievement. Such fortuitous ascent occurs, for example, when sudden wealth is made by gambling or mineral prospecting: areas in which the degree of rational control by the actor is relatively small and the activities more functionally autonomous within the whole economic system. Social mobility through entertainment and sport is also important: these avenues have, of course, traditionally been regarded as the substitute means of mobility, success depending here on the good fortune of innate talent rather than on the promise of reward through work.

A marked improvement in life-chances occurs very frequently in these stories. Indeed the existence of systematic connections of this kind between those of high and those of low status is probably a universal mythic structure. If we ignore the 'cryptoproletarians' whose 'real' nature is eventually recognised and their condition changed accordingly, and if we omit the 'hypergamous' Cinderella-like marriage, substantial changes of fortune still occur in over a third of the sampled stories. The distribution of such change is not random, it occurs much more frequently to men than women (a third of the heroes, but only a seventh of the heroines) since a 'good' marriage is the mechanism by which the pay-offs for women are obtained. Social mobility is also a premium awarded almost exclusively to approved characters: put simply, such mobility is a reward for virtue, although not all the virtuous poor end up with goodies bestowed upon them.

The most frequent means by which improvement is achieved 'institutionally' is by promotion at work, usually simply as a result of assiduous labour but sometimes as a reward for technical innovation. Educational channels are also seen as the bright boy's way out of the working class. What is strikingly absent is the linking of material improvement to fraternalistic solidarity. One of the crucial 'silences' of this genre of popular stories is precisely this missing mode of class action.

But what of those whose success depends on some obscure process of lucky chance or on the more open avenues of entertainment and sport (33 'luck' and 8 entertainment or sport)? The inheritance of property is a key factor in the 'luck' category: it is lucky rather than structural despite the key place of inheritance in the economy because in these stories it appears not as a customary expectation but as the unexpected consequence of a wayward whim or a little-known benefactor. Similarly dependent on chance is the gift of a job – the employer figuring here as a *deus ex machina*, intervening within the ranks of the unemployed to reward the good by acts of personal patronage. Poverty is further escaped from in this fiction by lucky finds, success in competitions, lucky encounters. A range of characters is depicted tapping rich veins of opportunity for glamorous achievement in film stardom, top golfing, composing popular songs, tap-dancing, etc.

In the stories, an undercurrent image of a society is presented in which opportunity is determined by impenetrable factors outside one's own control, a society which is far from being rationalised and calculable but is instead personal and arbitrary. Thus, paralleling the literary vision of an ordered industrial society there is an irrational world of arbitrary poverty and unhappiness, mediated on the one hand by magical escapes and on the other by a vague compensatory ethic of sacrificial acceptance.[15]

Portrayal of the Rich

As a group the rich are composed in the stories both of valued and of disapproved individuals. They are situated socially either in a landed gentry/aristocracy class or as prominent businessmen. The more middle-class the readership of a magazine, the more likely it is to contain stories about aristocrats rather than businessmen.

If one were to isolate the dominant structure of feeling connoted by the rich it would be that essentially the rich are like you and me. They may be conspicuous as consumers (perceived as acceptable and natural) but they are not fundamentally alien or remote. There is not to be found in this portrayal the élitist view that the rich develop modes of living, sensitivities, tastes and moralities superior to others as a consequence of their economic privilege.

The sense of an underlying unity between classes which is premissed on the democratic view of the rich is sustained by presenting the orbit of the rich firmly in the *domestic* sphere.[16] Class relationships rarely appear in work settings, thus tending to obviate the sense of deprivation or powerlessness which might be evoked in working-class readers. Secondly, wealth can be portrayed more as a *decorative trimming* than as a vital social difference, by focusing, as the stories do, on peaks of consumption – highly ritualised occasions like balls, hunting, dinner-dances – and on the acquisition of stereotyped objects (Rolls-Royces, mansions, diamond rings and nannies are the most popular). But it can be implied that these coexist with the same everyday experiences of life and the same values or interests as the readers and it is this interpretation which the stories present. Only in the case of those clearly demarcated as disapproved characters does money have any adverse effect on character. It is hardly surprising, given this image of the rich, that the paramount ethical and social problem discussed by these writers is snobbery – that particular corruption of wealth in which the rich are attributed a superior status-honour to others. This is one of the few areas in the stories in which a discrepancy between what is done and what ought to be done is overtly recognised and universally condemned. As such it totally eclipses all other possible subjects for critical thought, notably those ideas deriving from a distinctively radical or more profoundly egalitarian value-system. The critique of snobbery must thus be carefully distinguished from any deep-rooted attack on the distribution of material goods. Rather the reverse: its function must be seen as that of shoring up the legitimacy of the economic élite by portraying it as penetrable by low-status outsiders; the élite is democratic in its sympathies and hence the reverse of a monopolistic group.

Money is perceived individualistically as a reward for merit and so is status; the *ramifications* of this into status exclusiveness are radically rejected. Only in a tiny minority of stories (9 out of 103) is there any questioning of the legitimacy of sharp inequalities of wealth. Even in these cases the purity of the conflict view of class is usually destroyed by alternative, more benign, interpretations of the actions and interests of the dominant class. Consequently, poignant stories describing how the blocked lives of the poor contrast with the everyday luxuries of the rich are ended quite dissonantly, with the magical goodwill of a rich reformer, or the promise of beneficial class unity in the future. In this respect the small set of realist stories in the magazines carry on the hopes of the industrial moralists of the 1840s that ultimately the rich and poor need not inhabit different worlds.[17]

Sex Roles in Popular Stories

One element in the quest for romantic marriage in these stories is the competitive struggle between characters who represent different ideas of masculinity and femininity. It is here, *par excellence*, that natural/unnatural oppositions abound and where the confusions between culture (or history) and nature appear most starkly.

The sexual ideal types can be defined most clearly by their opposites, the signs by which the stories' villains are connoted. The possession of demonic magical powers is sometimes retained from the older fairy-story form to add a witch-like aura to the 'bad' female. Even without such magical capacity, such women invariably lack all values except that of sensual experience and possess passions which threaten all established, ordered domestic structures. The terms 'wanton women', 'snake', 'white witch', 'butterfly', a woman 'all out for [her] bit of fun', 'gold-digger', are unambiguous labels of such folk devils. Somewhat more subtly, women who find housework too restricting or who choose to combine work with having children are always castigated, though occasionally such rebellion is a transitory, pre-reform, stage for heroines.

The romantic love ethos of these stories needs to be carefully distinguished from any ideal of passionate love or eroticism. It is an ethic of paradox. It is held to be founded in the attraction of the whole personality, not on sensual, physical bonds. At the same time the heroines *have* no personality: their virtue lies in being unobtrusive, like good servants; they are pretty and highly functional adornments to the routine world of everyday life. More structural variation can be found in the depiction of male characters' personality and occupational patterns. Nevertheless, certain tabooed interests can be uncovered. Note, for example, how villains cluster in the sphere of the arts (jazz music, popular composers, dance-band players) and in the service sector (hairdressing, domestic service), not just in the more predictable role of professional criminal. The frequent choice of these occupations for the negative characters is probably linked to two factors. The first is the incongruity of the work ethic with jobs concerned to satisfy leisure interests. The second is the fact that the professional expertise of musicians, hairdressers, and so on links them to the world of sensual experience, emotion and appearance which is usually portrayed as being of feminine concern. The male domestic servant (a particularly frequent villain) is in a markedly ambiguous position in that there is a clash between the ceremonial and deferential roles legitimised for servants in these stories[18] and the autonomous, active character of valued masculinity. The male servant pollutes social classifications, which makes him the obvious candidate for dishonour.

The largest number of heroes are businessmen or their sons (22 stories) followed by doctors (18 stories). Since, unlike the treatment of doctors, the activities, objectives and dilemmas of businessmen are rarely described by the authors, the significance of the medical profession is perhaps worth commenting on here. Medical practice seems to provide the possibilities for very close analogies between the heroes of domestic fiction and those of the fairy-tale as studied by Propp. The doctor is invariably cast in a benign light, unlike, say, the complex treatment of Lydgate in *Middlemarch* where a struggle between scientific advance, commitment to patients' welfare and status interests is depicted. There are no evil doctors in this fiction. Essentially the doctor is the chivalric knight, like him he must pass various tests and demolish various obstacles before being rewarded with romantic marriage. The tension which appeals

to writers here is that between professional ethical rules and
worldly emotions. The doctor is committed to a discipline
which controls the enormous power he possesses. Thus he can
kill without the crude resort to tools of violence or brutality, so
an allegation of poisoning patients is a frequent complication of
these plots. Or more negatively, by not performing conscien-
tiously what was in his power to do he may potentially fail to
provide a cure for the illness of disapproved characters, hence
affecting the interests of hero or heroine. Thus the stories show
the commitment to professional rules reigning supreme over
other emotions (cash interests, emotional entanglements, and
so forth). The doctor in the magazine stories could be seen as
the reversed image of the chivalric knight who is the quintessential fairy-tale hero: where the latter has a disinterested duty
to kill, the doctor must disinterestedly save. The appearance of
the villain, however, allied the knight's professional duty to kill
with his emotional aims. The absence of any such reinforcement often characterises the tests of the doctor's character,
indicating the more purely ethical interests of the domestic
story.

The Rural Myth

One consistent element in the imaginative structure of these
stories which reinforces their interpretation as modern myths is
the connotation of the country with purity and the city with
constraint, artificiality, force and fraud.[19] Thus there is a
paradox that in magazines circulating extensively amongst an
urban working class, the advanced industrial society is symbol-
ically abolished. Instead valued characters live in cities only
under the spur of necessity. Urban life is fundamentally seen as
restless, atomised and mechanistic, its relations dominated by
the cash nexus. These elements are in turn systematically
removed from country life, which becomes the arena of moral
sentiment and understanding. Popular literature then continues to use a convention which has its roots in the major
literary tradition, most noticeably in the pastoral myth, which
is seen as using rural idealisation to 'attempt to reconcile some
conflict between the parts of a society . . . and . . . to reconcile
the conflicts of an individual in whom those of society will be

mirrored . . . .'[20] The rural myth is not just the product of writers but can also be found in wider cultural settings. For example, it was assumed prior to the rise of modern psychoanalysis that Nature possessed an order which would create harmony within the unbalanced being of the madman.[21] In these 1930s stories the rural characters are not clowns, fools or shepherds totally outside the main action as in the old pastoral but they have much the same purifying force: 'The simple man becomes a clumsy fool who has yet better "sense" than his betters and can say things more fundamentally true; he is "in contact with nature", which the complex man needs to be . . . [and] with the mysterious forces of our nature . . . .'[22] Signs of such idealisation in these stories are that moments of harmony (declarations of love, endings) tend to take place in the country, and that valued characters are countrymen or have their social roots in the country whereas this is much rarer for disapproved characters. Passages that explicitly celebrate the country are not uncommon while celebration of the city and dissatisfaction with the *constraints* of country life are both significantly absent. In the country stories it is particularly clear that if any conflict or strain does appear in such a setting it is invariably attributed to *individuals'* moral failings (greed, over-ascetism, and so on) and never to impersonal clashes of interest. This world is therefore overwhelmingly one of psychological reductionism.

It could be said, in summary, that the function of country life for the writer is to serve as an escape hatch from the full consequences of urban capitalism. As a further bulwark against despair or resentment it plays a role complementary to the widespread social mobility, frequent hypergamous marriage and hidden hands working cunningly on behalf of the good which are such prominent features of the story world.

In conclusion, it has been shown that the ideological structure of the domestic story is that of possessive individualism. The purity of this world-view is nevertheless inconsistently mitigated with two alternative images, first, that the deserving are rewarded by magical good fortune; second, that an organic social order can only be conceptualised in terms of the country. Furthermore, the nature of the realist plot demands some treatment of the consequences for individuals of the experiences of poverty, wage labour and status injuries. In a parallel fashion, the images of women are arranged around the valued ideals of domesticity, self-effacement and altruism, but the demands of realism precipitate the recognition of doubts, dissatisfactions and minor rebellions against the domesticated role. These popular stories are thus underpinned by a bourgeois consciousness. The distinctive contributions of working-class culture are portrayed in a negative light, if at all. The details of this dominant ideology neveretheless represent a particular combination of patterns which is historically variable rather than timeless. The emergence, additionally, of structures of feeling which are dissonant with the ideological recuperation of the ending undoubtedly explains in part the pleasure of these texts.

NOTES

1. See, for example, L. Goldmann, *Pour une Sociologie du Roman* (Paris: Gallimard, 1965), and P. Bourdieu, 'Intellectual field and cultural project' in M. F. D. Young (ed.), *Knowledge and Control* (London: Collier-Macmillan, 1971), pp. 161–88.

2. V. Propp, 'Morphology of the Folk-Tale', Supplement to *International Journal of American Linguistics*, XXIV, 4, part 3, Indiana University Research Center; and 'Fairy Tale Transformations', in L. Matejka and K. Pomorska, *Readings in Russian Poetics* (Cambridge: MIT Press, 1971), pp. 94–114.

3. This criticism was first formulated by Lévi-Strauss. See C. Lévi-Strauss, *La Structure et La Forme* (Paris: Cahiers de L'Institut de Science économique Appliquée, 99, 1960) Série M. No. 7, pp. 25–33.

4. Marx and Engels make this point with compelling clarity in their classic case-study of a popular novel in *The Holy Family*. See *Collected Works*, Vol. 4 (London: Lawrence and Wishart, 1975).

5. A. Swan, *My Life* (London: Ivor Nicholson and Watson, 1934).

6. T. Elsaesser, 'Tales of Sound and Fury', in (no ed.) *Melodrama in the Cinema* (Glasgow: Glasgow Film Theatre, 1977).

7. Ibid., p. 6.

8. G. Orwell, 'Boys' Weeklies' (1938), reprinted in *Collected Essays, Journalism and Letters*, I (Harmondsworth: Penguin, 1980) 505–31; R. Hoggart, *The Uses of Literacy* (London: Chatto and Windus, 1957), pp. 94–104; R. Roberts, *The Classic Slum* (Manchester: Manchester University Press, 1971) Chapter 8; A. Swan, *My Life*.

9. *The Hulton Readership Survey*, compiled by J. W. Hobson and M. Henry (London: The Hulton Press, 1947).

10. C. L. White, *Women's Magazines* (London: Michael Joseph, 1970), pp. 23–57.

11. *The Hulton Survey*, Table 4, pp. 13–15, shows that in 1946 2.4 per cent of men in income group AB read *Tit-bits*, 2.8 per cent of income group C and 3.6 per cent of DE. *Answers* had a similar, rather smaller circulation.

12. *The Hulton Survey*, Tables 7–9, pp. 17–19.

13. P. J. Keating, *The Working Classes in Victorian Fiction* (London: Routledge & Kegan Paul, 1971) discusses the use of 'cryptoproletarians' in Victorian novels.

14. T. Parsons, *The Social System* (New York: Free Press, 1951) Chapter X, uses this representation of illness.

15. R. Williams, *The Long Revolution* (Harmondsworth: Penguin, 1965) especially in Chapter II, 'The Analysis of Culture', notes the importance of magical escapes in Victorian popular literature.

16. See Lukács on this development in the nineteenth-century novel, 'The Intellectual Physiognomy of Literary Characters', in L. Baxendall (ed.), *Radical Perspectives in the Arts* (Harmondsworth: Penguin, 1972), pp. 89–141.

17. See, for example, Disraeli's *Sybil* or Mrs Gaskell's *Mary Barton*, together with the comments of Raymond Williams in *Culture and Society* (Harmondsworth: Penguin, 1961), pp. 99–119, and Alan Swingewood, *The Novel and Revolution* (London: Macmillan, 1975). It is worth emphasising that wealth may be portrayed in several ways without the social control implications of this fiction being significantly altered. For example, Evelyne Sullerot's analysis of contemporary novels presented in photographic form in magazines shows that many of the same features of the story world are shared with my 1930s sample, including the work ethic, heroes who are socially mobile, and heroines who frequently have menial jobs. Yet wealth is systematically presented as leading to unhappiness. She comments:

> What excellent remedies for poor and powerless readers to learn that money not only makes for unhappiness, but soils and corrupts; that their sensitivity and weakness are their trump-cards for this life because there is another aspect of life to success and power (their handicaps becomes their advantages, their weaknesses a strength . . .) . . . the reality of the heart transcends all this and makes a victory out of sacrifice and a triumph out of abnegation!

See E. Sullerot, *La Presse Feminine* (Paris: A. Colin, 1966), p. 123.

18. The inadequacies of the theory that popular literature reflects society are particularly apparent here, for the legitimacy of domestic service prevails untouched in the stories despite census records of the marked trend away from domestic service. Paradoxically, dislike for this form of work is evident even in the magazines' own 'problem page' correspondence.

19. R. Williams, *The Country and the City* (London: Paladin, 1975) has recently traced this theme running through the major literary tradition.

20. W. Empson, *Some Versions of Pastoral* (London: Chatto & Windus, 1950), p. 19.

21. See M. Foucault, *Madness and Civilisation* (London: Tavistock, 1967).

22. W. Empson, *Some Versions of Pastoral*, p. 4.

5. A Career in Love: The Romantic World of Barbara Cartland

ROSALIND BRUNT

Barbara Cartland is The Queen of Romance. This is what her publicity says, and it is amply justified. She has been in *The Guinness Book of Records* since 1976 as the most prolific author in the world and she is also the current all-time world bestseller of romantic fiction. In assuming the royal role, Cartland takes on a celebrity status which is promoted to quite 'camp' excess. At the same time, she readily undertakes to uphold the responsibilities she associates with celebrity. She firmly believes that she has a moral and educative duty to communicate the values of romance both to her immediate readership and to the public-at-large.

In this chapter I want to consider what those values consist of and what Cartland could be said to typify about contemporary romantic writing. Clearly she cannot be understood in terms of a norm or an average. But I would suggest that Cartland is 'typical' in the sense of embodying certain features that are 'characteristic' of romance, while at the same time remaining quite assertively unique and extraordinary as a writer and celebrity. Indeed, it is precisely that exaggerated individuality, and everything about Cartland that makes her an 'extreme case', which helps to highlight particular elements of the kind of romantic world she represents.

The title of the chapter refers to 'making a career' out of 'love' in two senses. First I want to consider romantic fiction in terms of authorship and production; particularly how it connects with the worlds of celebrity and the leisure industry. In this sense, Cartland will figure as an exemplar of the sort of career that modern romantic writers may make out of their work. Secondly, I want to look at how Cartland herself promotes 'love' as the main, or indeed, sole, 'career' for women – both in her fiction and also through a variety of non-fictional media in which she appears 'in her own person' as celebrity and opinion-maker.

In discussing Cartland's own 'career in love', I will draw attention to the context of commodity-production in which contemporary romance operates. Given that romantic fiction is now big business, questions of marketing strategy have become crucial, and the demands of rapid turnover and a short 'shelf life' require packaging and a brand-name. In the fiction market-place, readers are thus encouraged to buy romantic novels not primarily on the basis of their title-descriptions or contents but simply because they *are* 'Cartlands' or 'Cooksons' or 'Heyers' with trademark portraits or easily identifiable 'logos' on their covers. Furthermore, the authorial brand-names of romance are also celebrated in a number of leisure-and-publicity spheres apart from the novels themselves.

I believe it is important to examine these areas of marketing and publicity because readers do not come to romantic novels merely as if they were self-contained isolated texts. We bring to them a range of expectations built up around knowledge of their authors' personas as celebrities who are famous for uttering statements as 'themselves'. Thus in the case of Cartland, she follows a career pattern common to many romantic authors, comes from a journalistic background and then maintains her journalistic interests alongside the production of romantic fiction. It is through journalism that she assumes the public role of advice-giver, opinion-maker and self-promoter, both with by-line magazine and newspaper articles and with non-fiction books of an anthology and memoir type. At the same time she features as 'herself' through advertising, celebrity shows, broadcast and press interviews and merchandising promotions such as store openings and fashion shows.

Promotional effort of this kind is often understood as a matter of mere tautology, of individuals 'famous for being famous'. Where Cartland is concerned, I want to suggest that there is more substance to the celebrity image than that. When her opinions are offered for exchange in the media market, they do not belong just to some insubstantial or trivial persona. Rather, I think that the career Cartland has built for herself is based on views of the world which have some content and some consequence. As a celebrity she certainly provides entertainment value, often of a quite outrageous kind. But she also functions as a moraliser for the times, as an active contributor to the heterogenous cultural baggage that makes up contemporary common sense.

Since readers come to Cartland's fiction with some existing knowledge of the 'interventions' she makes in the public domain, I want to start by examining some of the components of the celebrity aspect of her romantic career. In particular, I will include a consideration of the main views and causes she supports and the production contexts in which they are promoted – with special reference to the 'empire' of romance that Cartland has established. Then I will look in more detail at her views about femininity and the way in which she understands and presents 'love' as *the* feminine vocation. From this perspective I will come finally to the romantic fiction itself and discuss how the narratives function both as entertaining diversions in the leisure industry and also as moral fables with a strong didactic purpose. And here I will suggest that maybe the messages which Cartland sends to her audience are based not so much on the ideal values of a romantic world as on the material conditions of the real one.

Cartland as Celebrity

On the back covers of her novels Barbara Cartland is literally on display, conspicuously made-up, wearing lavish jewellery and a sequinned ballgown. The cover portraits vary from head-and-shoulders to full-length versions which include a golden couch and cherubs bearing flowering cornucopias. Everything declares luxury and no-expense-spared and the pose is appropriately regal. These portraits crystallise a persona that readers of different generations are assumed to know something about already. They make an invitation to enter and inhabit a world that is clearly marked out as different from our own and therefore a diversion, an escape, a special treat for us in much the same way as Cartland lays on exquisitely rich teas for visiting journalists and tourists.

The component values of this different world were first assembled in the 1920s, the era when the Cartland persona was getting established. This was the Britain of the Bright Young People and not, primarily, of encroaching Depression and slump. Cartland entered 'Society' as a debutante, then became a Beaverbrook journalist doing gossip features about her own milieu and, at the age of twenty-four, a novelist. Her first novel, *Jigsaw* (1925) publicised as 'Mayfair with the lid off' established the characteristic Cartland story-theme. It is the tale of a naive heroine discovering London and the dangers of men; how she resists temptation from the wrong sort and eventually marries one of the best sort, a Duke. *Jigsaw* was a rapid success, translated into five languages and running into six editions. It made Cartland a celebrity who was identified with her own heroine's lifestyle and was described as the 'clever' or 'young' Society Girl Author. 'Celebrity' and 'author' came together from the first: 'Miss Barbara Cartland is one of the cleverest members of the younger set. She is not only well-known in Society, but is also making quite a name for herself in the literary world' (*The Sketch*, 14 October 1925).[1]

As her own romantic story goes, Cartland the partying socialite became the Mayfair hostess in 1927 when she accepted her forty-ninth marriage proposal from a scion of the largest private printing company in Britain, McCorquodales. Along with her new duties of drawing-room entertaining, organising charity balls, pageants and matinees, she continued to write and to develop a 'platform'. The idea of a 'platform' was inspired by Beaverbrook, who taught her the need for establishing a set of beliefs through which writers could make their marks as celebrities of substance.

Her first cause proved the most enduring plank of the Cartland platform: persuading women of the need to work harder at their femininity. Her debut as a celebrity advice-giver was in a series of radio talks started in 1929 called 'Making the Best of Oneself' and aimed at exhorting women to make more effort with their own appearance and homes so that they could bring greater happiness to others.

The 1920s are a 'touchstone' period for Cartland, not only because of personal associations of youth, courtship, happy early marriage and celebrity, but also because of the values she considers to be embodied in the era. When she recalls the 1920s it is in terms of dashing excitement and glamour, identified with reckless young men of the officer caste of 'Society' and young women, spirited and innocent, celebrating their class in the leisure interludes before marriage. The 1920s feature also as the most recent contemporary period for the location of Cartland romances. The appeal here is to naturalist authenticity. Since the topic of the heroine's virginity is central both to the narrative and to the moral conventions of her novels, Cartland feels that any location set in a later period would jeopardise the strong claims her novels make to factual accuracy. Moreover, her evocation of the 1920s, as exemplified in the autobiographical memoir *We Danced All Night* (1971), is that of the last Romantic Age in Britain.

But while this is the version that predominates in Cartland's insistent reworking of the period, there is an important subtheme that acknowledges the majority experience of the times and affords some glimpse into 'other people's lives'. It is what goes to make up the second plank of her platform of beliefs: namely, the idea that with Society privileges go public responsibilities and duties towards those less fortunate – together with a specific concern to make the world a better place.

The formative experience for Cartland was the General Strike of 1926, when along with many of her peers she became a strike-breaking 'volunteer'. Her duties took her to parts of London that shocked her with their poverty. In particular, an emotional encounter with a striker's wife led to a reconsideration of her position:

For the majority of young people in the twenties the strike seemed at the time an adventurous exercise; and yet looking back it meant far more than that. It was for me, and a great number of my contemporaries, a milestone. It was a moment when we ceased to be young and carefree and thoughtless, when we began to think . . . . We had always known that because we were born into a certain stratum of society we

had responsibility for those less fortunate. For those who had
lived in great castles on country estates it had been automatic
. . . . But for those like myself, who were poor, there was still
the idea that by the accident of birth one was, with or without
money, the 'Lady Bountiful', . . . I took this all as a matter of
course, just as once or twice a week I would walk beside my
brother's pram and go with Nanny to a cottage to hand over
soup or outworn clothing for those in need.

But in London, as I danced day and night, it seemed as if I
had no responsibility. Yet after the strike I began to think
about those dirty, mean streets, those ragged children, and
those men who had struck because they were denied what
they believed was just for themselves and their families.

Now that my brother was living at home I began to learn
about things that I had only vaguely heard my father
discussing before he was killed – the political implications of
poverty, the right of everyone, whoever he might be, for his
voice to be heard in the running of the nation.[2]

This episode in her life started Cartland on a specifically
political career in the direction of what might be called 'welfare'
or 'radical' Toryism – beliefs she developed in close collabora-
tion with her brother Ronald, whose own political career she
administered until his death at Dunkirk in 1940. Theirs was
the kind of Conservatism that is opposed to *laisser-faire*, places a
high premium on justice and fair play and at least entertains
the arguments of socialism before rejecting them, mainly on the
grounds of impracticability.[3]

Since the Cartland family had no inherited wealth and an
ugly divorce in 1932 left Barbara Cartland with reduced
financial means and a daughter to support, novel-writing and
journalism became an economic necessity, both to retain her
position as a Mayfair celebrity and in order to finance Ronald's
rise through the ranks of the Conservative Party. In the 1930s
her writing career took off in earnest as she learned how to
increase productivity; by dictating to secretaries she was able to
reach 10,000 words a day. Meanwhile, against heavy odds and
as a result of a massive campaign orchestrated by his sister,
Ronald Cartland was elected a Birmingham Tory MP in 1935
on a Christian and anti-appeasement ticket. In the same year,

Cartland published the first of her advice-books to offer a coherent philosophy of life – *Touch the Stars: A Clue to Happiness*. This book is about how to achieve and maintain an optimistic outlook. Its requirements are a lifelong effort at self-improvement and a reach that is always to exceed the grasp. The sustaining motivation in this philosophy is the concept of 'The Life Force'. In Cartland's view, the Life Force is a power which finds its highest expression in love, particularly the romantic and divine. And it is indeed through the agency of the Life Force that romantic love is combined with divine love and transformed by it.

Cartland's interest in the Life Force relates to the third plank in her platform, a developing concern with the whole area of the spiritual and the transcendent, ranging from comparative religious study, yoga philosophy and Eastern occultism to Coué-ist auto-suggestion and the paranormal. What has sustained this interest is Cartland's view that life is a mystical quest after truth which everyone should attempt to attain through the power of positive thinking. The approach is summed up in a recent autobiographical memoir, *I seek the Miraculous* (1978).

As established in the 1920s and 1930s, Cartland's triple platform of views about femininity, politics and spiritual well-being forms the ideological underpinning of her whole career. It constitutes a bedrock set of opinions which are then expressed and elaborated through the Cartland persona as it reveals itself in political activity and public works, in advice-giving journalism and in the fiction-writing which she insists must have some moral purpose beyond being 'merely fiction'.

The way these different aspects of Cartland cluster to make up a celebrity career only becomes fully apparent after the Second World War. Although a second marriage in the late 1930s to another member of the McCorquodale family restored her to the class of wealthy landed gentry, complete with Scottish estates and later a Hatfield stately home, a public life of writing and celebrity remained for Cartland a moral, if no longer an economic, necessity. After wartime service in welfare work and morale-boosting for troops and war-brides, she became an active officer and fund-raiser for St John's Ambulance Brigade and in the 1950s and 1960s served as a

Hertfordshire County Councillor, a Tory in a previously safe Labour seat. In this capacity, she campaigned for improved conditions for nurses, midwives and the elderly and was instrumental in winning government legislation for the provision of local council sites for gypsies. She opened the first such camp, Barbaraville, and ensured that Romany children were baptised and educated.

Electorally, this was a highly unpopular campaign and she consequently lost her seat in 1964, but she was already well embarked on her most celebrated public role as Queen of Health, and becoming known for her advocacy of the mental and physical benefits to be derived from natural food and vitamins. Starting her campaign in the late 1950s with the founding of The National Association for Health and with the multimillion seller, *The Magic of Honey*, she was instrumental in converting what was regarded as a cranky fad into what is now both part of the contemporary currency of common-sense wisdom as well as an expanding business. Consequently, many health products have received a personal Cartland endorsement message to help their marketing effort.

It was not until the late 1960s and 1970s that the Queen of Health finally came into her own as The Queen of Romance. She had kept up a consistent flow of writing since the 1920s, covering a wide range of opinion- and advice-offering books with a fictional output that reached its hundredth title in 1964. But it is only very recently that she made the conscious decision to expand her writing energies in the direction of romance.

In assuming the title, Cartland not only increased her output but also placed herself in a particular tradition of romance writers who place considerable importance on the moral content and public reception of their work. She claims that the strongest literary influence on her is Ethel M. Dell, one of the most popular and prolific romantic authors of her youth. Dell wrote in a religiose vein, with a strong valorisation of virginity as the essence of feminine purity, and a fictional framework of highly dramatised adventure. She was among the many writers of the pre-Second World War romantic boom who have recently been rescued in abridged form in *Barbara Cartland's Library of Love* series.[4]

But the idea of the Queen of Romance as a public celebrity

and advice-giver originates from another of Cartland's favourite authors of the same period, Elinor Glyn. It was she who
created the regal model by encouraging identification between
her fictional heroines and herself, developing an exotic appearance and public manner and publicising a Philosophy of Love
which she named 'It'. 'It' was based on a combination of the
Life Force, the occult and romance. In the 1920s, Hollywood
promoted 'It' as 'sex-appeal' but she meant by it something
more akin to magnetic energy, a 'charisma' that emanated from
certain beings who, like herself, could be open to spiritual and
erotic 'aspects'. By promoting 'It' around her own person,
fiction, films and journalism, with ever-widening claims for its
elixir properties, Glyn maintained a world-wide audience until
her death in the 1940s and ensured her place as celebrity
advice-giver.

Although Cartland's career lacks the notoriety that attended
Glyn's, it shares a romantic philosophy based on a similar
vitalism and is established around a persona with much of the
same outrageous *chutzpah* and élan. Cartland's famous public
appearances – the white Rolls-Royce, the royal appurte-
nances, the 'Cartland Pink' – owe much to Glyn's sense of
celebrity occasion which in her case went with hints of exotic
adultery, 'trademark' red hair and tiger-skin props. Both
careers are concerned with creating a deliberate style of the
Romantic Writer as extravagant of both material and spiritual
wealth; about creating a public for one's work by encouraging
an excess of interest in the larger-than life, but apparently real,
person behind it.

The latest manifestation of Cartland's celebrity has proved
to be a real royal connection: step-grandmother to the Princess
of Wales. Although Cartland has maintained a 'royal' silence
about all this and stayed away from the Royal Wedding in
1981, she could not inhibit widespread public comment and
speculation. One aspect of this is the projection of Cartland and
daughter in an Ugly Sisters role. They are presented as stealing
the limelight from the younger and prettier Diana and as
aiming to out-royal the Royal Family with their pretentious
manners and excessive lifestyles. But besides being seen as,
herself, the stuff of Cinderella legend, Cartland is also claimed
as the very author and producer of the actual Happy Ending

when the experienced Playboy Prince, the wealthiest and highest-born man in the land, discards the more sophisticated women he has dallied with to marry his teenage virgin bride. The Royal Wedding was repeatedly and publicly recognised as a fiction: a 'fairytale romance', a 'pure Cartland script'. Moreover, it was claimed to have the same social function that Cartland frequently ascribes to her own fiction: of providing an 'escape' from the miseries of recession Britain, while at the same time promising women that virtue still has its own reward.

A Cartland-inspired Royal Wedding, despite the accusations of vulgarity, has been the ultimate accolade of celebrity in a career spanning nearly sixty years. To have such a real public event described as if it were the work of her fiction is the culmination of the project Cartland started in the 1920s, of making herself over to her public. This self-production of the writer as a public figure is what contributes to the development of Cartland's career in terms, not merely of celebrity but also, in its latest phase of intensive fiction production, of industry.

The Cartland 'Empire'

The deliberate accentuation of the Romantic Writer side of Cartland came about as a combination of personal circumstances – widowhood in her sixties after nursing an invalid husband, a determination thereafter not to become a 'useless' woman – shrewd commercial acumen and a particular reading of 'signs of the times'.

In the early 1960s her publishers had warned Cartland that her romances were in danger of looking *passé*; their claims for virginity were dated. She was urged to be more 'permissive' and also less prolific in case she saturated a market with unwanted product. At the risk of losing her readership, she ignored their advice and decided to ride out 'the swinging sixties'.

Cartland has often said since that she always predicted a reaction to 'permissiveness'. She watched her sales figures closely and noticed that besides becoming a bestseller in Far Eastern countries where virginity was still prized, her figures were also climbing in 'permissive' Scandinavia in the late

1960s. Unable to persuade her publishers that this might be an advance indication of a potentially widespread reaction to contemporary mores, she finally took matters into her own hands.

In 1973 she signed with new publishers, Pan paperbacks, with a contract to write ten books a year. She then made the same deal with another British paperback house, Corgi. Through Corgi's link with Bantam, USA, she could now break into the American market which she had entered two years previously with little success under her old publishers. Bantam were cautious to start with: sales representatives were asked to check-out the market 'on the ground' and reported an enormous unsatisfied demand for romance. Here Cartland could make an offer that few, if any other, romance writers could better. She already had a stockpile of well over 150 novels never before published in the United States. In addition, there were the twenty annual titles she was now to deliver annually to Corgi and Pan. At the age of seventy-two, her time had come, and in the first year of the Bantam deal, fifty Cartland titles were issued in the United States on a weekly basis as a numbered series to encourage regular collection. By the end of the 1970s it was claimed that 18 per cent of all American women had read 'a Barbara Cartland' – and 39 per cent never read a novel anyway.

This combined project of ambitious productivity and recycling activity displays considerable financial *nous* and market calculation on Cartland's part. It serves to indicate the extent to which she must be understood, not only in terms of a writer as a celebrated individual and extraordinary person, but also as part – the key part still – of an elaborate set of social and economic relations. In the 1970s, Cartland, writer-and-celebrity, became the public front and mainstay of a rationalised Cartland *industry*.

The centre of this industry remains domestic and familial – albeit on a 'royal' scale. It revolves around the Cartland stately home, Camfield Hall, with its Elizabeth I associations. This is known to her associates and staff as 'The Factory' and is divided into areas for the production of fiction, for business transactions, living quarters and entertainment suites for tourists, guests and promotional interviews. One of her sons, already editor of *Debrett*, the society directory, has become her full-time business manager. The other son, a stockbroker, advises on the historical background for her fiction and reads drafts and proofs. Both are her business partners. Besides domestic servants, Cartland employs a staff of four full-time and six part-time secretaries to cope with the fiction output and the readership correspondence, mostly seeking health advice, of 10,000 letters a year.

Such figures are constantly recounted in any publicity about Cartland. They enumerate and quantify the Cartland success-story thus: 'She's the fastest writer of romantic fiction in the world with a total 100 million sales and 40 million in circulation at the moment' (BBC-2, 16 May 1980). 'I'm the best-selling author in the world. I have sold 200 million books and written lots of things besides novels' (*Women's Realm*, 11 July 1981). In 1976 she increased the annual fiction output to twenty-four novels a year, so that by 1982 she had gone over the 300 mark. Such productivity is achieved by the daily discipline of an afternoon's dictation of between 6000 to 7000 words recorded on tape and by a secretary's shorthand. Cartland reclines on a sofa and talks straight into a microphone without notes or pause for writer's block. The manuscript is typed, corrected and read for grammar by a retired public schoolmaster and members of the family. The whole 'processing' operation takes between two to three weeks, during which time another novel is being researched by Cartland after tea and in the early evening. In this way, not only does Cartland's writing become an intensively socialised practice, it also becomes powerfully implicated in 'commodity fetishism', literary value becomes primarily and proudly expressed in terms of an exchange of quantities in the marketplace.

As in all recently rationalised capitalist enterprises, the Cartland industry is keen to 'diversify' itself into an 'empire'. Hence the creation of Barbara Cartland Promotions, which has moved into the general leisure market with 'spin-off' products of romance. These include, in the USA: Romantic Tours to Britain (see the homes of the Cartlands and the Spencers), *World of Romance* magazine, retailing at 100,000 copies a month, *Barbara Cartland's Romances*, a strip cartoon recycling the novels and syndicated in seventy-two US papers (and in 1983 again recycled in the British *Mail on Sunday*) and 'Decorating with Love', Cartland home furnishings. There are plans for similar commodity expansion in the European and Australian markets, plus another form of recycling with film and video exploitation. In the British market, apart from the health product promotion, the Cartland name is branded on perfume, travelogues for British Airways and an album of lovesongs with the London Philharmonic. This type of commercially expansive operation relies on extensive organisational back-up and material resources, but at the same time its commodities are personalised and individualised on the basis of only one 'name' as if Cartland were the sole originator and producer of all 'her' output; as if it were 'all her own work'.

Of course, without a 'Queen of Romance' there could be no business empire based on her name in the first place. It is also the case that she adheres to an earlier, more individualist model of capitalist enterprise at variance with contemporary corporate and managerial practices. Hers is the very embodiment of the determinedly single-minded entrepreneurial achiever, the self-improver who embraces 'the spirit of capitalism' in the classic Weberian terms of work as a 'duty' and a 'calling'. Cartland's daily routine might be Weber's very ideal-type of 'rationalised conduct',[5] combining as it does an heroic individualism with a disciplined and dedicated involvement in work. Moreover, she invests her work with the qualities of an 'ethic'; in addition to its bringing economic rewards and social recognition, work is always for her '*the* work'. The productivity, prolific output and diversification of her empire has a purpose – a mission, a responsibility, to do good in the world.

Cartland as Opinion-maker

I have already outlined the 'purpose' of Cartland's career in terms of her platform of beliefs concerning femininity, politics and the need for spiritual and bodily well-being. Although the three 'planks' are closely linked, it is the first I would now like to consider in more detail, since her views on women, and their relation to men, are most relevant in examining what remains the centrepiece of her empire, the romantic fiction, and what she sees as the purpose of writing it, namely to provide models of behaviour appropriate to women and men.

'My heroines have always been virgins', says Cartland. But it was only in the 1960s and 1970s when her fictional output was intensified that this aspect of her work took on any special significance. It now features as the one thing 'everyone' can be assumed to know about Cartland novels, even unread. This is because she has become publicly identified in this period of romantic productivity as an active propagandist for virginity. On one level, 'virginity' constitutes a vulgar and cynically employed sales gimmick: the unique selling proposition in a 'permissive' era. As Cartland often remarks of her penetration of the American market: 'After all, I was the only author in the world with a hundred and fifty virgins lying around'. But 'virginity' is not simply being exploited in the interests of commodity production. Or rather, it *can* only be exploited in this way because it also acts as a resonant codeword for a stance taken towards contemporary moral conduct. Before considering how virginity works as a device in Cartland's fiction, I want first to establish some of the connotations of the term as they are elaborated through Cartland's own persona in the opinion-making role that is most familiar to her public.

Cartland's propaganda for virginity is based on the view that sexual divisions are irreconcilable and given for all time. Furthermore, a notion of 'gender', which would point to the differences between men and women as having social and cultural origins, is simply denied or collapsed into the eternal verities of 'the sexes'.

On this basis, Cartland's advice on what conduct is appropriate to 'the sexes' starts from propositions about the fundamental nature of *men*; women must first accept what a man essentially 'is' in order to be true to their own essences. So: 'What is nonsense from the word go is that women could ever be the equal of men' ('What Do Women Really Want?', *Guardian* Women's Page, 24 June 1977). Men are the superior sex not only biologically (stronger bodies) and intellectually (better brains) but also because their lives inevitably give them more 'experience'. The natural forces primarily governing a woman's life are instinct, intuition and emotion; all useful qualities for adapting to the needs of a man. The chief 'destiny' of a woman is to love one man, even if she considers herself emancipated and educated. In the process of courtship her sexual instinct will remain dormant until first awakened by the experienced man. In return, she should be 'worshipped, cossetted and adored' by a man.

This is not only a woman's reward; it is also her greatest achievement. Because although men are innately superior, there is one sphere of their activity, the arena of courtship, where their conduct inclines to the base. Here, in the erotic sphere, they are physical and animal ('all men are cavemen and philanderers at heart'), motivated by straightforward and undeviating lusts and drives. On their own, they cannot change what they 'essentially' are; nor are they able to comprehend that sexual conduct has moral implications – unless they are influenced by women's transformative powers. Given their base nature, it is a considerable feat for women to get and keep men through marriage. Because the only way to do this is precisely not to appeal to the 'cavemen' in them, but to transform their philandering into the transcendent category of enduring love. Transcendence involves redemption: women 'redeem' men by enveloping them in the spiritual purity and mystique that is symbolised first in the offer of their virginity to the future husband and then in the guarantee of chastity and faithfulness after marriage.

It is frequently remarked that this scenario preserves the double-standard iniquities of 'innocence' for her and 'experience' for him. Barbara Cartland has grown weary of such observations: that is precisely the point, she says. *Because* men and women are neither equal nor the same, someone has to be the teacher and someone the pupil 'and who better to teach than the husband?'

The double standard also pre-supposes two sorts of women: the ones who are true to their pre-defined natures and those who, fortunately for men's essential natures, are not. As well as the women destined to fulfil their vocation as wives, there must always be those destined to be the focus of men's 'experience'. This contradiction Cartland simply accepts as a fact of life: there have always been enough 'Liliths and Eves' for men to practise on; there always will be.

But what has changed in the current situation is that now *all* women risk reverting to the Lilith and Eve category. This is because permissiveness and feminism – identically twinned aspects of the sexual revolution – are degrading women and diverting them from the path of seeking men's respect. The need of the age is to make a return to the redeeming Virgin Woman, the only 'real' woman, in that it is she who guides and inspires men: 'In time we may produce a Superwoman, but in doing so we will lose the Superman, for he is only super, only at his greatest when his spiritual capabilities are accentuated by the pure, mystical perfection of his ideal – The Virgin Woman' ('Why Virginity is Becoming Fashionable Once More', *The Times*, 12 January 1977).

It is on the basis of these views that Cartland places her fictional contribution. She describes the social function of her novels as 'entertainments with a message'. And that message is primarily intended to advocate the values associated with femininity in its 'virgin' aspect – as represented in an enjoyable and diverting fictional form. Her novels are explicitly devoted to the cause of demonstrating that men's baser sexuality may be transformed into love, redeemed by the heroine's virginity. Additionally, the novels aim to link this transformation with Cartland's ideas on the spiritual importance of the Life Force (pure love involves the magnetic attraction of a man and woman 'meant' for each other and then transported to the plane of fate), and the reforming zeal of doing good (in the state of pure love, moral conversions take place, particularly in men). Virtue is thus doubly rewarded.

Cartland is well aware that when her messages are embodied in story form the conventional happy ending of romance will be the guarantee of such reward. Real life may not be so simply pleasant. Therefore the appeal of her books is not necessarily 'to reality but to what men and women really *want*'. The ultimate mission of the novels is the restoration of men's and women's (particularly women's) free and most authentic selves, undistorted by the currents of the present.

Such recourses to the fundamentals of human natures and needs are not of course original to Cartland; indeed, they have such a long history that they seem to have been permanently embedded in common sense. But they take on a particular cogency when being advanced by someone who is not just anybody, but who lays public claim to mass attention. It is indeed Cartland's sharp awareness that her messages represent values under threat and on the defensive that makes her the more combative in proclaiming them against what she sees as the prevailing temper of the times. Hence she explains the boom of all romantic fiction, and especially of her own in the 1970s, in terms of an antidote to 'porn, the kitchen sink and women's lib'.

This three-point condensation of what constitutes 'permissiveness' recalls the opinions of that other moral entrepreneur, Mary Whitehouse, spokeswoman for the National Viewers' and Listeners' Association in Britain. Both women attack similar targets from the standpoint of an earlier Britain when values seemed more clearly demarcated and secured. But there is a marked difference of style and class between them and Cartland is anxious to distance herself from the comparison: 'Well I hope I'm not seen as a Mary Whitehouse in a pink dress'. For the moralism of Whitehouse comes out of, and is primarily addressed to, a disaffected petty bourgeoisie, the scrimpers and savers and ratepayers. It deploys a rhetoric of right-wing populism that invokes Victorian values of self-help, evangelical religion and moral indignation. It would have no truck with the level of conspicuous consumption positively flaunted in the Cartland lifestyle. But that lifestyle is precisely Cartland's 'promise' in difficult times, part of her 'answer' to a permissiveness which is not only seen as subverting and degrading the natural relationship between 'the sexes', but is also, most importantly an offence to aesthetics, good taste and *savoir-faire*. Above all, 'porn, the kitchen sink and women's lib' lack style and poise.

If a return to any kind of 'protestant ethic' is to be accomplished, then for Cartland all the effort and self-discipline required for goodness must always be tempered by a positive assertion that pleasure and wonderful times can also be restored. Unlike Whitehouse, she insists that 'ethics' need 'entertaining' in every sense. Therefore Cartland says to her public: re-enter with me a past world of glamour and excitement, of aristocratic 'class' and extravagance. The tide of permissiveness will be stemmed because together we will 'usher in a new Romantic Age'. This is the promise embodied in her own persona as 'Crusader in Pink', in the assumption of the title 'Queen of Romance' which proclaims that the triumph of fantasy and idealism goes along with material and economic success, and in the declarations that her novels aim to purvey both 'morality and loveliness'.

If this is the promise, if such are the claims and expectations surrounding the Cartland name, what of the narrative consequences? Given that readers approach her romantic fictions with certain 'stocks of knowledge' about their author's career, how is it that they actually work *as* fictions? What is 'the story'?[6]

'Entertainments with a Message'

Two first impressions: because of my previous knowledge of Cartland, I approached her novels expecting both that they would contain explicit, 'attacking', propaganda on the theme of 'virginity' and that they would be 'romantic' in the sense of 'soppy love stories'.

On the first point, I was looking out for overt authorial intervention in the narrative, for instance, in the form of digression or caricature and 'linguistic intensification'.[7] These two latter features are commonly used devices in women's magazine fiction. They employ highly exaggerated metaphorical language to dispose of any characters who have been made to stand for values that the author strongly opposes. But I found that they tended to occur only when Cartland picked an historical background that offered explicit parallels with the present. For instance, in *Vote for Love* (1977), set in 1907 in the context of militant suffragette action in London after the defeat of the Women's Suffrage Bills, Cartland takes up a strongly engaged and partisan position against the women's campaign. This sorts oddly with the graphic descriptions in the novel about the suffering of suffragettes in prison and appears strangely excessive seventy years on – until it becomes clear that through 'women's suffrage' we are reading 'women's lib'. Hence, the most committed suffragette in the book is its most evil character, a thoroughly 'overdetermined' baddy who is the heroine's wicked stepmother, 'a large and aggressive-looking' man-hater, 'a strident, overpowering woman', 'shrill', 'frustrated' and 'fanatical'. It is she who forces the heroine, 'sweet', 'spiritual' and 'flowerlike' Viola, into the feminist movement, much against her 'innocent' and 'feminine' nature, and beats her up when she fails to bomb the home of her future MP husband. But in my reading of Cartland I found such obvious dice-loading a rare device unless, as here, there were very direct historical connections to be made with Cartland's own preoccupations with current sexual politics.

On the second point of 'romantic-ness': given Cartland's many expatiations on what heterosexual love may mean, I had imagined that the novel texts would be full of 'purple passages' in the manner, say, of Elinor Glyn. That is, that they would contain a number of discursive elements with no plot-function other than to convey by means of heightened rhetorical description that falling or being in love is a positive and benedictory state. But what is striking in a Cartland novel is the *absence* of such passages of powerful emotion, indeed the lack of any sort of 'love-interest'. It is as if 'romantic love' is almost external to the whole narrative enterprise.

In place of emotional intensity, Cartland's fictions rely upon pace of action, much plot-incident and scene-shifting. The concern with rapid and varied story-telling means that, in the first instance, 'virginity' has a narrative function. It serves as a plot-motivator, a mechanism for producing the key problem that the rest of the story will set out to solve. That problem is how a young woman will manage to maintain her virginity under a range of difficult and pressing circumstances until her wedding day.

Once this main narrative impetus is put in motion, the plot then proceeds according to a basic formula that is made up of a set of familiar elements which are constantly reordered and reworked in a process of 'bricolage'.[8] The formula is usually an assemblage of such elements as: establishment of period-location; introduction of virgin heroine in her teens or early twenties, depicted as in the courtship phase of her life and faced with a number of marriage options; ensuing complications based on competition between suitors, other women, or misunderstandings and misrecognitions of true feeling; resolution and closure of options when the-always-intended hero makes his intentions clear with a marriage proposal; conclusion of the courtship phase and ending of the story on a declaration of love between the couple either following the first kiss or the first orgasm of the wedding night.

Since readers come to expect such elements in some combination in any Cartland novel and, in this sense, if we have read one we have read them all, the question obviously arises as to what it is that sustains interest sufficiently to keep up, and increase, the purchase of new titles that replenish the stocks in batches every few months. I would suggest that the answer has much to do with the pleasures of 'bricolage'. Precisely because the story elements are familiar we are assured of entering a customary world. We 'know where we are', but also, since the familiar always combines in an unfamiliar arrangement in any particular book, we cannot exactly predict which of the heroine's options will lead to the predictable outcome, nor how each story episode will relate to the next. It is this 'how', the *treatment* of the story, with its reliance on an episodic structure full of action and historical detail, that upholds readers' interest in what-happens-next. Narrative suspense also implies 'waiting' and 'withholding' and I believe Cartland's fiction also appeals to a prurient curiosity of the kind: how, and how long, can the heroine 'hold out'? Feminist critics have often observed various similarities between the attractions of romance and pornography[9] and I would add that, in this case, narrative 'pull' is one of them.

Moreover, Cartland has the sort of story-telling facility that invites readers to become involved participants in the story-line. In the first place, her narratives have a sense of what I would call 'a continuous present' – a series of rapidly unfolding events conveyed *as if* they were immediately happening, even when they are related in the past tense. The 'continuous present' is most noticeable when the first-person-heroine-as-narrator device is used and the reader is addressed *as if* actually 'here' in the action. But even when the authorial third person is used, the reader is still 'drawn in' because the style of any Cartland novel is always predominantly oral: the text assumes the qualities of direct speech and takes the particular form of conversational anecdote. Since this is an approach that implies face-to-face intimacy, Cartland addresses her readers as personal confidantes.

Cartland's mastery of the oral style obviously relates to the conditions of production of her fiction – the afternoon sessions of intense and continuous dictation. But it is also a technique derived from journalistic practice. She often recalls Beaverbrook's advice at the start of her journalistic career about holding the audience's attention by means of the simple 'arresting' sentence and the short graphic paragraph. And indeed the novels are linguistically similar to the textual qualities of tabloid journalism. Combining with the overall conversational style of first or third person narrator, the recounting of individual episodes makes much use of direct quotation and reported speech between various of the story's characters; sentences are not prolonged with subordinate qualifying clauses, and paragraphs, while full of detail, are not of any discursive length but usually restricted to between one and three sentences.

Such stylistic effects contribute to the 'entertaining' aspect of a Cartland novel. They make for an easy and diverting read and hold attention and involvement without requiring much concentration or effort. But as has recently been remarked about Cartland's style, the 'simple sentence' is never just that; it is also an important and recognisable didactic construction.[10] Cartland herself makes the point when she says, 'You have to put [the] message across simply in "cat sat on the mat" terms. If young girls read a Barbara Cartland which is a "cat sat on the mat" as a romance, then they'll absorb the right ideals. Those ideals are all in my books and I really believe they're important' (*Woman's Realm*, 11 July 1981).

To return to romance-writing in terms of 'mission', to the central notion of what Eagleton has called 'texts as pretexts',[11] what is the moral tale that can be read off from the narratives? In the concluding section I want to suggest that the message has little to do with inculcating 'those right ideals' that relate to Cartland's belief in the transcendent essences of man- and womanhood. On the contrary, what emerges is a forcefully *materialist* account of gender relations and circumstances – a demonstration that gender aligns, not with innate sexual natures, but with many kinds of economic, social and cultural powers that go to construct patriarchy; and that what moves women into the sphere of romance is associated more with historical necessities than biological fate or Life Force destiny.

So that what a Cartland novel actually 'tells' its readers about the pursuit of love is that courtship is primarily about the real world of commodity exchange: it is *the* economically rational career for a woman under most forms of patriarchy. Indeed, the message is the more striking for being frequently expressed in terms of 'vulgar' materialism, as crudely and mechanistically determinist.

I suggest that how a Cartland novel works involves a process of what could be called 'narrative subversion', whereby the messages of Cartland the moralist are undercut by Cartland the story-teller. And finally I want to give one example of narrative subversion in operation.

Narrative Subversion

I have chosen an example of a novel relating to Cartland's touchstone era of the 1920s, the latest date for which she feels 'virginity' can be authentically mobilised as a central plot concern. *Love and Linda* (1976) is set in Britain in 1928. It is a first-person narrative told by eighteen-year-old Linda in the present tense, but with reference to the past mainly in terms of 'yesterday' as if she were confiding to a friend in a sort of episodic diary style.

Linda is the 'illegitimate' daughter of a chorus dancer and an unknown aristocratic father. Disowned by her mother, she is brought up as a charity pupil in a convent. Leaving school at eighteen with no means of livelihood she immediately lands a job in a chorus line after a chance encounter with a professional dancer, Bessie, with whom she goes to live. Bessie immediately becomes Linda's mentor in the ways of the world and men:

> 'Now listen to me,' Bessie said seriously, taking my arm, 'most men like something young, and they are prepared to pay for it. Don't you give them anything unless you have to. Don't kiss them, don't even let them hold your hand, until they have paid, and paid heavily for the privilege . . . You keep yourself to yourself, Linda Snell, and you make your price a wedding ring, and mind it's a platinum one too.'
>
> 'You're a gold digger, Bessie', I said.
>
> She laughed and replied:

'Of course I am, and what woman isn't? There are gold-diggers in every class . . . The less you give a man the more he admires you. You give them nothing, Linda, and they will come around after you like rats after aniseed.'

Unfortunately, Bessie does not take her own advice and dies after an abortion, deserted by her married lover. But Linda literally profits by it and embarks on a courtship phase of 'thrilling' encounters with wealthy suitors, each episode of which is narrated in a breathless ingenue style with colloquialisms of the period. She is now a top mannequin but enjoying a much more luxurious lifestyle than she could possibly sustain by her own income. For she has learned from other women that it is possible to exist on a man's 'presents' of furs, jewellery and gowns for some time before he will demand the 'price' Bessie had to pay. Whenever this looks likely she must look for another, and wealthier, man for support and respect.

After resisting mistress-status from several married men – 'If you think you can buy me you are much mistaken' – Linda encounters a famous air pilot, Harry, in an episode which provides the only romantic 'love-interest' in the book: 'Love isn't a bit like I thought it would be, all sort of wildly exciting and queer. it's just like absolute peace, and I never want to be anywhere else in the world except in Harry's arms'.

Soon engaged, they spend a 'pretend honeymoon' together during which Linda remains only technically virgin:

> Harry said, 'I won't make you finally mine until we are married. I'm old-fashioned Linda.'
> 'I am . . . too,' I answered. 'There has . . . never been . . . anyone.'
> . . . 'You are so sweet, innocent and perfect my darling.' . . .
> But although I would have done anything he asked of me and sometimes we seemed to burn with a wild and wonderful fire Harry never lost control of himself.

Harry has no income apart from his winnings at air-races, and therefore the couple plan to marry after the next race. Linda is concerned: 'Not that I wouldn't work my fingers to the bone for Harry, and I don't mind how poor we are as long as we

are together. But it is worrying'. The worries are resolved by
Harry's death and two days later Linda finds she has become
Lady Glaxly after marrying 'Pimples', a wealthy long-time
suitor, in a fit of drunken grief. Three weeks later she wakes up
in hospital to find her virginity still intact because Pimples had
crashed the honeymoon car. But now he wants a divorce,
believing that the honeymoon with Harry was not in fact
'pretend'. They separate; she receives a meagre allowance from
the Glaxly family and is left to her own resources.

Now that 'Society' believes Pimples' story that she is no
longer a virgin, it is harder for her to receive presents. She gets a
notice to quit her apartment. When the bailiff turns her out he
asks,

> 'Ain't you got no one who can help you? What about a
> young man?'
> 'I don't want a young man, I want some work,' I said in
> between my sobs.
> 'That's what we all want,' he said. 'I have got two sons on
> the dole, and my daughter is laid up with laryngitis on half
> pay. It is hard times for all of us, Missy. But there, such a
> pretty girl as you ought to be able to get along all right.'

Finally Linda does. After eviction, she bumps into a new
suitor, Sir Sydney Wrex, who lives in 'an enormous mansion
that positively smells of money'. After hearing of her career to
date and accepting that she is still a virgin, he invites her to
become his 'pretend' mistress because he respects her and is
himself still married to a mad wife.

> 'Are you . . . saying . . . that we could just . . . be together
> . . . without . . .' I stammered and couldn't go on.
> 'You shall do what you want to do,' he answered. 'I will
> accept any terms you suggest.'
> I felt like a business contract, but I replied:
> 'I would like to be with you . . . I would like it very . . .
> much but . . . if you could wait until . . . I am sure about . . .
> the rest . . .'

The terms are that she will brighten up his house and life so 'that I shall feel that I am earning my keep and that I am not entirely a debtor. All women fundamentally like to give'. In return, he will not only 'keep' her but lavish gifts on her without 'taking' her virginity.

Pimples dies in a Japanese earthquake before their divorce and Linda contemplates becoming Sir Sydney's mistress for real. But before she can propose this to him a strike breaks out in his Northern factory, and immediately 'the poor wretched children with white faces and sores came into my mind. They would be the ones who would suffer. If the union's money completely petered out what would happen to them?' Since Linda has been concerned for some time that Sir Sydney is not only one of the wealthiest men, but also 'the hardest landlord and most severe employer in the country', she races north, organises a soup kitchen for the strikers' families, and defiantly demands that Sir Sydney should buy back his presents to her of diamonds and sables to prevent further starvation.

This encounter proves to be the redemptive moment. In the few remaining pages of the novel, Sir Sydney accedes to the strikers' demands, improves their homes and, revealing that his wife died in an asylum three weeks previously, proposes marriage to Linda, when she is expecting to be evicted for her defiance, because he now wants a son. Having held on to her virginity through all her adventures, Linda now happy 'surrenders' it on the last page.

When summarised like this the plot may appear merely ludicrous – and indeed it uses the plot devices of 'happy coincidence' and 'deus-ex-machina' with excessive effect. But the narrative is intended as a *naturalistic* attempt to get into one young woman's mind and follow her thoughts as she 'awakens' to experience through a rapid series of adventures. At times the requirement of narrative pace overtaxes fictional ingenuity, but Cartland's respect for the mode of naturalism as expressed in her concern to 'locate' her characters with historical accuracy, together with her interest in reproducing spontaneous speech-rhythms in an almost stream-of-consciousness way, lays the ground for a transparently materialist understanding of what happens to the heroine in *Love and Linda*. Despite the intention to construct moral messages, the novel actually produces insights about the real-life chances of women and men and women's historically necessary involvement in a patriarchal commodity market.

With this one example I hope I have been able to give some indication of how the romantic formula generally works itself out in Cartland's fiction. What I think the novels all express, in some measure, is a kind of 'political economy' of love. The heroine is typically established as marginal to family life – an orphan, say, or abandoned by her parents – and the plot therefore highlights the importance of the phase of courtship as a means of 'moving back in' – forming a new family with a man in order to obtain the only secure place for a woman that will guarantee her both cultural recognition and economic reward. Moreover, a woman is clearly represented as in some way 'handicapped' in the very struggle for material existence and always at a disadvantageous class-position in relation to a man, whether her father or future husband. Even where she has access to wealth – as an heiress say – there is likely to be some problem about her ownership of property, and any economic power she may have never ensures social and cultural survival without the help of a man. And since it is also highlighted that, in any case, she has very little labour-power to sell apart from what she makes out of her own femininity, her story is pared down to one demonstrable choice: to turn 'love' into a career and to re-enter the patriarchal 'protectorate'. In the process her virginity is for barter as the only commodity she possesses with an adequate exchange-value on the sexual marketplace.

From this perspective it is appropriate that the language of commodity exchange should permeate all Cartland's fictional texts. References to 'money' are crucial throughout; the hero's worth is constantly calculated by the narrator in terms of wealth; the couple are described as striking 'bargains', making 'negotiations' and 'deals', 'getting a fair price', 'selling yourself'. There is also at least one significant 'waiting' episode in the books which depicts the heroine just managing to preserve her virginity before the time is appropriate for consummation. This takes such forms as the 'pretend' honeymoon, the housekeeper–master relationship, as in *Love and Linda*, or the chaste marriage. Besides providing a suspense function in relation to the plot, these 'waiting' episodes are intended to give the moral message that a woman's influence, as symbolised by her virginity, can effectively control the danger of men's sexuality. Some feminist commentators have also noted a striving for equality in such scenes and regard them as holding out the promise of 'the gentle man' and of 'a love without subordination'.[12] But while I agree that they could make a potent appeal to the 'if only' longings of women readers, I suggest that the primary narrative effect of these episodes is an enhanced recognition of women's subordinate position. For the Cartland heroine never inscribes 'virginity' with any values of her own, such as 'integrity' or 'independence'; for her it represents only the values imposed by men and their property, and when men have to hold back its asking price soars. The narrative resolutions which are consequent upon the 'waiting' show that the heroine's reward for conserving her virginity is always to win the one male character in the book who is by far the best placed, both culturally and economically: 'the wealthiest man in England', 'a future prime minister', 'from one of the oldest families in Europe'. As the heroine makes love her career, so she moves through the story on a path that is determinedly, albeit innocently, upwardly mobile.

But love is not 'supposed' to be, primarily or at all, about material reward in this world. If this is what the narrative is indicating, then it is clearly subverting Cartland's message that, *in the end*, marriages are made in heaven after the woman's virginity has 'redeemed' – in a spiritual sense – the man's sexuality and hence his whole nature. The conclusions of the novels therefore revert to the transcendent every time. The proposal kiss or wedding night orgasm must be shown to be both divine and an emanation of the benignant Life Force. *Love and Linda* ends thus:

> I pulled him towards me.
> 'Make me . . . sure . . .' I whispered.
> Then he got into bed, took me in his arms and kissed me slowly, passionately and very, very possessively.
> And it was as if he gave me all the most wonderful, beautiful things in the world – the sun, the moon, the stars, the sea, the flowers. They were all there and I was a part of them. I know now that love is divine and comes from God and while it's the most thrilling, rapturous sensation

one could ever imagine, it also makes me want to be good.

I'm sure now that Sydney loves me as I love him. I didn't know a man could be so gentle and yet so wildly exciting . . . .

For all the novels' variety of historical location and action, their endings are identical. The same story of unequal exchange and masculine possession is invariably invested with the same religiose rhetoric. Hence, the final words of *Vote for Love* are:

> He sought her lips.
> As his mouth, passionate, demanding and insistent, held her captive, she knew that he carried her into a special Heaven of their own where there was no fear, no anxiety, but only a love which was a part of God.

Or take this more recent example:

> The Duke looked at the sky for a moment. Then he said, and his voice was very moving:
> 'I asked for a woman pure and untouched, and that is what I found but I was also given someone so perfect, that I want to fall down on my knees in gratitude.' . . . Their kiss was as spiritual and ethereal as the moonlight.
> Then as he felt her body pressed against his, the fire that was never far from the surface rose within them . . . .
> 'I love . . . you . . .' Anoushka murmured against his lips. 'Show me how to make you . . . love me.' . . . He took one last look at the moon, the stars, the lights of the city, and he felt as he drew Anoushka below that their beauty went with them.
> It was all part, as they were, of the love of God which is purity itself.

This ending comes from *Pure and Untouched* (1981), the novel which achieved some notoriety when it won the pink marzipan pig award from the feminist group, Women in Publishing, in 1982. This was for the year's most 'outstanding contribution to sexism'. I am not so convinced, myself. I think the group misreads the full connotations of 'pure and untouched' virgin-

ity in much the same way as I have tried to indicate Cartland
herself does when she acts as ideologue for femininity. But in
her fiction, I suggest, Cartland the celebrity opinion-maker
gives way to Cartland the breezy story-teller who need never
pause for thought or writer's block.

And given that very self-assured and spontaneous mode of
composition, it is not really surprising that in all her novels the
ideologue's spiritual messages get overlaid with naturalist
detail and cannot resist the narrative drive towards the
representation of material circumstances. Hence the idealist
version of love remains as much an imposed and tacked-on an
ending as any 'magical resolution' and through her fiction
Cartland offers a stranger truth: the romantic writer as
inadvertent feminist.

NOTES

1. Quoted in *Barbara Cartland Scrapbook* (Bath: Royal Photographic
Society, 1980).
2. B. Cartland, *We Danced All Night* (London: Arrow, 1977), pp. 354–5.
3. See Cartland's reference to her discussions with Ronald:

Two years earlier, while still at Charterhouse, Ronald had written a long
and passionate letter on the injustices suffered by Labour. 'I have been
talking to some of the men working on the roads there,' he said, 'and they
have almost convinced me that Socialism is the right policy. Every man
should give to society as a whole more than he takes from it, and until that is
brought about England cannot be saved . . . .' But when we talked about
Socialism, Ronald could not reconcile himself to the overthrow of tradition.
He believed in Private Enterprise and in the freedom of the individual. He
thought that Socialism would not only prove restrictive in industry, but
that their centralisation of bureaucracy would prove impracticable and
expensive.

(B. Cartland, *We Danced . . .* p. 256)

4. This was a numbered series published by Corgi–Bantam Books
between 1977–81. It consisted of novels by, for example, E. Glyn, E. M. Hull,
E. M. Dell, P. Wynne, J. Farnol, 'condensed' or 'specially selected and edited'
by Barbara Cartland.
5. See M. Weber, *The Protestant Ethic and the Spirit of Capitalism* (London:
Unwin, 1970).
6. The sources on which this section is based include: B. Cartland, *Love,
Life and Sex*, revised edition (London: Corgi, 1973); H. Cloud, *Barbara
Cartland, Crusader in Pink* (London: Pan, 1981); M. Allison, 'Profile: Barbara
Cartland', *Health Now*, No 15, (1981); G. Burn, 'There's Pornography and

There's Barbara Cartland', *Honey* (January 1978); P. Yates, 'In the Royal Pink: The Princess of Punk weighs up the Queen of Romance', *Cosmopolitan* (July 1981).

7. S. Hall, 'Linguistic Intensification in "Cure for Marriage" ', stencilled paper for women's magazine project, Centre for Contemporary Cultural Studies (Birmingham University, 1967–68).

8. C. Lévi-Strauss, *The Savage Mind* (London: Weidenfeld and Nicolson, 1974), pp. 16–36.

9. See for instance: S. Firestone, *The Dialectic of Sex* (London: Paladin, 1972); Germaine Greer, *The Female Eunuch* (London: Paladin, 1971); A. Barr Snitow, 'Mass Market Romance: Pornography for Women is Different', *Radical History Review* (Spring–Summer 1979).

10. See the discussion on Cartland's 'elementary sentence' and its relation to English teaching in schools in 'Recent Developments in English Studies at the Centre' in S. Hall *et al.* (eds), *Culture, Media and Language* (London: Hutchinson, 1980) Chapter 19, pp. 235–68.

11. See the discussion on the moral and social aspects of novelist Samuel Richardson's work in T. Eagleton, *The Rape of Clarissa* (London: Blackwell, 1982) 'Introduction', pp. 1–39.

12. J. Batsleer, 'Pulp in the Pink, *Spare Rib* (August 1981). See also R. Harrison, 'Women and Romantic Fiction: Subordination and Resistance', paper to BSA Annual Conference, (Manchester, April 1982).

6. *Room at the Top*: The Morality of Affluence

STUART LAING

John Braine's *Room at the Top*[1] was published in March 1957 and was immediately exceptionally successful for a first novel by a largely unknown author. It sold 35,000 copies in the first year of publication (as opposed to an average for first novels of about 5000). It was serialised (drastically abridged) in the *Daily Express* and by the end of 1958 Braine was reported to have earned between £12,000 and £15,000 from the book.[2] During 1959 the potential market was greatly extended by the Penguin paperback edition and Jack Clayton's cinema film. These two proved mutually reinforcing and the Penguin edition was reprinted eight times in the first year and nineteen times by 1970. From the mid-1960s Penguin were proclaiming *Room at the Top* (alongside such texts as *The Odyssey* and *Lady Chatterley's Lover*) as one of their million-sellers. The edition continued in print through the 1970s and by 1981 was in its thirtieth reprint.

The film was also a commercial (and, for the most part, a critical) success. It was one of the first of a number of films which, from the late 1950s, replaced Ealing and Boulting Brothers' comedies with regional/working-class realism as the dominant style in British film-making. Many of these films were based on recent plays and novels – *Look Back in Anger*, *A Taste of Honey*, *Saturday Night and Sunday Morning*, *The Loneliness of the Long-Distance Runner*, *This Sporting Life*, *A Kind of Loving*. The novel and film of *Room at the Top* became situated at the forefront of a considerable cultural trend whose roots lay, in part, in the 'Movement' novels of Kingsley Amis and John Wain and the 'Angry' writers of 1956 – John Osborne and Colin Wilson. The

novels and films which appeared after 1956 markedly extended
the social range and size of the audience of these earlier works.
In retrospect it is possible to see, in the period 1957–64, an
unusual degree of overlap between previously (and subse-
quently) quite rigidly stratified cultural sectors in Britain. The
realist style (frequently with regional, usually Northern, and
working-class content) was simultaneously at the forefront of
serious artistic practice and available (and on offer) to a very
large popular audience. In novels, films and also on television
(in plays – ATV's *Armchair Theatre* and the BBC *Wednesday Play*
– and series, *Coronation Street* and *Z Cars*) the serious and the
popular converged. *Room at the Top*, which, in one sense, was a
conventional 'middle-brow' text (in the manner of such 1930s
circulation library stalwarts as Priestley and Howard Spring)
both received attention as a serious contribution to the 'English
Novel'[3] and became a mass bestseller to rival Ian Fleming's
James Bond thrillers.

During the 1960s the novel was kept in the public eye both by
its sequel *Life at the Top* (hardback 1962, paperback and film
1965) and by a television series, *Man at the Top*, running in the
late 1960s and early 1970s; Penguin covers of the period used
TV stills as a selling point. The novel has in fact become a
relatively unusual publishing phenomenon, being both an
instant bestseller and able to command regular reprints for a
period of nearly twenty-five years.

John Braine himself was thirty-five at the time of first
publication. His first synopsis for the novel had been rejected in
December 1951 (the novel at that time being called *Born
Favourite* and its hero Bob Mayne, not Joe Lampton). During
1951 Braine had abandoned his job as a librarian in Yorkshire
and attempted to earn his living as a writer in London. Despite
selling a few articles to the *New Statesman*, *Tribune* and other
journals (as well as some radio work) he was unsuccessful and
contracted tuberculosis. He was in hospital for eighteen
months and worked on the novel during that time; it was finally
accepted for publication in 1955.[4]

John Braine has given a number of accounts of the origins of
the novel. At one level the emphasis was on writing from
observation and experience – forsaking exotic 'literary' envi-
ronments for a less glamorous setting. At another level the

interest lay in the psychology of the hero – 'I saw a man sitting in a big shiny car. He'd driven up to the edge of some waste ground, near some houses and factories, and was just sitting there looking across at them. It seemed to me there must have been a lot that led up to that moment'.[5] The novel's form is itself clearly the product of a highly pragmatic approach to writing. In Braine's view there is no need to consider complex aesthetic issues since 'there is nothing you cannot say within the framework of the straightforward realistic novel'.[6] This was a position particularly suited to a mid-1950s Britain which rejected continental extremism in literary theory and practice as well as political ideology.

The novel itself is centrally concerned with the exploits of one character, Joe Lampton, who in the immediate aftermath of the Second World War has (as a reviewer summarises) 'come from Dufton to Warley, as it might be from Bolton to Leicester: from a spiritually dead-and-alive mill town to a mixed light-industry centre that has some pretensions to social elegance and cultural life. He is socially, economically, and above all sexually on the make'.[7]

The plot hinges on Joe's relationships with two women – Alice Aisgill and Susan Brown. Alice is married and in her mid-thirties (nine years older than Joe); Susan is nineteen, inexperienced and the only child of a wealthy businessman. The novel progresses by interweaving episodes from the development of the two relationships within a single year of Joe's life. As each relationship moves towards a climax of resolution or dissolution the opposing sets of values represented come into sharp contradiction and require Joe to make a choice between the two women and the ways of life they embody.

Alice, from Joe's first meeting with her, confounds his expectations. Her rejection of conventional compliments leads Joe to remark that 'she certainly wasn't succumbing instantly to my charm'.[8] The significance of charm has already been elaborated by Joe – 'Charm was a favourite object of discussion between Charles and myself; we had the notion that if only we could learn to use it our careers would be much benefited' (p. 19). Alice's imperviousness to charm is the first sign that she does not live her life according to the rules for social success. She buys her own drinks (beer) and actively subverts Joe's idea of how women ought to behave. He has to find new terms to understand her – 'I was talking as freely with her as I would with Charles', 'I can talk with you like a man' (p. 53).

As the relationship develops, however, Joe finds himself being offered other ways of seeing Alice. He is jokingly accused of 'boozing with married women' (p. 59) by his work colleagues and is then asked, 'Aren't you doing a bit for her?' (p. 114). Here two powerful areas of social discourse are called into play. First there is the code of accepted public standards. Here 'boozing with married women' implies behaviour on the edge of acceptability, with the implication of an underlying base of value (belief in marriage). Adultery, or an affair (as serious propositions), are unmentionable. Secondly there is the discourse of male society, particularly that of young unmarried men with 'normal appetites' – 'If you're hungry and someone's preparing a good meal, you'll naturally angle for an invitation' (p. 32). All women are regarded as fair game. This discourse, in the novel, is particularly related to the war experience and to all-male gatherings – the mess-room or the pub.

The implications of these ways of seeing begin to influence Joe as the relationship develops into sex. Alice is initially almost a mother-figure, certainly a friend, and Joe sees an opposition between sex and friendship – 'I could get sex at any pub or dance-hall, but not the friendship which Alice had given me . . .' (pp. 37–8). Sex is seen as involving almost antipathy to the partner. The threat it poses here is *not* social (because Alice is married) but emotional. It might trivialise or damage their relationship. It is this separation between sex and human relationship that Alice breaks down, while offering a new kind of definition to Joe – 'don't fall in love with me, Joe. We will be friends won't we? Loving friends' (p. 84).

This attempt to establish some intermediate point between the extremes of casual encounter and total commitment (falling in love) is precariously situated, as Joe's private reflections show – 'I was the devil of a fellow, I was the lover of a married woman, I was taking out the daughter of one of the richest men in Warley' (p. 84). Joe speaks here as a young unmarried man (with 'natural' sexual appetites) and Alice is reduced to a social category, '*a* married woman'. Ultimately Joe is persuaded to abandon Alice precisely by seeing her in this way – as the bit on the side which threatens his attempts to advance himself socially.

This view of Alice is, above all, 'sensible'. The word 'sensible' is repeatedly used to criticise the terms of the relationship. When there is a temporary rift over Alice's past as an artist's model she comments – 'We might as well be sensible. We did agree, didn't we, that there'd be nothing permanent about it' (p. 120). Joe tries to persuade himself to agree – 'it's all over now, the sensible part of me said, you're well rid of the neurotic bitch. You're out of the danger of scandal' (p. 121). These judgements from the realm of the sensible reappear after the climactic Dorset episode. Alice judges Joe's expression of love for Susan as 'very sensible', implying the lack of depth and spontaneity in Joe's feelings. Finally, after Alice's death, Joe's attempts to maintain control are 'sensible' – 'Joe Lampton was doing the sensible thing, keeping out of harm's way' (p. 223). This is the code of common sense, the appeal to the need to adjust to the reality, the norms, of the social world.

To be sensible Joe must reject Alice. Against this is a positive conception of the relationship – 'I was discovering that I had never really made love to a woman before or truly enjoyed a woman's body. The sort of sex I was used to was sex as it would be if human beings were like screen characters – hygienic, perfumed, with no normal odours or tastes' (p. 98). Here a concept of human authenticity ('really', 'normal') is invoked – not the 'natural' sexual appetites, but some notion of emotional depth. The reference to 'screen characters' creates a contrast with Joe's view of Susan ('conventionally pretty', 'like the girl in the American advertisement') and stresses the contradictions in his desires, one of which is precisely to live like men in advertisements.

This ambition is central to Joe's attitude to Susan. This relationship, unlike that with Alice, always has a clear goal – 'my intentions . . . were always those described as honourable' (p. 57). That Joe wants to marry Susan is accepted (if not welcomed) by all concerned; what are in question are his motives. Is he pursuing a romantic dream, a cynical manipulation or a class war? For Joe the image of the fairy-tale offers a mixture of these – 'Even apart from her money, she was worth marrying. She was the princess in the fairy-stories, the girl in old songs, the heroine of musical comedies. She naturally belonged to it because she possessed the necessary face and figure and the right income group. And that's how it is in all the fairy stories . . .' (p. 57). Joe then indicates how the romantic images (beauty, extravagance, exotic possessions) are all dependent on money. The fairy-tale comparison becomes a way of discrediting conventional moral stances. Susan sees only the fairy-tale's surface structure. Her innocence is shallow naïvety. She can be manipulated by Joe because she never realises how her own identity is based on a grading scheme whose sanction is not natural hierarchy (aristocracy, monarchy), but income-level. The fairy-tale analogy also stresses Joe's problems; he is 'the equivalent of a swine-herd'. With Susan he has always to mask his class-consciousness and avoid revelation of the true factors which structure both the fairy-tale and his own ambitions.

As the relationship develops Joe's consciousness becomes increasingly dissociated from his behaviour. Behind his formula of 'scraps of poetry, names of songs, bits of autobiography, binding it all with the golden syrup of flattery' (p. 229) lie his real thoughts – 'I've got her, I took my friend's advice, she's mine and I can do what I like with her. I've beaten that bastard Wales. I'll marry her if I have to put her in the family way to do it. I'll make her daddy give me a damned good job. I'll never count pennies again' (p. 137). The language of romantic courtship is crushed by the brutal short sentences which see life as a series of power relations ('got', 'beaten', 'put', 'make') and employ a deliberately reductive vocabulary ('bastard', 'family way', 'count pennies').

It is inevitable that the character of Susan never achieves the same level of complexity as that of Alice for Joe's choice is not between two women but between a place (Warley) and a person (Alice) – effectively between social values and authentic human values. This opposition between the social and the human forms the basis of the novel's presentation of different concepts of 'the real' – concepts which structure the whole of the text and determine its offered solutions. Four senses of 'the real' can be distinguished:

(1) *The Reality of Sense Perception.* The novel assumes the

non-problematic existence of a reality available through (common) sense perception. This is not so much challenged as reinforced by Joe's surreal perception of his surroundings after Alice's death since this merely serves as an index of the severity of his mental disturbance.

(2) *The Reality of Social Facts.* This refers to a comprehension of how the social world operates. Charles persuades Joe to leave Alice by telling him to 'face facts' (p. 195) (possible scandal, Alice's age and lack of money, her tendency to be unfaithful). Abe Brown defends his actions by saying 'I didn't make the world' (p. 210). Life (unfortunately) is not charming or agreeable. Society is a rigid hierarchy based on income-level.

(3) *The Really Human.* Joe feels that marriage to Alice would be 'real', not just 'a licence for sexual intercourse' (p. 173). The relationship is 'something . . . uncompromisingly real' (p. 99). In retrospect Joe judges that with Alice 'I had my chance to be a real person' (p. 124). The reference is to a level of feeling and experience too intense to be accommodated within existing social forms.

(4) *The Reality of Violence and Death.* 'I was jerked into that zone of unreality one would inhabit for seconds at a time in the R.A.F. watching a Wimpey scarcely a wing-tip away disintegrate into rather gaudy green and orange flames, knowing that the men inside, with whom one had been drinking a few hours ago were being fried in their own fat like bacon' (p. 21). In *The Social Construction of Reality* Berger and Luckmann argue that everyday reality is surrounded by a number of 'marginal' situations with which its explanations cannot cope.[9] In *Room at the Top* it is violent death which is marginal, hovering just below the surface of everyday life, particularly in memories of the war and, in Joe's case, of his parents' deaths through bombing – 'the invasion of the abbatoir, the raw physical horror suddenly becoming undisputed master' (p. 96). This area of reality/unreality dominates the whole text momentarily after Alice's death and dismemberment – 'a lump of raw meat with the bones sticking through' (p. 220) – as Joe's mental state is

destabilised. He has 'an attack of the truth'; the world is 'nothing but a storm of violence' (p. 221). Reality here resides neither in the disagreeable but manipulable 'facts' of social organisation nor in the possibility of becoming authentically human, but rather in the physical limits of individual existence – eventual death and bodily disintegration.

However, through most of the text this 'zone of unreality' is only latent. The greater part of the novel is devoted to the elaboration of a particular view of British society and contemporary history structured on the basis of (2) above. There is, first, a detailed and specific account of general social changes through a sketching of four distinct moments in Joe's life. *The Slump* (or the Thirties – the two terms are used interchangeably) is identified as a working-class experience (of Dufton, not Warley); it is the general image for the environment from which Joe is escaping. *The War* provides an experience for measuring all the male characters. Idealism is rejected (as in Joe's use of the prisoner-of-war camp for his own advancement). Emphasis is laid on the stripping away of normal civilised practice. *The Post-War Period*, the specific moment of the novel (1946–7), is insisted on, not only through the dates given but also through reference to two continuing experiences of the period, rationing and the Labour government. *The Present* (named on the novel's opening page as ten years later) is the moment from which the novel is narrated. Joe, in 1956, has become materially and socially successful; he looks back on an earlier and different self (one which is 'hardly touched by any of the muck one is forced to wade through to get what one wants' (p. 10).

In its construction of this historical model *Room at the Top* was situating itself as part of a more general attempt throughout the 1950s to make sense of what post-war Britain had become. In the early 1950s, for example, the contrast between the 1930s and the post-war period was a central topic within political rhetoric. The Labour manifesto for the General Election of 1950 'was principally notable for its emphasis on the contrast between full employment under the Labour Government and pre-war unemployment under Conservative Governments. In a few vivid sentences, the Labour "myth" of the thirties was

presented, of dole queues and means tests.'[10] Four out of five
Labour election broadcasts in 1950 made detailed comparison
with the 1930s and the day before the poll the *Daily Herald*
published a front-page picture of cloth-capped Stepney unemployed with the slogan, 'Life in the Tory Thirties'. In
photographic form the Jarrow marchers 'must have tramped
through several hundred thousand copies of Labour addresses'.[11] Conservative responses were to claim that Labour's
record of 1929–31 was the worst of all, to argue that Labour's
post-war full employment record was due solely to Marshall
Aid or to stress that the Conservative Party had itself now
changed. All these responses indicated that they were unable to
contest the fundamental images of the contrast.

By the 1955 election this historical model had altered
radically. Labour had been defeated in 1951 not through the
loss of their own support but by the collapse of the Liberal vote
(between the 1950 and 1951 elections the number of Liberal
candidates fell from 475 to 109 and their total vote from 2.6m.
to 0.7m. – the Conservatives were the main beneficiaries,
although the total Conservative vote was still nearly a quarter
of a million less than that for Labour). The Labour response to
the situation was then remarkably complacent. In the immediate aftermath of the election the *New Statesman* commented:
'Supporters of Labour who have long suffered from Tory jibes
as they waited in queues are now going to have a quiet bit of
fun. The Tories have actually persuaded many middle-class
people that all our post-war difficulties are due to the incompe-
tence – or worse – of the Labour party. They expect the
butchers' shops to be filled with succulent steaks at prices they
can afford.'[12] By 1955, however, Labour's problem in trying to
construct a plausible rhetoric was an inability to deny that such
'steaks' had indeed arrived.

During 1953 the post-war consumer boom got fully under
way as income tax was cut by 6d; between 1952 and 1953
expenditure on consumer durables rose from £531m to £678m.
In the 1950s decade as a whole such expenditure doubled as
against only a 25 per cent increase in expenditure on food. In
1953 500,000 new cars were sold in Britain (300,000 in 1952) –
and 1.1m television sets (700,000 in 1952). In 1953 the
Conservatives achieved their much vaunted annual housing

target of 300,000. Unemployment was held at the same level as under the 1945–51 Labour government while between 1952–4 food rationing was finally ended with tea, sugar, sweets, butter, meat, bacon and cheese becoming freely available.[13]

In the 1955 election the key historical contrast was no longer Thirties unemployment/Forties social welfare but rather Forties Labour austerity/Fifties Conservative affluence. The Conservative manifesto stated that 'a Party must not only be judged by what it says. It must be judged even more by what it does – therefore we ask the British people to make this comparison now: Which were better for themselves, for their families and for their country? The years of Socialism or the years of Conservatism that have followed?'[14] Rationing was a prime target. One poster had the caption – 'queues, controls, rationing – Don't risk it again', while the *Daily Express* argued that 'Socialism without rationing is like Wormwood Scrubs without walls. It cannot be done'. The same paper also provided the other term of the comparison – 'the British people never had it so good . . . higher pay packets, lower taxes, full shops and nice new homes'.[15]

The late 1950s saw concerted attempts to consolidate this new consumer society as the dominant British self-image. By 1957 television sets were in over 50 per cent of homes and over half of these could receive the new commercial channel. The numbers of private cars rose, between 1955 and 1959, from 3.5m to 5m. These two objects were central in the symbolic representation of modern Britain. In July 1957 (four months after the publication of *Room at the Top*) Macmillan, putting the Conservatives back on course after the Suez fiasco, made his two famous 'never had it so good' speeches, referring to 'a state of prosperity such as we have never had in my life-time – nor indeed ever in the history of this country'.[16] Between June 1957 and September 1959 the Conservatives spent an estimated £468,000 on press and poster advertising. In the summer of 1959 a fall in unemployment and a tax-cut coincided with the distribution of posters proclaiming – 'Life's Better with the Conservatives. Don't Let Labour Ruin It'. Two of these showed family scenes – one with a family washing a car, the other with family members eating an abundant meal with a television set strategically placed in full view.[17] These images denoted the achievement of the transition from Thirties Depression (poverty) and Forties austerity (sufficiency) to Fifties affluence (luxury).

Room at the Top offered itself as a commentary on this transition in a variety of ways – most obviously through the changes in Joe himself. His Thirties experience of the Slump in Dufton and his subordinate position in the post-war period (when 'one was always hungry . . . for profusion, hungry for more than enough' (p. 129) give way to his achieved entry into the world of the Top. By 1956 we hear of Joe's expensive dressing gowns and of his descriptions of himself as like 'a brand-new Cadillac' (p. 124) and a 'character in a magazine advertisement' (p. 183). Joe's material success is precisely a matter of car ownership, sumptuous meals and an ability to fulfil the dreams of the world of advertising (increasingly prominent through the late 1950s with the penetration of commercial television). His success is, however, clearly simultaneously a material gain and a human loss – 'I look back at that raw young man sitting miserable in the pub with a feeling of genuine regret; I wouldn't, even if I could, change places with him, but he was indisputably a better person than the smooth character I am now, after ten years of getting almost everything that I ever wanted. I know the name he'd give me: the Successful Zombie' (p. 123). *Room at the Top* thus may be read, in terms of Joe's progress, as a critical assessment of the morality of affluence, of the human cost of its achievement. The extent to which such an assessment could be taken seriously, however, would depend on how far Joe could plausibly be taken as a representative case.

It is here that the relative lack of information given about the situation of Joe in 1956 (Joe as narrator) is crucial. For it is this lack which allows Joe's progress to serve as an illustration both of the rise of a new managerial class and also of the alleged 'embourgeoisement' of the working-class as a whole – both these apparent social changes being much debated in political, journalistic and academic attempts to describe the new composition of post-war British society during the 1950s.

Orwell's wartime essay 'England Your England' (1941)[18] had contained a brief concluding section in which he sketched the current and future patterns of British society. The discussion assumed the probable continuation of 'the upward and downward extension of the middle class'. Orwell noted two constituent elements of this movement. First there was the structural requirement of modern industry for an increasing number of 'managers, salesmen, engineers, chemists and technicians of all kinds'. Secondly there was, more importantly for Orwell, 'the spread of middle-class ideas and habits among the working-class'. In the post-war period, particularly in the 1950s, both elements appeared with increasing frequency in all forms of social description.

Initially the problem was how to assess the period of Labour government. In 1945 Britain was the only major European country to emerge without wholesale internal destruction (either physical or cultural). However, although British society had suffered no internal rupture (all its major pre-war institutions continued to function uninterrupted), important social changes had taken place on a scale very different from those of the Great War. Both civilian bombing and the degree of social mobilisation had made the war very much a 'People's War'. Civilian evacuation, direction of labour and the concentration of Allied troops within the country resulted in a considerably increased exposure of different social groups to each other. The experience of being in the Armed Forces for up to seven years meant that in the late 1940s a large number of men re-entered the labour market, or entered it for the first time, in their early and mid-twenties. The War thus transformed and deflected set social patterns and careers. This period of transition is crucial for Joe. The prisoner-of-war camp provides 'the only chance I'd get to be qualified' (p. 118) as an accountant, giving him his first step on the ladder. The War kills his parents and also the Thompsons' son, allowing Joe (who is 'the image' of the dead Maurice Thompson) to break with his background and move into a vacant space (literally – the dead son's bedroom) in a middle-class household.

Such social changes did not, however, require the emergence of a transformed political culture. Labour was elected as a party of change but also as one led by ministers who had already been governing for five years. Their declared long-term aim, nevertheless, was to establish a 'Socialist Commonwealth' and the key-notes of its programme (welfare and public ownership) were clearly intended to benefit the working class in particular. Following the programme's implementation (in the National Insurance scheme and the nationalisation of transport and power) there arose an inevitable and recurrent question (both for Labour supporters and critics) of what achievements, in terms of greater social justice, these changes had produced. Had poverty, unemployment and privilege been abolished? The new 'affluent society' of the 1950s was incessantly interrogated for answers.

One set of answers developed Orwell's observations on the necessity of an expanding technical and professional stratum whose status and income were not necessarily related to property ownership. In *New Fabian Essays* (1952) Labour 'revisionists' (the later 'Gaitskellites') proposed a new political analysis for a new situation. Antony Crosland argued that in the new mixed economy 'decision-making and economic control have passed to the new class of (largely) non-owning managers'.[19] According to Austen Albu – 'The habits, experiences and behaviour of these salaried officials are in a different world from those of the small masters of true private enterprise and much nearer those of some branches of the Civil Service and of public industry'.[20] This version of the managerial revolution thesis is perhaps too benevolent to fit Joe's character but his arrival at the Top is marked by a salaried position in Brown's with the brief to 're-organize the office' because the owner is 'not interested in the administrative side' (p. 210).

A rather different set of issues was generated once the focus switched to the individual origins of the members of this 'new class'. The keynote here was frequently the growth of educational opportunity and the belief that innate ability was now being rewarded. In *Encounter* (July 1956) Charles Curran argued that the Butler Education Act was successful in creaming off the cleverest working-class children – 'Britain in fact is very close to the point where it will be true to say that there is a general correlation between social status and mental ability'.[21] This assertion became, for a time, one of the truisms of post-war social analysis. Young's *Rise of the Meritocracy* (1959) summed up the implications while it was frequently suggested that 'success has replaced heredity as the basis of class affiliations'.[22]

The 'new class' were then the sons (and, less often, daughters) of the working class and lower middle class who had risen through education. They moved through the improved State education system to qualify for professional or white-collar jobs, the reward coming in salary and career prospects rather than in property ownership. A crisis of identity and origins was one consequence of this achieved social position as formal education offered a diametrically opposed *cultural* context to that of working-class families. In a letter to *The Times* in January 1958 (during a correspondence about class and education), Winston Fletcher, a Cambridge student with 'a cockney accent' commented – 'This predicament is quite common under our present educational system . . . . The working class boy far from worshipping at the shrine of his parents' income-group finds himself dissociated, despises the ignorance of those who were once his friends'.[23] The dissociation then led to an aggressive acceptance of the idea of meritocracy and its goal of individual advancement. It was in relation to this aspect of the 'new class' debate that two articles appearing within a year of the novel's publication cited *Room at the Top* as an illustration of this area of social change.

Geoffrey Gorer's 'The Perils of Hypergamy' appeared in the *New Statesman* on 4 May 1957.[24] He argued that Braine's novel could be placed alongside *Lucky Jim* and *Look Back in Anger* in terms of the central relationship between a hero 'of working-class origins' and 'a middle to upper middle-class woman'. For the hero a tension developed between the working-class background ('emotional values', 'types of sex identification', 'patterns of domestic life') and the acquired middle-class habits ('intellectual interests, social horizons, accent and vocabulary'). This tension appeared most clearly at the moment when the members of this rising class attempted to fix their new status through marriage. The plots which focused on romantic/sexual episodes were then effective representations of more general cultural problems.

Frank Hilton in *Encounter* (February 1958)[25] started from social analysis rather than literary texts. His article, 'Britain's New Class', considered 'the emergence of the British working-class from the sweat-shops of the last century and its disintegration as a class in the process'. Education was crucial in allowing a significant number of the children of the old working class to become social climbers, 'the elevated underdogs' – 'Our underdogs are on the move today. Remember they are ambitious, intelligent, and they come from nowhere. They have no inhibitions. They have nothing to lose that they have not already automatically lost by the simple fact of their intelligence and education.' Again the heroes of Amis, Osborne and Braine were cited as exemplary figures. Joe Lampton was singled out for particular criticism because of his 'violence and ruthlessness' and 'anachronistic behaviour'.[26] This attack reflected the degree to which Braine's hero embodied the less acceptable face of the 'new class' – the drive to material success, the rejection of origins, the echoes of the Victorian self-made man rather than the more admirable qualities of those who had been refined through liberal education – the Hoggartian 'scholarship boy'.

Room at the Top recognisably addressed the issue of class changes at this level of individual mobility. Equally, however, it offered itself as a comment on the more general 'embourgeoisement' thesis which considered status not so much as a product of occupation as of domestic lifestyle and patterns of consumption. Irrespective of job, the new welfare provisions and possession of consumer durables were presumed to be affecting general living standards, behaviour and attitudes. In 1941, Orwell had written of 'the germs of future England' already emerging – 'it is the same kind of life that is being lived at different levels, in labour-saving flats or council houses . . . . It is a rather restless, cultureless life, centring round tinned food, *Picture Post*, the radio and the internal combustion engine'.[27] During the 1950s there were many similar statements concerning the advent of 'mass culture' in Britain, although television was characteristically substituted for *Picture Post* and the radio. Orwell himself went on to argue that, 'in tastes, habits, manners and outlook, the working class and the middle class are drawing together'.[28]

At first the Labour victory of 1945 appeared to have rendered such speculations about the disappearance of the working class temporarily irrelevant. Indeed attention in the late 1940s was rather directed at the situation of the middle class. Austerity, rationing and increasing standardisation of welfare and education seemed to threaten a proletarianisation of the middle class rather than the reverse.

The implications of these changes were, however, always ambivalent. By 1952 the proportion of people describing themselves as 'working class' was significantly smaller than in 1946. One contemporary analysis suggested that 'six years of rising wages had enabled an appreciable number of working-class people to attain what they regarded as a middle-class standard of living with the result that they now *feel* middle-class'.[29] The apparent continuation of this trend through the 1950s pointed to a paradoxical situation for the Labour party. Had Labour rendered itself obsolete by setting right all the grievances of the working-class poor and underprivileged? Behind 'embourgeoisement' lay the Thirties, dole and depression, memories of which were crucial for the 1945 victory. If *Love on the Dole*, *The Road to Wigan Pier* and the Jarrow march represented the quintessential characteristics of working-class experience then anything which brought security and prosperity was clearly middle class.

The perspective of historical contrast was, as already noted, basic to the idea of a classless, affluent Britain. When the *Sun* (as the 'middle-market' successor to the *Daily Herald*) was first launched in September 1964, it situated itself firmly within the terms of this accepted social analysis. The front-page editorial of the first edition read:

Look how life has changed.
Our children are better educated. The mental horizon of their parents has widened through travel, higher living standards and T.V.
Five million Britons now holiday abroad every year.
Half our population is under 35 years of age.
Steaks, cars, houses, refrigerators, washing-machines are no longer the prerogative of the 'upper crust', but the right of all. People believe, and the *Sun* believes with them, that the division of Britain into social classes is happily out of date.[30]

Class is here seen, by implication, as directly determined by the attainment of a certain material standard of living (steaks, cars). The point was that, as Wayland Young wrote in *Encounter* in July 1956 'since George Orwell published *The Road to Wigan Pier* in 1936, Wigan has changed from barefoot malnutrition to nylon and television'.[31] When the facts of material advance were put alongside the scale of the Labour electoral defeats of 1955 and 1959 the thesis seemed confirmed; as Douglas Jay remarked after the 1959 defeat – 'we are fighting under the label of a class that no longer exists'.

Room at the Top inserted itself into this debate in a more indirect way than in the case of the 'new class' thesis. Here the novel's reticence about the details of Joe's social position at the time of narration is particularly important. Joe's material success is essentially measured against both the working-class conditions of the 1930s and his own situation at the beginning of the novel. It is not compared to the standards of others at the time of writing (1956–7). Indeed the remarks about rationing imply that readers may not even remember the experience of post-war austerity. The focus is on the transition from deprivation and consequent ambition to attainment – an attainment fundamentally material in character. It is in this way that Joe's individual advance offers itself as representative of a general material improvement (and its 'human' costs).

It is important here to recognise the text's specificity in presenting social models. It does not merely reflect already formed opinion or ideologies; it actively produces its own constructions which are then available as a further irreducible element in the general social process of creating meanings to make sense of experience. The novel, within the general framework already outlined, develops its own particular language for representing forms of social stratification. 'World' is used to evoke the general atmosphere of a particular lifestyle. Two 'worlds' are set against each other – 'The world of worry about rent and rates and groceries, of the smell of soda and blacklead and No Smoking and No Spitting and Please Have The Correct Change Ready and the world of the Rolls and the Black Market clothes and the Coty perfume and the career ahead of one running on well-oiled grooves to a knighthood, and the party in the big house at the end of the pine-lined drive' (p. 126). Each world is composed of stereotypical figures in a fixed tableau – Dufton and Warley, poor and rich, working class and middle class.

'Class' itself, as a term, is used more flexibly and frequently. 'Working class' and 'middle class' are opposed in describing the gap between Joe's past identity and future aspirations – 'I was wearing my shirt for the second day. I had the working-class mentality' (p. 151). Elsewhere, however, 'class' is used more loosely to denote a range of levels of social status – 'The ownership of the Aston-Martin placed the young man in a social class far above mine; but that ownership was simply a question of money' (p. 28). This implies a plurality of classes and is an indication of how the novel moves from the use of a common way of describing social difference (which is, however, ambiguous in its implications – how much collective agreement is there on precisely what determines class?) to a textually specific thesis about social structure. The shift is most clearly accomplished through Joe's tendency to substitute 'grade' for 'class' in his own vocabulary.

The term 'grade' is introduced by Joe as his private way of understanding society (and, in particular, women's social positions). Unlike 'world' or 'class' it has no presumed endorsement by general social usage, but derives from the distinctions of rank and income made within the local government service (in which he works). Early in the novel Joe explains the idea of grades to the reader with the comment – 'This no doubt all seems very cynical but the fact is that Charles and I could eventually work out husbands' incomes to the nearest fifty pounds. There was a time when the accuracy of our system profoundly depressed me' (p. 37). The 'system' itself is based on the proposition that the appearance and character of any given woman will be an accurate guide to her husband's income. Three levels of persuasion are used to gain the reader's assent to this. First there is an appeal to a general reality ('the fact is'). Secondly Joe's depression provides a further guarantee; like the reader Joe finds the facts distasteful but is forced to admit their truth. Finally there is the proof of the novel itself. Joe can only get Susan by being well off. He then turns this to his own advantage. By getting Susan he becomes wealthy – thus demonstrating that beautiful women and material success are inseparable.

The 'grading system' then operates to offer a vulgar materialist account of social structure; income-level determines all. However, there are ambiguities here. At one level this is a matter of relative income, but it can also imply absolute material standards – if wearing the same shirt two days running is working class then changing your shirt every day is middle class, even if everyone does it. This can be directly linked with the underlying assumptions of the embourgeoisement thesis. Even Raymond Williams was moved, in 1961, to comment that – 'There are many signs that money, in the form of conspicuous possession of a range of objects of prestige, is rapidly driving out other forms of class distinction'.[32] Joe's own analysis pushes this to its logical conclusion in arguing that 'social class . . . is simply a question of money'.

Room at the Top clearly offers a particular account of social structure and class formations which has connections with similar contemporary accounts in political, journalistic and academic analysis. It would, however, be inadequate to see the novel as simply endorsing a reductive view of human relations and social organisation. *Room at the Top* also offers an alternative view of 'reality' – one based on the 'human' qualities found in Joe's relationship with Alice and, in a different way, on the world of his working-class origins. Joe's parents and his aunt represent 'traditional' working-class values and his father's comment 'There's some things that can be bought too dear' (p. 95) is in direct opposition to the world-view which Joe's success with Susan endorses.

This idea, that the pre-war working-class community had embodied a set of values at odds with those of the 'you never had it so good' affluent society, was developed in a whole range of cultural sociological and political studies in the late 1950s. Perhaps the most notable was Richard Hoggart's *The Uses of Literacy*, published only a month before *Room at the Top*, also dealing with the West Riding and discussing the same range of historical moments. Hoggart examined 'the possible interplay between material improvement and cultural loss'. Mass culture was 'less healthy' than the older culture; mass entertainments were 'what D. H. Lawrence described as anti-life'.[33] Hoggart's arguments as a whole are complex but the element of nostalgia for a more authentic way of life and set of values which material progress had apparently destroyed is clearly present, as it is in *Room at the Top*.

In the novel these values are specifically linked to those which Joe finds in his relationship with Alice – 'It was possible; it was real; I could be with her all the time, we could become as firmly rooted and as good as my father and mother' (p. 173). This possibility is revealed as illusory since these 'real' values can no longer be accommodated with the social structure (in fact they never could – Joe's father could retain his integrity only by refusing all forms of individual advancement). At one level the authentic values of the Joe/Alice relationship can only exist by virtue of standing outside the social system (the 'grading' system).

Nevertheless the novel is a social realist text and Alice is a representative character within it; she has a particular class position and background. She is middle class but not 'bourgeois'[34] – rather bohemian. She is a skilled actress, a former drama student who tried to succeed professionally. She was once a nude model for an artist and has her roots in London. The flat in which she and Joe meet denotes a particular kind of social milieu – the world of professional theatre. Alice's values and allegiances are thus in many ways as different from Susan's solid upper-middle-class respectability as they are from Joe's working-class roots.

This location of authentic human values in a representative of a particular marginal fraction of the middle class is not accidental nor as insignificant as a casual reading of the novel might imply. Indeed the moment of the appearance of Braine's novel saw the rise of a movement, with a significant level of membership drawn from this fraction, whose absolutist view of political morality was just as much in conflict with the dominant values of pragmatic materialism, as were the values of Joe and Alice with those of the 'grading system'. CND (effectively launched towards the end of 1957) was a movement whose political goals were 'expressive' (psychological and emotional) rather than 'instrumental' ('economic and material'); its members believed that 'principles' were more important than 'power'.[35] It was an oppositional movement not so much in terms of proposing an alternative form of social organisation as of trying to make society live up to its own professed ideals. Its members held 'unusually high expectations of their society' and expected it 'to adhere in international affairs to the kind of strict moral code relevant to the conduct of individuals'.[36]

The movement's membership was predominantly middle class, in particular the educated middle class working in the professions – teachers, clergymen, medical and social workers, architects and scientists. Intellectuals and artists were prominent and 'the archetype figures of the unilateralist movement were actors and playwrights'.[37] John Braine himself became a member, an occasional speaker and was later reported as a supporter of the more militant Committee of 100.[38]

The appeal of CND in the late 1950s and early 1960s (both within and without the Labour party) can be partly understood in terms of its providing a focus for oppositional opinion at a time when the problem of material provision appeared to have been solved. Social criticism then re-formed around the rejection of society's moral standards and behaviour rather than its material inequalities. Parkin argues that 'CND provided the one single political movement in which "progressive" values were fully represented in their pure form, and where they could remain untarnished by the demands of electoral expediency'.[39] *Room at the Top* greatly extended the scope of its analysis and appeal by offering a representation of such absolute human values, at odds with a materialist society, and (in the book's terms) indicating how people 'ought' to be rather than how the world is.

The novel itself pulls together all the different aspects of these 'real' human values through Joe's reflections (from his 1956, narrator, position) on how he has changed – 'I don't of course care whether that young man looking at the theatre bill was wiser or kinder or more innocent than the successful Zombie. But he was of a higher quality; he could feel more, he could take more strain. Of a higher quality that is, if one accepts that a human being is meant to have certain emotions to be affected strongly by all that happens to him' (p. 123). The 'higher quality' is a matter of intensity of feeling and response since the language of conventional virtue is compromised. Susan's innocence, for example, is mere naïvety and a simple reflex of her father's money and mother's aristocratic ancestry. Instead a different set of positive terms is developed – 'real', 'alive', 'human'. The recurrent image of 'Zombies' is an extension of this – a way of judging social success by different criteria.

Alice's death forms the novel's climax and here, finally, the primary level of reality engulfs both the social and human scales of measurement. Both, however, have already been presented as vulnerable. Violent death is an integral element of the memory and meaning of the war (Joe's parents and comrades, the WAAF girls, Mrs Thompson's son), a collective experience too recent to be suppressed. Equally the commitment to the values of 'life' in Joe's relationship with Alice ('I'm alive now, all of me's alive' (p. 98)) and implicit in the Zombie image, is open to a reversal, as in Joe's comments on his 1956 self – 'I wouldn't say that I was dead; simply that I had begun to die. I have realized, you might say, that I have, at most, only another sixty years to live. I'm not actively unhappy and I'm not afraid of death, but I'm not alive in the way I was that evening I quarrelled with Alice' (p. 123). The two meanings of death – the metaphorical death of Zombiedom and the literal physical death of all individuals – are here fused. The logic is remorseless. By structuring human values on the metaphorical axis life/death and then transporting this into the physical world, the novel presents human values as inevitably subject to destruction, frequently of a violent and total kind.

The amoral social order (based on the struggle for material gain) is then justified, as a necessary adjustment to the facts – as Abe Brown advises – 'Don't worry about the way the world's run. Enjoy yourself' (p. 164). Joe's progress is precisely the process of discovering that the 'human' and the 'world' cannot be reconciled – 'I wanted to be in Warley. Alice didn't belong to Warley. I couldn't have both her and Warley: that was what it all boiled down to' (p. 214).

In a late revision of his concept of world-vision Lucien Goldmann argued for the recognition of a 'critical' element in many works of art. This would consist of 'an awareness of the values rejected and even repressed by the vision which makes up the unity of the work, and an awareness of the sacrifices which men have to suffer because of the refusal and repression of these values'.[40] In *Room at the Top* the 'human' (as embodied most clearly in Alice, but also in Joe's parents) is the critical element which has been refused and sacrificed. Through the recognition of this the novel is then able to present itself as an oppositional account of contemporary society (aligning itself with New Left cultural critics, with mythologisers of 'traditional' working-class culture and with the desire for a humanitarian, idealist politics as embodied in CND), while simultaneously ultimately endorsing as 'realistic' the ideology of affluence and individual material gain, of embourgeoisement and political pragmatism.

This conjunction of apparently contradictory positions within a single text goes a long way towards explaining the central cultural position enjoyed by *Room at the Top* in the late 1950s and early 1960s. It seems a remarkable achievement to be able to offer such opposing views simultaneously, although perhaps not so remarkable as it first appears since both views are simply direct reversals of each other within a single ideological field. The dominant view evacuates morality and idealism to the spheres of the past or the extra-political (art, personal relations); the alternative positions in effect accept this definition and develop their value-systems and strategies in the margins of social and political life. Joe's choice of Warley is regrettable and deeply regretted, but inevitable.

The novel version of *Room at the Top* is the original and, in literary-critical terms, the definitive text. Nevertheless it is very probable that, in the period 1959–63/4 it was the film version which constituted the dominant form in which *Room at the Top* was received. Perhaps even more likely is that, for many, both versions existed side-by-side, perhaps merging into each other (for some the film of the book, for others the book of the film). In this context it is necessary to ask how far the film offered a different set of messages and what different factors of determination were involved.

The film (not scripted by Braine) inevitably compressed the events of the novel considerably. Some characters, such as Mrs Thompson and the original Charles (who remained behind in Dufton in the novel) disappear altogether; others, such as Eva, are less prominent. Structurally the most striking change is the complete loss of narrative perspective; there is no narrator looking back on a younger self. Such a loss was by no means inevitable – indeed in many ways film as a medium can handle flashbacks and time-shifts more economically than print. The result, for this film, however, is the avoidance of any elements which would detract from an emphasis on direct pictorial realism – something which gives its audience unmediated contemporary experience.

This loss necessitates the development of alternate strategies for making Joe sympathetic. The form of the novel is what Raymond Williams has characterised as 'the fiction of special pleading' – 'The stress is really this: the world will judge me in certain ways if it sees what I do, but if it knew how I felt it would see me quite differently'.[41] The novel depends heavily on Joe's private explorations and justifications – almost buttonholing the reader – to maintain sympathy. Without this, the film places a much heavier emphasis on the nastiness of Joe's adversaries – particularly Jack Wales. Three new incidents are added. Jack now overhears Joe's social blunder in mispronouncing brazier as brassiere and is shown laughing exaggeratedly and raucously. A completely new scene is inserted, consisting of Joe gazing at Susan through the window of a women's clothes shop and being discovered by Jack who proceeds to insult him in a variety of ways. Finally Joe's first date with Susan is interrupted by Jack's sudden appearance in the restaurant and Joe's subsequent retreat. Jack's additional vindictiveness thus compensates for the loss of Joe's special pleading.

The main lines of the Joe–Alice–Susan triangle are preserved, although some of the emphases are altered. In the film the sexual relationship with Alice begins only after Hoylake has warned Joe away from Susan (this scene is much later in the novel). Conversely the sexual relationship with Susan starts much earlier in the film. Indeed in the film Joe's reason for going back to Alice (after their break-up over her past as a model) is his depression at his lack of fulfilment following his sexual success with Susan and not, as in the novel, depression at his *lack* of success because of her family's opposition. Again the emphasis is on developing strategies for ensuring sympathy with Joe's predicament. The final decision to leave Alice is also made more sympathetic. To Brown's ultimatum are added two new scenes. George, Alice's husband, comes to Joe's office to tell him that he will not divorce Alice and will sue him for enticement. A further scene is added in which Susan tells Joe that the wedding is off unless he never sees Alice again. It is, however, the role of George (making actual what in the novel are only potentialities voiced by Charles) which makes Joe's active decision to leave Alice almost superfluous – simply a recognition of factors outside his control.

The most striking change in the film, however, is the casting of Simone Signoret as Alice. Alice is now French and given a new social background (came over to England as a teacher in 1937 – Joe is likened by her to 'a boy I used to know in the University of Paris'). Alice's French qualities do not alter her structural position, rather they are a different way of signifying similar values. In the film accents naturally assume greater prominence – Joe's Northern working-class against Jack Wales's Standard Oxbridge or Abe Brown's Yorkshire against his wife's virtual self-parody of aristocratic elegance. Here Alice's distinctive French accent denotes her as apart from all others, outside social categories. Frenchness becomes a way of representing Alice's freer attitude to sexual relations as supported by a whole 'other' value-system not simply a matter of loose morals. In the novel much of this, again, is achieved by Joe's narrative commentary.

The scenes of Joe and Alice together are central to the film's articulation of the oppositional values contained in their relationship. Authenticity is again the key-note; much of the novel's dialogue is retained, but with extra emphasis on the idea of 'being yourself'. Alice is the chief proponent of this. On their holiday she tells Joe that 'you've been damaging yourself as a person . . . you don't ever have to pretend, you just have to be yourself'. A particularly interesting addition is the citing of the 'First to thine own self be true' passage from *Hamlet*. Joe starts the quotation but Alice is needed to finish it. This reference offers a validation[42] of their position in terms of artistic truth and cultural tradition, also indicating Alice's unusual position as a woman with intellectual capabilities. This theme of selfhood is retained in their final meeting with further new dialogue as Alice reproaches Joe – 'you just had to be yourself . . . with me you were yourself, only with me'.

The emphasis on authentic self is a simplification of the more complex ideas of the novel but not an alteration of the basic opposition between the human and the social. In the novel

Joe's regret and sense of defeat are conveyed through retrospective commentary; the film adds one extra closing scene – the wedding of Joe and Susan (with Joe still in a state of shock). As the honeymoon car drives away Susan reminds Joe that they are now together 'till death us do part'. She interprets Joe's subsequent tears as proving that he is sentimental after all; he is of course weeping for the death of Alice. Here Joe is clearly the victim rather than the culprit.

The film thus finds alternative ways of presenting Joe sympathetically. This allows the deletion of the narrative commentary and a consequent emphasis on the direct 'reality' of the characters, events and, particularly, setting. In the context of British films of the period it is not surprising that reviewers emphasised the film's realism – 'lively and local in its accents (Yorkshire); it cuts into the social layers'; 'at long last a British film that talks about life here today . . . in the middle of the dissolving and reforming social patterns of our time and place'.[43] One effect of the removal of the narrative commentary seems to have been that the moment of the film's events was registered less precisely. It now became post-war in general – 'life here today'. The film looked at everyday events and settings of contemporary life; this was innovatory and radical in itself. This aspect of the film provided a bridge towards the sequel *Life at the Top* and the TV series *Man at the Top* both of which were set much closer to the moment of their appearance. In these texts the centre of interest shifts to an examination of the good life itself, of the operation of power and the world of executives and management – characteristic 1960s themes. The novel version of *Room at the Top*, however, also survived as a steady seller and considerable cultural presence through the 1960s and even the 1970s – Joe Lampton's success, and its costs, continuing to provide a paradigmatic instance of the working-class hero on the make:

> There is room at the top they are telling you still
> But first you must learn how to smile as you kill
> If you want to be like the folks on the hill
> A working-class hero is something to be.[44]

NOTES

1. John Braine, *Room at the Top* (London: Eyre and Spottiswoode, 1957). Page references given below are to the subsequent paperback edition.
2. Kenneth Allsop, *The Angry Decade* (London: Peter Owen, 1958), pp. 23, 90.
3. John Holloway, 'Tank in the Stalls', *Hudson Review* (Autumn 1957), 139.
4. Graham Turner, *The North Country* (London: Eyre and Spottiswoode, 1967), p. 401.
5. Allsop, *Angry Decade*, p. 90.
6. John Braine, *Writing a Novel* (London: Eyre Methuen, 1974), p. 16.
7. G. S. Fraser, *New Statesman* (16 March 1957), p. 358.
8. *Room at the Top* (Harmondsworth: Penguin, 1959), p. 48.
9. P. Berger and T. Luckman, *The Social Construction of Reality* (London: Allen Lane, 1967).
10. H. G. Nicholas, *The British General Election of 1950* (London: Macmillan, 1950), p. 116.
11. Ibid., p. 213.
12. *New Statesman* (3 November 1951), p. 481.
13. G. Worswick and P. Ady, *The British Economy in the 1950s* (London: Oxford University Press, 1962).
14. D. Butler, *The British General Election of 1955* (London: Macmillan, 1955), p. 18.
15. *The Popular Press and Social Change*, unpublished report for the Rowntree Trust, University of Birmingham, 1968, p. 5:24. An edited version published as A. Smith, E. Immirzi and T. Blackwell, *Paper Voices* (London: Chatto & Windus, 1975).
16. Anthony Sampson, *Macmillan* (Harmondsworth: Penguin, 1968), p. 159.
17. D. Butler and R. Rose, *The British General Election of 1959* (London: Macmillan, 1959), p. 136 (facing).
18. George Orwell, 'The Lion and the Unicorn', *The Collected Essays, Journalism and Letters of George Orwell* Volume 2 (Harmondsworth: Penguin, 1971), pp. 74–99.
19. Antony Crosland, 'The Transition from Capitalism' in R. Crossman (ed.), *New Fabian Essays* (London: Turnstile Press, 1952), p. 37.
20. Austen Albu, 'The Organisation of Industry' in *New Fabian Essays*, p. 131.
21. Charles Curran, 'The Passing of the Tribunes', *Encounter* (June 1956).
22. R. Miller, *The New Classes* (London: Longman, 1967), p. 19.
23. *The Times* (29 January 1958).
24. Geoffrey Gorer, 'The Perils of Hypergamy', *New Statesman* (4 May 1957), pp. 566–8.
25. Frank Hilton, 'Britain's New Class', *Encounter* (February 1958), p. 60.
26. In a letter published in *Encounter* (April 1958) John Braine replied to this criticism by an appeal to reality. Compared with 'what goes on in business every day' Joe was neither violent nor ruthless – Hilton was merely being sentimental.

184   *Popular Fiction and Social Change*

27. Orwell, 'The Lion and the Unicorn', p. 98.

28. Ibid., p. 98.

29. R. Lewis and A. Maude, *The English Middle Classes* (Harmondsworth: Penguin, 1953), p. 17.

30. The *Sun* (15 September 1964).

31. Wayland Young, 'Return to Wigan Pier', *Encounter* (July 1956), pp. 5–6.

32. Raymond Williams, *The Long Revolution* (Harmondsworth: Penguin, 1965, p. 349; originally published London: Chatto & Windus, 1961).

33. Richard Hoggart, *The Uses of Literacy* (London, Chatto and Windus, 1957), pp. 24, 277.

34. Alice tells Joe 'Don't be so bourgeois' when Joe tries to end their embrace because Elspeth has come into the flat (p. 104).

35. Frank Parkin, *Middle Class Radicalism* (Manchester: University of Manchester Press, 1968), pp. 2, 36.

36. Ibid., p. 30.

37. Ibid., p. 99.

38. Christopher Driver, *The Disarmers* (London: Hodder and Stoughton, 1964), p. 115.

39. Parkin, *Middle Class Radicalism*, p. 39.

40. Lucien Goldmann, 'Criticism and Dogmatism in Literature', in David Cooper (ed.), *The Dialectics of Liberation* (Harmondsworth: Penguin, 1967), p. 145.

41. Raymond Williams, *The English Novel from Dickens to Lawrence* (London: Chatto & Windus, 1970), pp. 73–4.

42. This is a common trait of middle-brow cultural products; the 1960s TV Western series, *The Virginian*, for example included an episode entitled 'To Thine Own Self Be True'. What tends to be forgotten however, in this appeal to a supposedly timeless human truth, is that in *Hamlet* the words, spoken by Polonius, are clearly to be received ironically, given the context of the whole speech of stereotyped parental advice and Polonius's subsequent death while spying.

43. W. Whitebait, *New Statesman* (31 January 1959), p. 144; I. Quigly, *The Spectator* (30 January 1959), p. 144.

44. John Lennon, 'Working-Class Hero' (1970).

7. Utopia and Fantasy in the Late 1960s: Burroughs, Moorcock, Tolkien

DAVID GLOVER

Introduction

I want to begin with a disagreement – but one situated at some little distance from the youth culture of the late 1960s with which I will chiefly be concerned. In November 1963 a fierce controversy broke out in the letter columns of the normally august *Times Literary Supplement*, a controversy occasioned by a hostile review of William Burroughs' first published novel in Britain, *Dead Fingers Talk*. Leading literary figures of the day sided for and against the author in what proved to be an unusually protracted and acrimonious debate: 'we have never had a keener correspondence', observed the concluding editorial. Amongst those springing to Burroughs' defence were Michael Moorcock and Burroughs himself. For Moorcock the significance of Burroughs' work was apparently metaphysical, 'concerned with Space and Time, its nature, its philosophical implications, the place of the individual in the total universe'. 'A moral message', he confidently asserted, 'is not its prime concern.' In his own defence, however, Burroughs chose to emphasise precisely this moral message, since it 'should be quite clear to any reader . . . and I say it is to be taken as seriously as anything else in my work'.[1]

This disagreement between Burroughs and Moorcock seems to have passed unacknowledged, and I think it worth pausing to ask why this should have been so. I would suggest that it was not merely accidental and that at least part of the reason for this lies in a shared set of assumptions which undercut the surface differences between these two writers, providing them with a common universe of discourse. This ideology can best be understood as a kind of moralised or politicised aesthetics nicely epitomised in a favourite remark of Burroughs': 'I think that the most important thing in the world is that the artists should take over this planet because they're the only ones who can make anything happen'. As he asked David Bowie: 'why should we let these fucking newspaper politicians take over from us?'[2] On this view the regenerative power of the artist is believed to extend beyond the aesthetic sphere proper and is assigned a capacity and obligation to reshape the human order, or at the very least to provide a privileged key to its workings. Despite his disclaimers on 'social criticism' Moorcock's support for Burroughs appears to rest on just such a belief, as when he depicts modern science and modern literature converging on an investigation into the fundamental character of the social and natural cosmos, 'the paradox of the individual occupying the universe and the universe occupying the individual'. Thus Burroughs' work constitutes a 'scientific as well as [a] literary experiment', and this is said to be further corroborated by his ruthless exposé of the socio-political perversions of science.[3]

Because of the attribution of master status to the aesthetic attitude it has in this context the character of a totalisation, tending to integrate and subordinate all other perspectives within its own frame of reference, and hence has profoundly political implications. In its strongest form aesthetics is simply substituted for politics, offering, at one level, aesthetic answers to political questions; while at a minimum it merely takes over some of the functions of politics. In Britain a number of factors can be identified as pushing aesthetics into a key societal position in the immediate post-war period. Firstly, there was a redrawing of social class boundaries during the course of which the middle classes developed their distinctively 'separatist mass media and commercial or cultural institutions; most visibly in the "class" newspapers and periodicals'. As Eric Hobsbawm has further observed: 'a marked emphasis on "culture" was probably the most important innovation in the newspapers which appealed to the middle class in the post-war period, and which now fed their readers with book reviews, and pages on the theatre and the arts to an extent unusual before the Second World War'.[4] Here 'culture', whether confirming or challenging the canons of bourgeois art, operated as a means of defining and defending status. Secondly, there were developing significantly new strata, notably intellectuals and youth, their material preconditions clearly lying in the expansion of the educational system; for example, by 1956 the number of university students was almost double the pre-war figure, and three-quarters of them were being assisted by state grants.[5] And thirdly, providing a context and an occasion for these changes, the experience of a qualitatively new phase of economic prosperity and expansion associated with technological and managerial innovation, particularly via forms of state intervention. The range of cultural response engendered by these changes was complex and varied and included a cultural criticism which repeated the already well-worn themes of a descent into a mass society, uniting voices from left and right in a chorus against the impact of affluence, social reconstruction and equal opportunity.[6] In the late 1950s, however, one particular strand brought together all of the factors mentioned above in a single formation – that discontent amongst the new (predominantly lower-middle and working-class) intellectuals known as the Angry Young Men. Symptomatically, Osborne's play *Look Back In Anger* opens with an attack on the arts pages of the Sunday papers.

Such statements echoed much of the post-war critical consensus on cultural matters, so that it should come as no surprise to see these same themes – revolt against 'the assumed conformities, bland hypocrisies and comfortable conceits of modern society' – carried forward into later thinking.[7] The Underground or hippie counter-culture in fact displayed a large measure of continuity with the Angry Young Men who were in many ways its most articulate precursors. This in itself indicates an important attribute of Underground ideology, namely its syncretistic ability to weld together a variety of disparate and often historically prior texts and ideas into a new bricolage. By way of illustration I want to look briefly at the programme outlined by the Scottish poet and novelist Alexander Trocchi, himself a writer who came of age in the 1950s, had been cast as ' a central figure in the beat movement', and who subsequently passed into the ranks of the Underground.[8] His 'revolutionary proposal' for an 'invisible insurrection' first appeared in the early 1960s, apparently partly inspired by Situationist writings, but then resurfaced later in the decade as Project Sigma in the Underground paper *International Times*, alongside his attacks on credit, banking and the corporate state. One of its central axioms was that 'there is in principle no problem of production in the modern world' and correlatively that the real problems of distribution could easily be handled by international agencies like the United Nations, thus initiating the displacement of the modern nation-state. The description of factory life given here and the diagnostic use which was made of it are particularly revealing:

> Man has forgotten how to play. And if one thinks of the soulless tasks accorded each man in the industrial milieu, of the fact that education has become increasingly technological, and for the ordinary man no more than a means of fitting him for a 'job', one can hardly be surprised that man is lost. He is almost afraid of more leisure. He demands 'overtime' and has a latent hostility towards automation. His creativity stunted, he is orientated outwards entirely. He has to be amused. The forms that dominate his working life are carried over into leisure which becomes more and more mechanised; thus he is equipped with machines to contend with leisure which machines have accorded him.[9]

The comparison here is between a technological principle around which social reality might be organised and an aesthetic one. But most importantly it depends upon the pervasive assumptions of mass society theory with its origins in conservative and Romantic thought: of isolated, atomised individuals, increasingly alienated from the society which they comprise, passive, manipulable, culturally blinded and impoverished for 'the psychological wear and tear of our technological age' is alleviated by nothing more than 'ENTER-TAINMENT' (ibid.). Industrial labour is therefore at the heart of the problem. As Trocchi later wrote:

... many of the younger generation now know, one is not NECESSARILY unfortunate to be unemployed; any misfortune resides in the ways in which society still, partly unconsciously, insists on twisting the arms of those who are. And a considerable percentage amongst the young are more and more concerning themselves with intuitive good sense almost entirely with the problem of tomorrow's leisure which they have decided to live experimentally now ... We must put down that unctuous rectitude of whatever trades' union official is still fool enough to say his members want work, 'not doles'. We want doles, not necessarily work.[10]

Trocchi is self-evidently addressing a demystified élite, 'that one million (say) here and there who are capable of perceiving at once just what it is that I am about', whom he inclusively calls 'we the creative ones everywhere' who 'cannot afford to wait for the mass'. His notion is one of 'cultural revolt', not 'the *coup-d'état* of Trotsky and Lenin' because 'political revolt is and must be ineffectual'; rather, we need a '*coup-du-monde*, a transition of necessity more complex, more diffuse' which 'must seize the grids of expression and the powerhouses of the mind'. In the final analysis 'history will not overthrow national governments; it will outflank them' and it is therefore the task of the new élite to create 'the necessary underpinning, the passionate substructure of a new order of things'. Here aesthetics borrows from existing political rhetoric and gives it a new inflection in order to provide the groundwork for specifically cultural solutions to the modern malaise, solutions centred on a radical communalism ultimately to be initiated in 'a vacant country house (mill, abbey, church, or castle) not too far from the City of London' wherein 'we shall foment a kind of cultural "jam session"; out of this will evolve the prototype of our *spontaneous university*'. This is arguably one of the earliest adumbrations of counter-cultural ideology in Britain.[11]

Within contemporary youth culture the rise of the hippie Underground was a major new development which was able to provide a more general social base for these ideas. Many of the sociological analyses of this phenomenon have been formulated in terms of a subcultural model of collective response or solution to problems experienced in particular parts of the social structure, but it is important to see such a movement as a set of signifying practices having their own level of determinacy, its ideological representations being articulated with class locations in a complex way rather than merely expressing them in a simple one-to-one correspondence. This would help account for the fact that this kind of formation is 'more diffuse, more conscious of an international cultural influence', with 'a longer influence over [its] members' life cycle'. Its ideologies arise in part out of 'the development of the Underground press which presents a political and cultural critique of the establishment', at the same time elaborating and publicising the notion of the counter-culture itself;[12] certainly in their heyday papers like *International Times* and *Oz* enjoyed peak circulations of 100,000.[13] Following this line of argument, it is important to note the capacity of the counter-culture to recruit and mobilise its members from a variety of class fractions and to impact quite substantially upon the wider society.

While debate as to the precise status of subcultural theory continues, there does now exist a fair measure of agreement upon the focal concerns of hippie ideology: passive resistance, movement and the search for new experience, disaffiliation, spontaneity, ego-expressivity, short-term hedonism, subjectivity and the cultivation of the self.[14] What I want to underline here is its profoundly anti-bureaucratic and anti-organisational emphasis; as one writer declaimed: 'bureaucracy is the big bad wolf'.[15] Or as another had pointed out slightly earlier: 'even to call it [i.e. the Underground] a new "movement" is to create a false impression. This new thing is just people coming together and grooving. If you haven't yet understood what grooving means then you haven't yet understood what is going on'.[16] Some members of the Underground felt that organisation in itself led to an 'extreme lack of communication between its members and a tendency towards mystification and formalism of most basic operations' deriving from 'a morbid fascination for the structures of the normal business world'.[17] The prospect of children who would be 'free, unprogrammed and completely unidentified with the state' meant, according to 'one child's young father, who delivered the baby himself, and told no one except the Underground press', that there would be 'no birth certificate, no schooling unless the child wants it, no taxation, no official record of his existence. These children will be tranquillised by hash, lullabied by rock and roll, educated by the community' thus side-stepping 'the bureaucracy'. 'How long', asked one prominent Underground figure rhetorically, can the establishment 'withstand the impact of an alien culture? – a culture that is destined to create a new kind of man?'[18]

At one level the alienness of this culture was due to that extremely wide-ranging syncretism already noticed: 'British mythology (Glastonbury, Arthur, etc.), race relations, community experiments, India, Gandhi, William Blake . . . all . . . turning up and interpenetrating as matters of Underground concern, with no feeling of oddity at all', Tolkien and McLuhan rubbing shoulders with Marcuse and Mao.[19] These items were subject to considerable reinterpretation in order to function as ideologemes; thus Arthur was hailed as 'the People's King, the King who was and once again shall be', ruling over a 'a very green land, a land of trees and hills and castles . . . a human yet spiritual land'.[20] One effect of this ecumenicalism, therefore, was that texts having their origins and drawing their sense from quite distinct historical periods were rediscovered and assigned a new significance – the vogue for H. P. Lovecraft's work is just one example of this kind of process, and certainly this was the case for Tolkien and Burroughs, and even, to a lesser extent, Moorcock.

At the same time there was also the development of a taste for fantasy amongst Underground audiences, a marked preference for anti-realist genres, fictional worlds whose sense was conditional on the acceptance by the reader of supernatural or extra-scientific elements in their narratives. This anti-realist/fantasy taste was at one extreme highly responsive to experimental forms of writing, and the actual format and style of counter-cultural journalism was in part a reflection of this, often taken to the point of unreadability. Such forms of writing and presentation were sometimes seen as a kind of literary equivalent to the alteration of consciousness, and there seems in fact to have been a good deal of support for this sort of work within the general literary culture of the time – it is worth recalling, for example, that it was possible for an innovating writer like B. S. Johnson to hold 'an almost unique contract' with Secker & Warburg in the late 1960s which guaranteed him a three-year 'living salary' conditional on the delivery of two novels.[21] A good example of this trend in a more popular genre was the rise of a 'new wave' in science fiction writing, which began to consolidate in the mid-1960s, most importantly, of course, in Moorcock's magazine *New Worlds*. While this must qualify any simple equation between the Underground and the readership for fantasy and utopian writing, nevertheless the sense of collective identity generated by the hippie movement did serve as the focus for a wider interest in new values and anti-traditional themes.[22]

It was widely and confidently felt during this period that the relationship between high and popular art and their publics had changed decisively, and that old barriers were breaking down. As Frank Kermode reported in an investigation conducted in 1970: 'few doubt that there *is* a new audience'. The beginnings of this new popular audience was usually dated from the early 1960s and it was perceived as being a large and 'primarily . . . young audience', one that 'has been trained not on past art but on the violence, discontinuity and novelty of a modern environment', ultimately the product of technological advance. The 'familiarity with very rapid transitions, new juxtapositions, the environment of movies and advertising' identified in this kind of McLuhanesque rhetoric was taken as constraining and modifying the role of the artist, particularly the literary artist, rendering the traditional conventions of such forms as the novel no longer acceptable.[23] Burroughs was frequently chosen as an illustration of these alleged changes, a writer who was concerned to recognise and take into account the character of the new audience in his work; for example, in an interview with Kermode he claimed an overlap between the audience for pop music, notably the Beatles (arguably then at the height of their own experimental period), and the readership of his books. Appropriately enough, bands life Soft Machine, Steely Dan and Dead Fingers Talk did take their names from Burroughs' writings, a connection mirrored in the dedication of the early (though not the later) editions of Moorcock's novel, *The Final Programme*, 'to Jimmy Ballard, Bill Burroughs and the Beatles, who are pointing the way through'. The link was far from idiosyncratic. For the 'warm, total and all-involving' counter-culture took artistic experimentalism in general and anti-realism/fantasy in particular as its ally in subversion, as signalling 'a new culture which is alive, exciting, fun, ephemeral, disposable, unified, unpredictable, uncontrollable, lateral, organic and popular', opposing the old as 'infinitely divisible, élitist, remote and detached', an outmoded pattern which was 'earnest, drab, puritan and anti-play'.[24]

These ideas need to be understood against the background of social and political debate in the 1960s which had become increasingly preoccupied with the need to modernise Britain, to update its culture and technology in order to bring into existence the good society, at once more prosperous and humane. Political opinion united around this diagnosis so that it became possible to speak of a 'social-democratic consensus' in which social welfare and economic advance were to be reconciled. Closely bound up with this was a series of legislative changes involving both major parties which explicitly aimed to liberalise the spheres of public and private morality, ceding whole areas of 'sexual and social conduct and freedom of expression' to personal decision – what has been termed 'the legislation of consent', a legal revision in the status of sexuality, morals and aesthetics felt to be appropriate to a more advanced type of society.[25] The Underground provided a further exploration of these themes as an integral part of its social practice, and hence is only fully intelligible as a response to the modernising discourses of the post-war period. Indeed it might be said that these discourses provided the very conditions of possibility for hippie ideology: they prepared an ideological space for the Underground to occupy and supplied a social object against which hippie ideology could offer itself as a critical commentary, a commentary that highlighted the limits of liberalisation and the repressive role of the State.

William Burroughs

I want now to turn to the work of three exemplary writers for this counter-culture in order to produce a reading of those ideological moments in their texts that are of special relevance to it. At first sight Burroughs, Moorcock and Tolkien might seem to make an oddly disparate collection; yet their works rapidly achieved canonical status amongst Underground readers and provided a vocabulary of reference for its journalism, correspondents signing themselves with such names as 'Bradley Martin' and 'Bilbo Baggins'. Each contributed, that is to say, to the formation of Underground discourse and its background assumptions. The advertisement for *The Lord of the Rings* which appeared in *Oz* makes this plain: 'Take *your* trip to Middle Earth with *The Lord of the Rings*. Tolkien's psychedelectable monsterpiece now in paperback 30s at any old bookshop everywhere', as does that for the 'mystical scene magazine' *Gandalf's Garden*, named after Tolkien's wizard and described as 'a crack in the cosmic egg', and this vision found its natural complement and extension in the artwork of Martin Sharp and John Hurford which graced the pages of *Oz* throughout this period. However, more specific personal connections and stylistic influences exist between these writers and will help place them in their proper context.

Tolkien's *Lord of the Rings* has been reckoned 'the main influence for the tremendous growth of fantasy and private-world fiction', in its turn underwriting the success of other fantasists, including Moorcock's sword-and-sorcery writing and the Gormenghast trilogy of Mervyn Peake.[26] Tolkien and Peake, very different writers, both crested on the same wave of popularity and were marketed on almost identical lines. Ballantines, the American paperback publishers, issued *Lord of the Rings* with 'pseudo-gothic illustrations' and also 'employed the same artist to prepare the dust-covers of the Titus books' making them look 'as if they were about the adventures of King Arthur and the Lady of Shalott'.[27] Moorcock, as editor of the magazine *New Worlds*, had not only employed Peake as an illustrator, but was instrumental in widening the boundaries of SF towards fantasy and experimental writing from the late 1950s on – pioneering the multiple-authored Jerry Cornelius series, for example, as well as making it a matter of deliberate policy to 'put stuff in the magazine which would gradually help people understand Burroughs' such as some of his own work and that of J. G. Ballard.[28] The Jerry Cornelius adventures were themselves significantly influenced by Burroughs, and both Moorcock and Burroughs became contributors to Underground papers like *International Times*, the Jerry Cornelius stories appearing there as a strip cartoon drawn by Mal Dean.

The immediate point of entry into Burroughs' work for many counter-cultural readers was the lore of narcotics. His two best-selling books, *Naked Lunch* and *Junkie*, each of which has sold over half a million copies since first publication, are those which deal most closely with the drugs milieu, whilst the covers of the paperback editions of the bulk of his work have alternated between images of the mainlining addict and psychedelic surrealism. At the same time, the rhetoric of consciousness-expansion was pressed into service in the marketing of his texts to suggest (in the words of one blurb) that 'reading Burroughs is like taking the ultimate trip to the outer limits of the contemporary nightmare', clearly paralleling other revelatory experiences then on offer.[29] Yet power and dependency within the junk world of the 1940s and 1950s served only as an initial metaphor for Burroughs, and whilst being amongst the most willing friends of the Underground he was often an intransigent critic of it. He was resident in London throughout this period and his own archives show numerous contacts with key Underground figures, if rather sceptical support for their activities.[30] In his utterly uncompromising opposition to what he called the three 'formulas' of nation-state, family and reproduction he sharply crystallised a number of strands in hippie ideology, pushing certain features of it to their logical limits; and he extended this to an equally uncompromising practice of writing. The primary characteristic of his texts, both in terms of form and content, is of structures rigidified to the point of incoherence and reactionary brutality, precipitating their own cataclysmic breakdown and transcendence. Thus, in the imaginary state of Annexia:

> every citizen . . . was required to apply for and carry on his person at all times a whole portfolio of documents. Citizens were subject to be stopped in the street at any time . . . . On subsequent inspection the citizen was required to show the properly entered stamps of the last inspection. The Examiner, when he stopped a large group, would only examine and stamp the cards of a few. The others were then subject to arrest because their cards were not properly

stamped . . . Documents issued in vanishing ink faded into old pawn tickets. New documents were constantly required. The citizens rushed from one bureau to another in a frenzied attempt to meet impossible deadlines.[31]

This growing feeling of frenzy is ready to erupt at any moment: 'And you can see the marks are wising up, standing around in sullen groups and that mutter gets louder and louder. Any minute now fifty million adolescent gooks will hit the street with switch blades, bicycle chains and cobblestones.'[32]

Burroughs has long held that 'the antiquated social structures we have now cannot support' what he sees as an 'escalating rate of change' and that 'writers must take a very definite stand'.[33] These views have roots deep inside the contradictory formation of the Beats and reflect the profound influence of Nietzsche and, more specifically, of Spengler within that milieu. Spengler's distinction between 'culture' and 'civilization' and the identification of 'civilization' with decay and dislocation has played a key part in Burroughs' work; a similarly negative evaluation of modern civilisation has also, of course, served as a mainstay of hippie pastoralism (although Burroughs has been highly critical of the new arcadianism because of its ultimate dependency on present-day industrial society).[34] Throughout his writing there is a powerful denunciatory rhetoric at work which aims at wising up the marks, 'to make people aware of the true criminality of our times'.[35] The tone is one of sarcasm, desperation and menace: 'Listen to my last words any world. Listen all you boards syndicates and governments of the earth. And you powers behind what filth deals consummated in what lavatory to take what is not yours . . . . These words may be too late. Minutes to go.'[36]

Historically speaking, Burroughs' work has rested on the use of two main technical and stylistic devices: the 'routine' and the 'cut-up' or 'fold-in' method, and these function to compromise any clear narrative order in his texts. The former has its origins in the 'spontaneist' ideology of the Beats, set out in Kerouac's 'Essentials of Spontaneous Prose' and restated in *Naked Lunch* in the assertion that 'there is only one thing a writer can write about: *what is in front of his senses at the moment of writing* . . . I am a recording instrument . . . I am not an entertainer'.[37] A 'routine'

is a sketch, a kind of exaggerated or highlighted burlesque
with vivid theatrical qualities, originally devised to be read
aloud or acted out before others, pieces with a strong oral
dimension, reflecting the Beat preference for public perfor-
mance and black humour. In the 'cut-up', on the other hand, as
its name suggests 'pages of text are cut and rearranged to form
new combinations of word and image', and from the mid-1960s
onwards all Burroughs' texts made use of this technique, even
to the extent of rewriting some of the earlier ones. What both
devices share is their critical, liberatory edge; their purpose is to
disrupt and discredit a status quo which is felt to be literally
unbearable. In the case of the 'routine' the target is those who
command and exercise power in one way or another, together
with their lackeys, and the attack is by means of fanciful and
even hallucinatory projection and distortion into horrendous
farce. More radically, in the case of the 'cut-up' the enemy is
language itself, conceived as the prime instrument of domination, as part of a veritable will to power through the 'absolute
barrage' of word and image, particularly from television and
newspaper; hence 'if you start cutting these up and rearranging
them you are breaking down the control system' and may be
able 'to some extent to nullify them'.[38] The lines of story and
sentence are fractured and fragmented so that the taken-for-
granted character of familiar discourses, whereby 'words have
lost meaning and life through years of repetition', yet which still
rigidly define and delimit the subject's life-world, are exposed
and their certainties placed in doubt.[39]

    This is, however, no simple liberal humanist vision. The crea-
tive power of language is no distinctively human capacity that has
been perverted and needs to be restored. Language is transitory
and impermanent, not even a necessary evil, for 'words are . . .
awkward . . . and they will be laid aside eventually, probably
sooner than we think'.[40] In *Naked Lunch* the words 'spill off the
page in all directions',[41] while in *Nova Express* we are warned
that 'to speak is to lie – to live is to collaborate'.[42] Nor is
language expressive of a human essence, since, as he emphasised in one interview, 'human beings are so diversified that
they are not even of the same species'.[43] The texts are littered
with references to mutant beings ('He caught the twittering
chirping sound of the tree-frog people . . . . It was about two feet

in length of a translucent green colour – The obsidian eyes were all pupil and mirrored a pulsing blood suction to rhythms of a heart clearly visible in the transparent flesh') part of a representation of the variety and continual proliferation of life-forms in an unregulated and abandoned way.[44] Moreover, the repulsive succession of 'identity transfers' and the dizzying metamorphoses of apparently human characters like Bradley the Buyer, the narcotics agent who turns into a horrible mutant junkie, parasitic on others 'like a vampire bat' or 'a gorged boa constrictor' and becomes 'a creature without species', all serve to undermine any confidence in humanness.[45] This is very different from the kind of oppositions found in most SF where the contrast between humanness or the human-like and other alien forms is usually paramount. Yet this facet of the texts was glimpsed only as psychedelia or as part of Burroughs' 'report' from his 'look at hell'. What was more easily picked up was the selective emphasis of another much-quoted dustjacket blurb which offered his work as 'an absolutely devastating ridicule of . . . the abuses of power, hero worship, aimless violence, materialistic obsession, intolerance and every form of hypocrisy'.[46]

Burroughs' depiction of control is virtually total. Whether it is the priestcraft of 'The Mayan Caper' or the corporate 'Trak Board' with its sinister product that 'never leaves the customer' creating the 'precise need of Trak servicing', 'Control's control' is massively dominant over its 'human cattle', except for the existence of minor criminals at the margins.[47] It is a condition of 'total emergency', demanding 'total resistance'; the alternative horizons are the destruction of the planet in nova explosion or the liberation of the biologic film by storming the reality studios. The machinery of control whose co-ordinates are the nation-state, family and reproduction leaves its supports perfectly vulnerable, locking them into the '*is* of identity': 'human activities are drearily predictable. It should now be obvious that what you call "reality" is a function of . . . precisely predictable because prerecorded human activities . . . a prerecorded biologic film'. The problem is that any escape or transcendence involves leaving this condition, but 'to really leave human form you would have to leave . . . the whole concept of word and image'.[48] What is at stake is the ability to chart psychic areas and explore inner space which has as its precondition the destruction of all forms of conformism and control. At one point in *Naked Lunch* a comparison is made between bureaucracies and co-operatives:

> Bureaus cannot live without a host, being true parasitic organisms. (A co-operative on the other hand *can* live without the state. That is the road to follow. The building up of independent units to meet needs of the people who participate in the functioning of the unit. A bureau operates on the opposite principle of *inventing needs* to justify its existence.) Bureaucracy is wrong as a cancer, a turning away from the human evolutionary direction of infinite potentials and differentiation and independent spontaneous action, to the complete parasitism of a virus.[49]

Burroughs rejects politics as a means of achieving change since he identifies it with the conventional mechanisms of the nation state and hence part of the very problem. But he does designate youth as a revolutionary vehicle for social change, 'the only effective challenge to established authority' capable of displacing the state and all its pathologies by violence and disruption since 'bureaus die when the structure of the state collapses'.[50] However, Burroughs has always been profoundly suspicious of political revolution as this is usually understood, and especially of the leftist variety, because it merely replaces one élite by another. Disruption via lifestyle and cultural innovation (including artistic and quasi-scientific experimentalism – hardly separate categories in his eyes): these are for Burroughs at least as important as organised violence. He has even argued that the real significance of revolutions may be that they create the type of chaos which is most favourable to change, change which must in the final analysis be at the level of life-forms; ultimately 'it is more necessary to change the world than society'.[51] Thus the importance of a cultural revolution whose most powerful weapons are new forms of consciousness.

Michael Moorcock

In terms of age, background and experience Michael Moorcock has by far the most direct claim to membership of Underground society, a society which is often affectionately satirised in his work, along with the straighter manifestations of swinging London. His output is prodigious and it is obviously impossible in this chapter to do full justice to that vast corpus. But from this period two of his most popular and successful creations stand out: Elric of Melniboné and Jerry Cornelius. Whilst these figures are drawn from rather different genres they are in fact closely related thematically, and the Cornelius stories actually rework some of the Elric material; indeed, according to the author 'Jerry Cornelius began as a version of Elric of Melniboné when, in late 1964, I was casting around for a means of dealing with what I regarded as the "hot" subject matter of my own time – stuff associated with scientific advance, social change, the mythology of the mid-twentieth century'.[52] Both protagonists are profoundly ambiguous figures, their strangeness physically marked out by the kind of stigmata which would qualify them for villain status in an Ian Fleming novel: Elric with his skin 'the colour of a bleached skull', his shoulder-length 'milk-white' hair and 'moody', 'crimson', 'slanting eyes' and 'brooding nature'[53] and Jerry Cornelius, his skin 'as black as a Biafran's', 'his hair not blond but milk white', but elsewhere appearing as 'slim, with large dark eyes and large, long-fingered hands' and 'long, fine black hair that flowed to below his shoulders'.[54] As in the Burroughs' texts, the world depicted here is one of civilisation in eclipse: Melniboné, a kingdom either waning or lost, 'ravaged, at last, by the formless terror called Time', and a latter-day Europe at the crossroads, 'ahead of the world' but 'soon to be shaken to pieces in the imminent pre-entropic wash of crisis'.[55]

The hero seeks to negotiate this world and its pitfalls, to kick against its destiny, to discover, as Elric says, 'what rules above the forces of Law and Chaos'; but these efforts turn out to be self-destructive much of the time and his knowledge and reserves of power are never quite under control.[56] It is of little avail to Jerry Cornelius that he has authored such books as

Time-Search Through the Declining West and *Toward the Ultimate Paradox*, for he is, like Elric, a struggling captive of his condition, mirroring 'the conflicting time streams of the second half of the twentieth century . . . and it seemed that the mind behind cried forward while the mind in front cried back'.[57] Both figures, for example, undertake that sword-and-sorcery cliché the subterranean journey in search of arcane and secret knowledge, 'the complete objective truth about the nature of humanity', a search that ends in dust and derision.[58] In the end both must return to the realisation that in their declining universe 'there is no new morality . . . there is no morality . . . there are no values!' and must resolve to 'live my life without ever knowing why I live it – whether it has purpose or not', in existential revolt against all established codes.[59]

Moorcock has stated that his books seek to demystify/ denaturalise the hero 'by leading always to final statements where gods and heroes and grand designs are shown to be pointless', an attempt to provide a corrective to 'a tendency towards fascism, towards thinking in terms of social pyramids' present in all fantasy, thus giving his audience a good read by preventing them going off 'with the wrong ideas'.[60] Moreover, the alternative to the hero principle is 'peace and love . . . basic hippie philosophy . . . if two people can love each other they create the foundation on which this perpetual process of disintegration can be overcome, or stalled', perhaps by fusing into a new hermaphrodite like Cornelius Brunner at the end of *The Final Programme*, 'the world's first all-purpose human being', a celebration of 'the central ambivalence of sex'.[61]

Yet notwithstanding this retrospective claim, the effect of Moorcock's texts is to encourage a deep sense of subjectivism on the part of the reader, eluding any clear meaning or message. This is particularly noticeable at the level of individual sentences, passages or episodes, in the spaces between the overarching structures of the main plot. There is a slackening of tension and a turning inwards which stands at odds with Moorcock's undoubted skill at conveying action and building up narrative pace. Here social relationships are interiorised, resulting in an exploration of the self through fantasy, dwelling particularly upon the constitutive moments in the formation of the personality, which probably reflects the influence of Peake.

Sometimes this serves to effect a simple libidinal release, the male fantasy self in brutal omnipotence so typical of hippie ideologies of sexual liberation; thus, suddenly, in the middle of a meeting with a client, 'Jerry reached up and pulled the girl to him. They kissed each other firmly and pulling off their clothes lay down on the floor and fucked with hot and hasty passion'.[62] Elsewhere the use of symbols points not merely to the desire to transgress, to break taboos, to violate the limits of the social, but towards tensions and conflicts within the self which the text fails to resolve. Under the thrall of his runesword Storm-bringer, which vampirically sucks the 'life-force' from its victims, Elric slaughters both the cousin he loves and his comrades and allies; as he warns his alter ego Moonglum: 'be wary of this devil-blade . . . It kills the foe – but savours the blood of friends and kin-folk most'.[63]

In *The Final Programme* this interiorisation is even more explicit. At one point Jerry Cornelius leads a raid upon 'his father's fake Le Corbusier chateau', in which 'Old Cornelius had exhausted and killed himself searching for the ultimate hallucinogenic device', a house which 'symbolised the very spirit of transcience' and afforded a pleasure like 'listening to last year's hits'. The chateau fatefully concentrates Jerry's biography within its walls, since it 'strongly . . . resembled his father's tricky skull' and the very purpose of the attack is to rescue his sister Catherine, whom he incestuously loves, held captive by his evil brother Frank, and liberate his father's microfilms. But the attack goes hideously wrong: Jerry acciden-tally shoots Catherine and as a result of her death becomes momentarily 'unaware of who or where he was' and subse-quently has to be hospitalised. Even the microfilms finally turn out to be meaningless, and matters are only resolved with the demolition of the chateau at the end of the book by Jerry's new 'bi-sexual self'.[64]

As this suggests, the writing here is allusive, heavily symbolic and at times portentous, holding out the feeling of a meaning just beyond the reader's grasp. This radical subjectivism is precisely Moorcock's intention for whereas his early writings were allegorical, appearing 'to say one thing on the surface and another thing beneath', his later books transform this into 'irony' since this 'allows for more than one interpretation on the part of the reader'. No 'key' is possible in these later 'ironic fables' for 'the effect of randomness . . . is achieved by a tightly controlled system of internal reference, puns, ironies, logic-jumps which no single reader may fairly be expected to follow'.[65] What we are left with is a contradictory movement between an individualism in which the hero is never clearly demystified and a fatalism as to the possibilities of the existing social milieu, a tension between self-aggrandisement and karma, itself depicted as a kind of acid-dream. Despite his failures the hero is constantly indulged, a central focus even when this self is at its most submerged: on a club dance-floor 'the sense of being part of the mass was a delicious feeling. He and the girl and the others around them seemed fused together with a total absence of individual identity', yet this only turns out to be Jerry's cue to go on stage and instrumentally dominate the rock band.[66] Communal togetherness only fades into its opposite, a heightened individualism, and there is nothing in the early texts to rival the demolition of illusion in the final Cornelius volume *The Condition of Muzak* (1976). Jerry Cornelius, a self without proper limit, is always at the centre of a conspiracy, in a futile world consisting largely of conspiracies, where the breakthrough to community is never quite made, and style is the only resource, a perfect (if unwitting) dramat-isation of the hippie dilemma to which Moorcock's texts are so closely tied.

J. R. R. Tolkien

The astonishing success of J. R. R. Tolkien's *The Lord of the Rings* has sometimes been felt to be puzzling, but as Giddings and Holland have recently pointed out it always received strong backing in the review pages of the middle-class 'quality' press.[67] Much of its power comes, of course, from the absorbing parallel world it creates for the reader, a world which has been claimed as close to SF.[68] But apart from this generalised appeal, why were so many within the Underground and beyond it so ready to take this 'trip to Middle Earth' in the late 1960s? Clearly its Arthurian resonances fitted well with that highly syncretistic version of tradition constructed by the counter-culture to which I have already pointed. However, the ease with which it could be assimilated also derives from the structural features of a narrative which could be read as a transformation of Underground concerns, and in turn helped to define these more closely.

In the first place, this parallel world is one which is thoroughly humanised, in the sense of being well-adapted to social needs without having to be mastered by a developed technology: it contains hostile forces, but is not itself hostile. The Shire is 'rich and kindly', a 'pleasant corner of the world' in which the hobbits can ply 'their well-ordered business of living'; despite their vaunted ability to 'survive rough handling by grief, foe, or weather' it is the sheer cosiness of hobbit life which strikes one, with its gardens, pipe-weed and uniformless policemen, and even Tolkien himself has written of their 'bourgeois smugness'.[69] It is a world, however, which is already beginning to experience the reverberations of crisis, 'rumours of strange things happening in the world outside'; as a sign of this instability, territories are starting to lose their recognised character and populations become disordered and displaced: 'elves could now be seen . . . passing . . . through the woods in the evening and not returning', 'dwarves in unusual numbers' and 'trolls were abroad . . . cunning and armed with dreadful weapons'.[70]

The source of this disruption is Sauron, the hidden adversary, an incarnation of evil of Gothic provenance whose malevolence is practically incomprehensible, the more so because barely glimpsed: 'Frodo looked into emptiness. In the black abyss there appeared a single Eye that slowly grew . . . So terrible was it that Frodo stood rooted, unable to cry out or to withdraw his gaze. The Eye was rimmed with fire, but was itself glazed, yellow as a cat's, watchful and intent, and the black slit of its pupil opened on a pit, a window into nothing'.[71] So powerful is this force that it cannot be defeated until counter-magic is mobilised against it; in reality when its own magic, the Ring, is turned on it, knowledge of which is only vouchsafed to the Baggins family and mediated by the wizard Gandalf.

In depicting the solemnity of this struggle the use of language sometimes has an almost Biblical cadence to it; the accounts of battles, for example, sound like incantations: 'and then all the host of Rohan burst into song, and they sang as they slew, for the joy of battle was on them, and the sound of their singing that was fair and terrible came even to the City'.[72] But notwithstanding this and the enormous amount of detail weighing down the text, the narrative generally moves along in a manner reminiscent of a Buchan adventure.[73] Despite some creakiness in the plotting, this is a narrative in which heroism and destiny are integrated rather than dissociated as in Moorcock's work. Frodo deserves to be chosen by the Ring which 'itself . . . decided things'. It is 'an evil fate' for the defeat of Sauron exacts a terrible price in death and injury, but it is Frodo's exemplary actions in the context of this destiny which demonstrate the possibility of ensuring that 'the Quest is achieved'.[74]

The vehicles of this evil are various, from the sinister Black Riders to the turncoat wizard Saruman. Of special importance though are the orcs since they are the main instrument of Sauron's domination and a central obstacle in the path of Frodo's journey into Mordor which is the core narrative of the book; indeed there is some evidence of readers skipping the fifth book in order to follow through this thread.[75] The very first reference to them is revealing: we learn that 'orcs were multiplying again in the mountains'.[76] Thus the essentials of the image: fecund, pestiferous, horribly sexualised in contrast to the orderly delayed marriages and bachelordom of the hobbits. With their ugliness, strength, foul smell, filthy jowls, long hairy arms and bow-legs the militarism of the orcs is insect-like in its organisation, 'like black ants going to war' in their black cloaks, iron-rimmed black caps with 'beaklike noseguard' upon which 'the evil Eye was painted in red'.[77] Their very names and voices are harsh, much given to cursing and swearing as befitting a lower order, and their speech reflects both their origins and their legendary cruelty: 'Nar – this little filth . . . beyond feeling sick for a bit, he'll be all right'.[78] They represent a world of 'great slave-worked fields', of 'great roads . . . to tributary lands, from which the soldiers of the Tower brought long waggon-trains of goods and booty and fresh slaves'; from these 'mines and forces' come 'the musterings of long-planned war . . . the Dark Power, moving its armies like pieces on the board'.[79] In such a world the suffering of one's fellows invites only laughter. It is the stark antithesis of hobbit life, its machiavellian political calculation the very opposite of the momentary initiative and bravery of Frodo and Sam; it represents in extreme form the threat of a rational nation-state whose time has not yet come, for, despite all the paraphernalia of maps, Middle-earth depends upon only a loose sense of territory, its boundaries primarily natural ones, mountain ranges, forests and the like.

This antithesis is crucial for Tolkien; as C. N. Manlove has observed: 'his picture of the alliance of the peoples of Middle-earth against Sauron is one of a co-operative effort by different races, each with a separate identity in which the author at least goes through the motions of taking a delight. It is precisely that they retain their generic individualities in coming together that should define the good; and under Sauron and the power of the Ring that identity should fade'.[80] The significance of the transformation of the Shire at the end of the book lies in this same point. It is not merely the occasion for an attack on the horrors of industrial desecration – the fouling of streams, the removal of trees, the monstrosities of modern architecture; it is also an account of the violation of the spontaneous order of the hobbits, the brutalisation of its populace, and their subordination to an external principle of organisation in which new laws are promulgated and enforced and power centralised in the person of 'the Chief' and his machinery of repression, under whose orders even beer-drinking and smoking are outlawed.

It has plausibly been suggested that such scenes owe something to the 'backward-looking nostalgia' typified in the Distributionism[81] of Chesterton and Belloc with its anti-industrial utopia of yeoman farmers and small craftsmen, thus supplying content to Tolkien's justification of 'Recovery' as a recuperative escapism, what he called the 'Escape of the Prisoner'.[82] Once again it is the function of the writer to safeguard and disseminate this aesthetic vision, the redeemability of the world from its present condition. 'Recovery' was Tolkien's term for 'regaining . . . a clear view' of 'things as we are (or were) meant to see them', that is as radically different from the distortions introduced by 'scientific theory'. This function of fairy-stories allows us to retrieve 'the wonder of the things, such as stone, and wood, and iron; tree and grass; house and fire; bread and wine', and the ideal environment for this appreciation is a restored communal pastoralism.[83]

Conclusion

For each of these writers the late 1960s was the period when, to borrow a phrase from Pierre Macherey, a public came to find itself in their work, tying that work to their own historical moment, with each author reaching maximum exposure and circulation through the medium of mass market paperbacks.[84] To be sure, for each of these writers the sense of an audience has been acute, even if not always unequivocally welcome. Tolkien was highly sceptical of his new readership in spite of his advocacy of the need for escapism in the face of the modern world. Deploring the initial American enthusiasm responsible for his late-won success, he sought to distance it from his own preferred reading of his texts, and regarded such youthful response as immature: 'Art moves them and they don't know what they've been moved by and they get quite drunk on it. Many . . . are involved in the stories in a way that I'm not'.[85] Burroughs too, notwithstanding his defence of the counter-culture and being much fêted by it, was critical of many of its beliefs and practices in a way that was never really recognised or acknowledged. He derided the hippie love ethic because 'the people in power will not disappear voluntarily, and giving flowers to the cops just isn't going to work'. Though youth constituted a revolutionary force, it had 'been lied to, sold out and betrayed' making the writer's task of 'mass deconditioning' more urgent than ever.[86] Again what is being signalled here is a gap between an authorial ideology and a culturally operative reading. Only Moorcock fully embraced the new Underground, regarding his 'most intelligent' appreciation as coming 'from that section of the public most at ease with what's these days called the "alternative" society'.[87] And he appears still nostalgically to regard this period as his own 'imaginative area', one of 'dirty cellars, three o'clock in the morning, looking for a dog end . . . that whole seedy romanticism, or romantic seedyism . . . the attraction of contemporary bohemianism'.[88] Though his muse is often treated ironically, Moorcock seems caught between the twin poles of individualism and communalism in hippie ideology and his debunking of the hero figure was only effectively accomplished, appropriately enough, as the counter-culture began to go into decline. With all these reservations and absences the work of all three authors was centrally caught up in the general mood of affirmation and social optimism of the late 1960s and benefited from the institutional support of Underground journalism, publishing and commerce. The enclosed worlds of their texts provided a touchstone for a critique of existing social structures and the construction of alternatives, social models prefigured in the achievements of literary technique. If the Underground's key political tract was, significantly, Herbert Marcuse's under-focused book *One Dimensional Man*, its fictional templates were drawn from Annexia, Melniboné and Middle-earth.

Postscript

In a recently published pamphlet decrying the erosion of the liberal gains of the 1960s Michael Moorcock has claimed that his early books were widely misunderstood. Far from being taken in the spirit of 'deep scepticism' which was apparently intended, Jerry Cornelius was adopted as 'a model by the very same young men whose euphoria and ambitions' the novels had satirised. While writers like Moorcock have had a central role in defining the key concerns of ideological and cultural discourse for their time, they have never been the final arbiters in the struggle over meaning. As Moorcock himself notes, it was 'probably inevitable' that Jerry Cornelius should have been transformed into 'a kind of hipper James Bond'. And, we might add, it was perhaps only fitting that the 1973 film of *The Final Programme* 'was directed by a man originally involved in the first *Avengers* TV series'.[89]

NOTES

1. For the full correspondence, see the *Times Literary Supplement*, 14 November 1963 to 30 January 1964.
2. W. S. Burroughs and D. Bowie, 'Beat Godfather Meets Glitter Mainman', *Rolling Stone*, 28 February 1974.

3. M. Moorcock, 'Letter to the Editor', *Times Literary Supplement* (21 November 1963).

4. E. Hobsbawm, *Industry & Empire* (Harmondsworth: Penguin, 1969), pp. 279–84.

5. P. Lewis, *The Fifties* (London: Heinemann, 1978), p. 160.

6. D. Hebdidge, 'Towards a Cartography of Taste 1935–1962', in B. Waites *et al.* (eds), *Popular Culture: Past and Present* (London: Croom Helm, 1982), pp. 194–218.

7. *Protest 1958*, cited in R. Neville, *Play Power* (London: Paladin, 1971), p. 18.

8. See the cover of A. Trocchi's *Cain's Book* (London: Jupiter Books, 1966).

9. A. Trocchi, 'A Revolutionary Proposal', *City Lights Journal*, No. 2 (1964), p. 17.

10. A. Trocchi, 'Watch that Gnome!', *International Times*, No. 58 (1969).

11. A. Trocchi, 'Revolutionary Proposal', pp. 14–22.

12. M. Brake, *The Sociology of Youth Culture and Youth Subcultures* (London: RKP, 1980), pp. 86–7.

13. I. Taylor and D. Wall, 'Beyond the Skinheads: Comments on the Emergence and Significance of the Glamrock Cult', in G. Mungham and G. Pearson (eds), *Working Class Youth Culture* (London: RKP, 1976), p. 115.

14. S. Hall, 'The Hippies: An American "Moment" ' (University of Birmingham: Centre for Contemporary Cultural Studies Stencilled Papers, 1968).

15. R. Durgnat, 'Is the Muse of Satire the Midwife of Corruption?', *Oz Newsprint Section* (April–May, 1968).

16. T. McGrath, 'Bust', *International Times* (13–26 March 1967).

17. B. Miles, 'The Phragmented Philosophy', *International Times*, No. 38 (1968).

18. R. Neville, *Play Power* (London: Paladin, 1971), p. 56.

19. G. Ashe, 'Letter from an over 30', *International Times*, No. 38 (1968).

20. *International Times*, 98 (1971).

21. For details, see *Transatlantic Review*, No. 21 (Summer 1966), p. 163.

22. On the changing nature of utopian thought and literature, see R. Levitas, 'Sociology & Utopia', *Sociology*, 13, No. 1 (January 1979), 19–33.

23. F. Kermode, 'Is an élite necessary?', *The Listener* (29 October 1970).

24. Neville, *Play Power*, pp. 52, 225.

25. S. Hall, 'Reformism & the Legislation of Consent', in National Deviancy Conference (ed.), *Permissiveness & Control: the Fate of the Sixties Legislation* (London: Macmillan, 1980).

26. See B. Aldiss, *Billion Year Spree: the History of Science Fiction* (London: Weidenfeld & Nicolson, 1973), p. 265.

27. J. Watney, *Mervyn Peake* (London: Abacus Books, 1977), p. 172.

28. A. Burns and C. Sugnet (eds), *The Imagination on Trial* (London: Allison & Busby, 1981), p. 118.

29. See the 1968 Panther edition of Burroughs' *Nova Express*.

30. W. S. Burroughs, *A Descriptive Catalogue of the William S. Burroughs Archive* (London: Covent Garden Press, 1973).

31. W. S. Burroughs, *The Naked Lunch* (London: John Calder, 1964), p. 31.

32. W. S. Burroughs, *Nova Express* (London: Panther Books, 1968), p. 18.

33. F. Kermode, 'Is an élite necessary?'.

34. See Burroughs' *Snack* (London: Aloes Books, 1975), p. 29.

35. W. S. Burroughs, 'Interview 1965', in A. Kazin (ed.), *Writers at Work: Third Series* (London: Secker & Warburg, 1968), p. 174.

36. W. S. Burroughs, *Nova Express*, pp. 9–10.

37. W. S. Burroughs, *The Naked Lunch*, pp. 218–19.

38. W. S. Burroughs, *The Job* (London: Jonathan Cape, 1970), pp. 18–19.

39. W. S. Burroughs, 'The Cut Up Method', in L. Jones (ed.), *The Moderns* (London: Mayflower Books, 1963), p. 315.

40. W. S. Burroughs, 'Interview 1965', p. 153.

41. W. S. Burroughs, *The Naked Lunch*, p. 226.

42. W. S. Burroughs, *Nova Express*, p. 12.

43. W. S. Burroughs, *Snack*, p. 27.

44. W. S. Burroughs, *The Ticket that Exploded* (London: Calder & Boyars, 1968).

45. W. S. Burroughs, *The Naked Lunch*, p. 27.

46. See for example the Panther edition of *Nova Express*. This comment and that in the preceding sentence are by Terry Southern and Anthony Burgess respectively.

47. W. S. Burroughs, *The Soft Machine* (London: Calder & Boyars, 1968), p. 34.

48. W. S. Burroughs, *White Subway* (London: Aloes Books, 1973), pp. 36–7.

49. W. S. Burroughs, *The Naked Lunch*, pp. 135–6.

50. W. S. Burroughs, *The Job*, p. 74; *The Naked Lunch*, p. 136.

51. W. S. Burroughs, 'Interview', *Le Monde* (18 January 1974).

52. M. Moorcock, *Sojan* (Manchester: Savoy Books, 1977), p. 150.

53. M. Moorcock, *The Stealer of Souls* (London: Granada, 1968).

54. M. Moorcock, *The Final Programme* (Glasgow: Fontana, 1979), p. 25 (orig. publ. 1965); *A Cure for Cancer* (Glasgow: Fontana, 1979), pp. 18–19 (orig. publ. 1971).

55. M. Moorcock, *The Stealer of Souls*, p. 9; The Final Programme, p. 101.

56. M. Moorcock, *The Stealer of Souls*, p. 69.

57. M. Moorcock, *The Final Programme*, p. 66.

58. Ibid., p. 15.

59. M. Moorcock, *The Final Programme*, p. 135; *The Stealer of Souls*, p. 71.

60. Quoted in Burns and Sugnet, *Imagination on Trial*, p. 113.

61. Ibid., p. 116; *The Final Programme*, pp. 101 and 222.

62. M. Moorcock, *A Cure for Cancer*, p. 37.

63. M. Moorcock, *The Stealer of Souls*, p. 111.

64. M. Moorcock, *The Final Programme*, pp. 66–96, 221–3.

65. M. Moorcock, *Sojan*, pp. 144–57; *The Golden Barge* (Manchester: Savoy Books, 1979), pp. 16–17.

66. M. Moorcock, *The Final Programme*, pp. 111–12.

67. R. Giddings and E. Holland, *J. R. R. Tolkien: The Shores of Middle Earth* (London: Junction Books, 1981), pp. 4–9.

68. J. A. Sutherland, 'American Science Fiction since 1960', in P.

Parrinder (ed.), *Science Fiction: a Critical Guide* (London: Longmans, 1979), p. 164.

69. J. R. R. Tolkien, *The Lord of the Rings, Part One* (London: Allen & Unwin, 1954), pp. 15–16; Giddings and Holland, *J. R. R. Tolkien*, p. 20.

70. J. R. R. Tolkien, *The Lord of the Rings, Part One*, p. 52.

71. Ibid., p. 379.

72. *The Lord of the Rings, Part Two* (1955), pp. 112–13.

73. Interestingly, Giddings and Holland have argued for precise parallels between Buchan's *The Thirty-Nine Steps* and *The Lord of the Rings*, claiming the former as one of Tolkien's 'three main source books' (the others being *King Solomon's Mines* and *Lorna Doone*).

74. *The Lord of the Rings, Part One*, pp. 64–5; *Part Two*, p. 252; *Part Three*, p. 225.

75. C. Wilson, *Tree by Tolkien* (London: Village Press, 1974), p. 17.

76. *The Lord of the Rings, Part One*, p. 53.

77. Ibid., *Part Two*, p. 244; *Part Three*, p. 189.

78. Ibid., *Part Two*, p. 350.

79. Ibid., *Part Three*, p. 201.

80. C. P. Manlove, *Modern Fantasy: Five Studies* (Cambridge University Press, 1975), pp. 200–1.

81. The Distributionist League was a predominantly Roman Catholic body which appeared between the wars, taking its name from its advocacy of a wider distribution of property. It was totally hostile to industrial society, and envisaged a return to small-scale local communities consisting of agricultural smallholders and independent craftsmen.

82. C. Wilson, *Tree by Tolkien*, p. 16; C. P. Manlove, *Modern Fantasy*, pp. 158–70.

83. C. P. Manlove, *Modern Fantasy*, pp. 164–5.

84. P. Macherey, *A Theory of Literary Production* (London: RKP, 1978), p. 159.

85. H. Carpenter, *J. R. R. Tolkien: A Biography* (London: Allen & Unwin, 1977), p. 231.

86. W. Burroughs, *The Job*, pp. 67–74.

87. M. Moorcock, *Sojan*, p. 154.

88. Burns and Sugnet, *Imagination on Trial*, p. 115.

89. M. Moorcock, *The Retreat from Liberty* (London: Zomba Books, 1983), p. 20.

8. *Watership Down*: Rolling Back the 1960s

CHRISTOPHER PAWLING

Watership Down has been one of the publishing triumphs of the 1970s. In his review of that decade, Christopher Booker notes that, 'its total sales to date, in the Puffin and Penguin editions alone, are around three million – and its world-wide sales are several times that'.[1] On the cover of the 1976 edition of the Penguin paperback it is described as a 'world number one bestseller', and though such claims are notoriously hard to substantiate, it is evident that *Watership Down* has sold exceptionally well both at home and abroad. When Macmillan of New York paid $800,000 for the American publishing rights, this incorporated 'the largest sum of money ever paid for paperback rights',[2] and the revenue from both book and film has allowed the author to retire from the Civil Service and to pay for the construction of an impressive residence on the Isle of Man. All in all, then, a considerable success, and one which cannot just be measured in terms of simple cash transactions. Richard Adams has received literary prizes and widespread critical acknowledgement, and, to quote Booker once more, *Watership Down* is accepted as 'one of those classics of children's literature which speak to readers of all ages, fit to be mentioned in the same breath as, say, *The Wind in the Willows*, *The Lord of the Rings*, or even *Gulliver's Travels*'.[3]

However, things looked rather different to Adams, the civil servant, in the late 1960s when he was trying to persuade various publishing houses that his tale about rabbits was worth marketing. At that time the answers were decidedly negative: 'Some felt it was too long; others challenged the strong anthropomorphism of his rabbits. One agent was even put off by the names of his characters: "To give a male rabbit a name like Hazel is surely absurd".[4] After seventeen rejections a small firm, Rex Collings, agreed to publish, although the novel did not appear until a further two and a half years had elapsed.[5] This was hardly an auspicious beginning, and one feels inclined to accept Adams' claim that he was as 'amazed as anyone' when the novel eventually became a bestseller.[6]

It is clear, then, that we cannot account for the popularity of *Watership Down* in terms of mass marketing and publicity. Or, to be more exact, it was only promoted as a bestseller when it had already built up a substantial readership. After having sold steadily in hardback, it was taken up by Penguin in 1973, but was handled initially as a children's story under the Puffin imprint. Even when positive reviews and word of mouth recommendation had led to its reclassification as a tale for adults as well as children, it was still not marketed in supermarkets or newsagents (this only happened after the film had opened up a potentially wider readership). Thus, *Watership Down* is different in kind from a bestseller such as *Jaws*, where the publishers purchased an idea for a substantial sum (Benchley sold them the book on the basis of a half-page draft) and were determined from the outset to make their investment pay off.[7] In Adams' case the promotion drive was a rather belated *post hoc* response by Penguin which consolidated the success of the film rather than the book.

How can these facts help us to account for *Watership Down* as a cultural phenomenon? How did it make its appeal, and what was the composition of its readership? In attempting to answer these questions we will of necessity be moving in the world of hypothesis and speculation for some of the time, as it would be manifestly impossible to find 'hard' data on the social background of every purchaser of *Watership Down*, let alone every reader. Nevertheless, we do possess a body of evidence (including the text itself of course) which allows us to hypothesise that *Watership Down* in its first phase (i.e. prior to the film) appealed almost exclusively to a middle-class readership. Positive responses from educationalists alerted the attention of the middle-class parent searching for guidance on his/her child's reading, and the accolade of the Carnegie Medal consolidated Adams' reputation as a 'good writer for young readers'.[8] Even a cursory glance at the text will show that *Watership Down* was designed to appeal to the young reader who was already in possession of a number of cultural reference points (such as Shakespeare, the Bible, *The Odyssey*, *Pilgrim's Progress*) and was likely to discourage the average working-class child. Moreover, even when Adams' novel was taken up by an adult readership, it comprised in the main students or ex-students.

So any analysis which attempts to trace the 'fit' between the text *Watership Down* and its readership must concentrate on the values and 'sensibility' of a particular cultural milieu – the middle class, plus what one might term 'ancillary' groups. In particular, I am interested in the crossover appeal of Adams' novel, and the way in which it managed to strike a chord with the largely middle-class youth culture of the early 1970s. Here we need to explore a number of related questions. For instance how did a morally uplifting tale for children come to have a significance for this youth culture? How can we account for the apparent contradiction between Adams' conservative political outlook, with its celebration of social élites, and the egalitarian approach of a student subculture? Why were such readers able to derive pleasure from a text which was seemingly so opposed to the 'anti-authoritarian' credo which they had adopted? Was *Watership Down* simply one in a long line of children's tales from *Alice in Wonderland* onwards, whose appeal to the adult world is based on a whimsical view of childhood, or did it manage to voice more fundamental fears and desires in the 'collective consciousness'[9] of its readership?

In attempting to answer these questions I am starting with the presupposition that it is possible to demonstrate a 'correspondence' between Adams' novel as a 'relatively autonomous' literary structure, and the socio-cultural context of its inception and reception.[10] However, it is important to qualify this remark in two ways. Firstly, I would maintain that a complete 'understanding' of the text will require an explanation of both form and content. An exclusive concentration on content is rarely justifiable, but it is clearly inadequate in the case of a fable, such as *Watership Down*, where the relationship between text and context is not immediately discernible. Here I would agree with Lucien Goldmann, when he argues that one should seek out the interconnexion between artistic creation and social consciousness in terms of 'the categories which structure one or other of them': 'The same categories and the same consistency may govern worlds with completely different contents so that transposition by the imagination is no longer an obstacle to the existence of a close relationship between culture and society.'[11] Clearly the content of Adams' fable deals with a different 'world' from the one inhabited by his readers, but the formal properties of the novel (narrative strategies adopted by the author, and so on) are circumscribed by the author's need to answer, or perhaps evade, crucial conceptual problems which are generated by the social milieu in which he 'moves and has his being'.

My second qualifying remark really forms a corollary to the above. It is clear from what I have just written, that we would be wrong to restrict ourselves to an examination of the way in which Adams' novel *reflects* a pre-given 'reality'. The novelist works on his/her raw material in an *active* manner, and the resultant text must be seen as a 'transformation' or 'restructuring' of observed reality, including the writer's own *relationship* to that reality. So we need to examine the way in which *Watership Down* recreates the world through the medium of an heroic quest, thereby allowing the reader to 'experience' that world in a new guise. In the process of identifying with Adams' characters during the course of their adventures, or seeing nature through his descriptions, the reader participates in an imaginative enterprise which produces certain aesthetic pleasures. At the same time, this process of identification with a fictional realm exposes the reader to the author's social and political attitudes to *existing* reality. It is worth noting that, although *Watership Down* ostensibly deals with the animal kingdom, it also manages to celebrate the values of 'tradition' and 'natural' hierarchies, against the implied misdemeanours of 'modern man'. In other words, one would be foolish to discount Adams' stake in the contemporary world by arguing that *Watership Down* is merely a fantasy, for it is also a *didactic* tale in which the author intervenes to *shape* consciousness.

One way of accounting for the popularity of *Watership Down* is to argue that it caters for a wide variety of tastes/interests. This is the line which Fred Inglis follows in his essay 'Spellbinding and Anthropology: The Work of Richard Adams and Ursula LeGuin'.[12]

> There is, as they say, something for everyone. For the intellectual child or adult there is the rabbit lore . . . and there are the makings of other cultures. Crossing into this territory, there is the ecology and the heady stuff of the conservation polemic, lapsing at times into an involuntary parody of *The Observer Book of Wild Flowers*. Woven into this thick technicolour, with all its living detail . . . is the war thriller.[13]

Clearly the fact that Adams' novel mixes a number of genres and themes can only have worked in its favour. At the same time, Adams' success derives from the fact that he was able to 'hit the right moment with this cultural recipe', as Inglis rightly comments. Unfortunately, although Inglis recognises that this timing is important, he does not go on to analyse the nature of the 'moment' itself. Thus my cultural reading of *Watership Down* will take up where Inglis leaves off, and attempt to explain why such a 'cultural recipe' should prove to be so popular *when* it did. This will involve an examination of the major subsets – the pastoral, the war story, and the mythic quest – which together constitute Adams' conservative utopia.

The Pastoral

Adams' version of the pastoral draws on a vein of thought which emerged in the nineteenth century and has played a large part in shaping the culture of the English middle class. From the Romantics onwards, 'nature' is presented as a utopian alternative to the world of industrialism and commerce. In the more radical versions of Romanticism nature becomes a repository for those values which are associated with an unalienated 'human essence', recalling a pre-industrial world in which labour and art are unified activities.[14] Frank Musgrove has pointed out that the 'counter culture' of the late 1960s reworked many of the themes of early Romanticism, in particular the attack on a technology which was not harnessed to 'use' values and meaningful human goals.[15] We find this 'ecological' variant of latter day Romanticism in the following comment from *Watership Down*: 'It comes from men [said Holly]. All other elil do what they have to do and Frith moves them as he moves us. They live on the earth and they need food. Men will never rest till they've spoiled the earth and destroyed the animals.'[16]

In *Ecstacy and Holiness* Frank Musgrove notes that 'naturalism' is one of the most distinctive 'value clusters' in the 'world-vision' of the counter-culture: 'naturalism leads to a concern for environment, a conservationist attitude to the countryside, opposition to unrestricted urban growth, and frequently a distaste for urban life'.[17] All these elements are evident in *Watership Down* and the text is studded with attacks on man's pollution of his world, thus echoing the fears of the counter-culture:

> Few places are far from human noise – cars, motor cycles, tractors, lorries. The sound of a housing estate in the morning is audible a long way off. People who record bird-song generally do it very early – before six o'clock – if they can. Soon after that the invasion of distant noise in most woodland becomes too constant and too loud. During the last fifty years the silence of much of the country has been destroyed.[18]

Adams' critique of a world in which our senses are assaulted and brutalised is set off against the delicate pleasures of the countryside. It is worth noting that the above quotation is followed by the sentence, 'But here, on Watership Down, there floated up only faint traces of the daylight noise below', for Watership Down is a utopian enclave which has not yet been ravaged by modern man. We can see this most clearly in the passage of extended natural description which opens Part II of the novel.

> The north-facing escarpment of Watership Down, in shadow since early morning, now caught the western sun for an hour before twilight . . . The red rays flickered in and out of the grass stems, flashing minutely on membranous wings, casting long shadows behind the thinnest of filamentary legs,

breaking each patch of bare soil into a myriad individual grains. The insects buzzed, whined, hummed, stridulated and droned as the air grew warmer in the sunset . . . . The larks went up, twittering in the scented air above the down.[19]

I have quoted at length from this passage because it is one of the most vivid examples of the 'pastoral' strain in *Watership Down*. Adams evokes a quality of fragility in his description of the natural world ('membranous wings' and 'the thinnest of filamentary legs'), thereby underlining the vulnerability of that world in the face of man's insensitivity and his technological armoury. Passages such as this may help to explain the appeal of *Watership Down* to the student-based subculture of the early 1970s, as well as highlighting some of the unresolved contradictions within that culture. One detects a late Romantic vein in Adams' writing which unites his work with the sensibility of the era, as expressed for example in some of the poster art where nature often acquires a tremulous, dreamlike sheen. Adams' version of pastoral betrays a rather fey obsession with nature which characterises the more retreatist, Arcadian side of the counter-culture. In the passage quoted above the language emphasises the limitations of a tired romanticism in over-worked poetic conceits ('scented air') and there is a wistful air which smacks of Tennyson and Swinburne. The overall effect is one of sentimentality and Adams offers nature as a consolation for the trials and tribulations of an urban existence. In this kind of literature, to quote Raymond Williams, 'The loved places are the "unspoiled" places, and no group agrees with this more readily than those who live in the "spoiled" '.[20] In *Watership Down* we are presented with a rural landscape which is lovingly described, both in terms of its cartography:

They had come to the line of the Portway – only intermit-tently a road – which runs from north of Andover, through St. Mary Bourne with its bells and streams and watercress beds, through Bradley Wood, on across the downs and so to Tadley and at last to Silchester – the Romans' Calleva Atrebatum.[21]

and a taxonomy of nature:

The rabbits sheltered in dim-green, sun-flecked caves of grass, flowering marjoram and cow parsley: peered round spotted hairy-stemmed clumps of viper's bugloss, blooming red and blue above their heads: pushed between towering stalks of yellow mullein.[22]

Passages such as the above seem to be 'neutral', and do not immediately connote any particular 'world vision'. However, it is worth pointing out that we are offered a landscape which is imbued with a certain history and traditions. If we were asked to describe this landscape we would probably come up with adjectives such as 'orderly', or 'comely'. We might also note the way in which the historical connection with 'classical' civilisation is invoked ('the Romans' Calleva Atrebatus') in an almost Arnoldian manner.[23]

The landscape which confronts us in this novel and in *The Plague Dogs* is noticeably walker's country (the Berkshire Downs in *Watership Down* and the Lake District in its successor) with 'pastoral' overtones. Under Adams' contemplative gaze the natural world tends to be domesticated and appropriated as an object for the consumption of the reader. At times the author indulges in a rather fetishistic classification of natural life which degenerates into 'an involuntary parody of the *Observer Book of Wild Flowers*', as Inglis so aptly remarks. (One wonders how many countrymen would recognise 'viper's bugloss', if they saw it.) One senses that this is an attitude to nature which tells us more about the desires of the city dweller, than of the person who actually works on the land.

Although the 'country-based fantasy'[24] of writers such as Adams and Tolkien has been much in vogue over the last decade and a half, it is not an entirely new phenomenon. Thus Raymond Williams' description of the 'Georgian' period in English literature (just before, and during the First World War) has an almost eerily familiar ring:

There was that uncritical, abstracting literary anthropology, within which folktales and legends became part of an unlocalized, unhistorical past; or the uncritical interest in myth, which made the land and the people a scene and characters into which anything could be projected . . .[25]

As Williams notes, the Georgians developed a poetic discourse which abstracted the countryside from any concrete history or social relations, allowing the suburban middle class to use rural England as 'an image for its own internal feelings and ideas'.[26] But this discourse did not die out with the Georgians; indeed, as the rural population has dwindled and the relative importance of agriculture in Britain's economic life has declined, the attraction of the rural myth has grown, offering an image of a golden age which invariably has its origins in an idealised version of feudalism. This 'country-based fantasy' can be traced down to Tolkien, where the hobbit is 'almost the archetype of the sturdy little yeoman',[27] and Adams draws explicit comparisons between the world of his rabbits and the everyday existence of the mediaeval village: 'For rabbits, winter remains what it was for men in the middle ages – hard, but bearable by the resourceful and not altogether without compensations'.[28] In *Watership Down* the emphasis is on continuity and tradition rather than change, and once evil in the form of General Woundwort has been expelled from this world, Hazel's band establish a warren which is markedly similar to the semi-feudal homeland of their youth.

I want to explore Adams' attitude to politics in more detail in the next section. However, I hope I have been able to show that the way in which he approaches nature is not entirely divorced from political considerations, and that the pastoral element is important for an understanding of the text as a whole. Whilst *Watership Down* gives expression to protests against the destruction of nature, it also lends a particular inflection to the ecological theme, covering it with a late Romantic/Georgian gloss. Thus, the English countryside has arguably more than one meaning in the text: in the main it is presented as a rural retreat, but it also has connections with a hierarchical world of feudal tradition.

Contemporary War Story or Archetypal Quest?

We have seen that *Watership Down* draws on the pastoral tradition in order to establish a framework of stability and continuity. However, this world of emotional security is counterposed to a narrative based on the adventure formula, in which a group of young male rabbits who have been made homeless are forced to encounter a number of tests on the way to establishing a safe haven. Adams pits his band of young bloods against a hostile environment in which they encounter men, foxes, dogs, crows and other hazards, as well as the totalitarian regime of a giant rabbit, General Woundwort, before they are able to establish a new home on the tranquil slopes of Watership Down. (There are clear parallels with an earlier 'country-based fantasy', *The Wind in the Willows*, where the water rat and his friends are involved in a desperate struggle to rid Toad Hall of an evil mob of stoats and weasels who are engaged in an orgy of desecration. Both tales invoke the opposition, order/stability versus mindless destruction.)[29]

When we first encounter Hazel and Fiver, they are members of a long-established warren which has not been exposed to danger for a number of years. The old chief is a tried and tested figure, but he has become rather detached from the everyday life of the warren, and he does not respond to Fiver's Cassandra-like prophecy of impending destruction. Having failed to persuade the elders that their home is in danger, Hazel and Fiver recruit a small band of rabbits who leave with the vague aim of establishing a new home, but are unaware of their exact destination. Later, after they have reached Watership Down, we learn that the original warren has been dug out and the rabbits gassed, in order to make room for a new housing estate. From this point on it is clear that Hazel's group are on their own, and so the remaining three-quarters of the book deals with the search for a set of does – an unnecessary appendage for a nomadic warrior, but indispensable if Hazel and Co. are to continue their line!

It is not hard to see that although *Watership Down* is a fantasy set in the animal kingdom it is also a reworking of an important cultural archetype, the Quest:

. . . the story is remarkably similar in outline to other, more celebrated Quest stories, such as *The Aeneid*, describing how Aeneas and his friends leave the burning city of Troy to found their new city in distant Italy, that of the Children of Israel escaping from bondage and threatened destruction in Egypt to set up a new home in the Promised Land, or

Christian in *Pilgrim's Progress* leaving the 'city of destruction' (which he has a premonition is about to be engulfed by fire) to set off on his perilous journey to the distant Celestial City.[30]

Christopher Booker's comparison is illuminating and he is correct in pointing out that *Watership Down* is based on the classic Quest narrative structure, right down to the fact that the journey itself occupies only one part of the tale. 'The worst ordeals of all await the hero and his companions when they have already come within sight of the goal, and face the obstacles which will stand in their way of winning it and securing it for the future.'[31] As Booker remarks, what matters in the Quest is 'not mere arrival at a goal, the winning of a treasure, or whatever, so much as the securing of a Kingdom, and usually, simultaneously, the winning of a Princess into the bargain'.[32] Just as the second half of the *Aeneid* is preoccupied with Aeneas' battle to secure his new home in Italy against the tribes who already live there, so most of the second half of Adams' tale deals with the daring rescue of the does from Woundwort's clutches and a final siege on Watership Down in which Hazel and Co. come tantalisingly near to defeat. It is only the expulsion of the enemy general and his alien hordes which can guarantee the peace and security of Hazel's utopian enclave.

The problem with this sort of comparison is that it seems to border on the ridiculous, since *Watership Down* is patently not constructed on the same scale as a classical myth. 'It is all very well to decry these heady similarities with the *Odyssey* or the *Aeneid* but the fact remains that *Watership Down* is not about great mythic heroes, cosmic enlargements of our own human nature. It is about bunny rabbits –'[33] Yet, this seemingly absurd paradox may actually help to account for the popular appeal of Adams' contemporary reworking of the Quest. As Booker remarks, the use of cuddly bunnies as heroes allows Adams to place the narrative in 'a pre-mechanical world, where the hero and his friends can only survive by their direct exercise of a balance of our primary, innate functions – physical strength, intuition, a courageous heart and all the rest'.[34]

By escaping the confines of the modern world in this way

Adams is able to produce a 'magical resolution'[35] to a problem which was first posed by Marx in the *Grundrisse*: namely, how is it possible to produce 'epic' literature in a world dominated by technology?

> Is the view of nature and social relations on which the Greek imagination and hence Greek (mythology) is based possible with self-acting mule spindals and railways and locomotives and electrical telegraphs? What chance has Vulcan against Roberts & Co., Jupiter against the lightning-rod and Hermes against the Credit Mobilier?'[36]

Marx argued that the function of mythology was to allow early man to dominate the forces of nature 'in the imagination and by the imagination'.[37] Once man was able to exert mastery over the forces of nature in a practical manner by means of technology, the cosmos of classical mythology was bound to lose its original function and meaning. Booker makes essentially the same point in a rather simpler fashion: 'There are virtually no more "boundless, unknown realms" left. The world has shrunk to a tiny, over-populated, over-explored, over-mechanized backyard.'[38] This is a somewhat platitudinous statement but, still, one takes the point. In order to be able to reproduce the world of the epic hero one either attempts to transcend our time or planet altogether (viz. some forms of SF fantasy), or one creates 'pseudo-mythic landscapes', à la Tolkien or Adams, which are not bound by the scale and the complexities of a modern technological environment. By presenting a rabbit's-eye view of the world, Adams 'transforms a stretch of our own, familiar, Home Counties countryside into a vast, seemingly mythic, realm'.[39]

> It takes a great feat of the imagination to transmogrify the contemporary English countryside, with its broiler farms, barbed wire fences, motorways and housing estates, back into a 'faery-realm' of romance and high adventure. But by diminishing his heroes to rabbit size, it is that which Adams has achieved – thus creating the most successful 'pseudo-mythic' landscape since the imaginary world conjured up by Tolkien.[40]

Whether or not one agrees that Adams' 'imaginary world' is on a par with that of *The Hobbit* and its successor, Booker is surely correct in focusing on this aspect of the text as a way of explaining an important aspect of its popular appeal. Moreover, 'one of the great advantages of having animals as your heroes, rather than human beings, is that you can invest them with purely *human* qualities, as opposed to all those dehumanizing distortions of human qualities which are unavoidable when you set an adventure story in our modern world of motor cars, aeroplanes, space rockets, telephones and all the rest of the gadgetry.'[41] Instead of being overshadowed by technology, Adams' heroes are shown in a direct, unmediated relationship to their environment. Even when technology of a kind makes an appearance (Hazel's group astonish General Woundwort by escaping on a raft), it has a comforting effect on the reader, evoking a pre-industrial world in which an invention such as the boat uses one portion of nature to extend man's control over the rest of his environment. This manageable technology does not have any of its contemporary connotations (as of a force out of control); instead, we are transported to the world of the children's encyclopedia, where human history is the narrative of enterprising individuals harnessing nature by means of a 'neutral' technology.

To return to Christopher Booker's article, I would argue that he has some interesting points to make about the relationship between Adams' pseudo-mythic landscape and what one could loosely term the 'ecological' response to technology (of course, one should remember that the ecological movement is a loose federation, and that Adams belongs to its conservative wing). But having said this, I think that Booker's final explanation of the meanings in the text, and its cultural function, is misleading. Although he does not have the space to put forward an elaborate theoretical argument, Booker is obviously preoccupied with a Jungian concept of the 'archetype' in which myths are seen as expressions of the fears or desires of a 'collective unconscious'.[42] So we are told that, 'at the deepest level' *Watership Down* is 'yet another of those countless fantasies of escape thrown up by the unconscious of modern man – escapes from the unspeakable, inhuman world we are creating for ourselves by technology . . .'[43] Explanations of this kind have become notorious, and the notion that myths emerge from the womb of some all-embracing 'collective unconscious' (with or without the aid of the writer as midwife) has to be rejected. Myths are cultural products which are designed to appeal to particular audiences/readerships at specific points in time. If we see *Watership Down* as just one more variant on a universal theme (the 'quest' of 'modern man' for escape from a nightmare world of technology), then we will inevitably overlook the more culturally specific aspects of the text.

One of the most interesting aspects of *Watership Down* is the way in which Adams draws on his experience in the War: 'In a sense . . . the book is about my war. I must confess that it was the high point of my life, and the rest has been little more than an aftermath.'[44] Like the British in 1940, our heroes survive their Dunkirk against General Woundwort's totalitarian hordes through a combination of courage, enterprise and superior leadership. In pure boys' adventure style, Hazel's band manage to outwit an enemy which is superior in numbers by employing secret weapons such as Kehaar the seagull who provides air cover at crucial moments, and a little mouse who leads resistance behind the enemy lines. Richard Boston sums up this comic book atmosphere in the following humorous but pointed manner:

> Hazel did a good turn to a mouse once. As a result we have the local population on our side, providing crucial intelligence about enemy troop activities. This underground resistance movement is made up of comic little foreigners who speak what is either organ-grinder Italian or onion-seller French. 'Is a plenty good a rabbits 'ere, is all my friends,' says the mouse who must surely be wearing a blue beret.[45]

Watership Down is a tale which focuses on the values of male comradeship and leadership in wartime. Therefore the narrative deals with the period between the defeat of Woundwort and the death of Hazel in a perfunctory manner, since it is clear that Adams is not interested in describing the mundane details of the rabbits' peace-time existence. Hazel is the born chief (apparently, he is based on Adams' commanding officer in the war), and Bigwig is the classic second in command:

Hazel realized wearily that Bigwig was probably going to be troublesome. He was certainly no coward, but he was likely to remain steady only as long as he could see his way clear and be sure of what to do. To him, perplexity was worse than danger; and when he was perplexed he usually grew angry.[46]

Adams' tale traces the way in which Hazel's 'natural' qualities of leadership cause the 'rank and file' to turn to him, rather than to the physically superior Bigwig, and the subtext is a thinly disguised political allegory which asserts that élites are vital to the survival of *any* species. The rank and file will function well enough, given proper guidance, but always need 'superior intelligence' to steer them on to the right path – 'Acorn, Hawkbit and Speedwell, decent enough rank-and-filers as long as they were not pushed beyond their limits'.[47]

In a recent study of Fantasy, Rosemary Jackson has argued that 'faery' stories, such as *Watership Down*, betray markedly conservative tendencies in the way that they anthropomorphise nature:

From Walter de la Mare, Beatrix Potter, A. A. Milne, to Richard Adams and J. R. R. Tolkien, a tradition of liberal humanism spreads outwards, covering with its moral, social, and linguistic orthodoxies a world of bears, foxes, wolves, rabbits, ducks, hens and hobbits. George Orwell's *Animal Farm* usefully translates animal into man for purposes of political allegory, but these romantic fables are more sentimental and nostalgic. They reinforce a blind faith in 'eternal' moral values, really those of an outworn liberal humanism.[48]

There are always dangers in making global judgements of this kind; after all, one might want to argue that there are important differences between the approaches adopted by, say, Tolkien and Adams. (*Watership Down* is a fairly overt allegory, whereas Tolkien was rather suspicious of any politicisation of fantasy.)[49] However, Rosemary Jackson is surely correct in her assessment of the 'ideology' of Adams' novel, particularly if one substitutes the term 'conservative' for 'liberal'.

Watership Down is offered as an adventure story, but it also operates as a parable about a certain form of society. During the course of the narrative Hazel and Co. triumph over the 'anarchy'/'decadence' of Cowslip's warren, and the 'totalitarianism' of Woundwort. They win through because their group is a 'meritocracy' which harnesses the energies and talents of each individual member in a productive and rational manner. Whereas General Woundwort has imposed his leadership on the rest of his group by means of sheer brute force, Hazel is not the most physically commanding member of his own band, and he has to win the loyalty and respect of the others through a series of tests. But Adams is no libertarian (his idea of democracy is clearly founded on a combination of 'breeding' and 'intelligence'), and it is obvious that Hazel is a 'natural leader' from the outset: 'Although he was a yearling and still below full weight, he had not the harassed look of most "outskirters" – that is the rank and file of ordinary rabbits in their first year, who lacking either aristocratic parentage or unusual size and strength, get sat on by their elders and live as best they can . . . .'[50]

In this microcosm of a meritocratic society, Hazel has to earn his place as chief. However, he has the gods on his side and in crucial episodes such as the crossing of the common (Adams' version of the wilderness) the narrative has the function of revealing and confirming Hazel's divine right to lead:

'Oh, Hazel', said Blackberry, coming up to him round a puddle in the gravel. 'I was so tired and confused, I actually began to wonder whether you knew where you were going. I could hear you in the heather, saying "Not far now" and it was annoying me. I thought you were making it up. I should have known better. Frithrah, you're what I call a Chief Rabbit!'[51]

It is true that Hazel's journey to the top is not all plain sailing (at this point in the narrative Bigwig is openly scathing about his companion's pretensions to the title of 'Hazelrah' – Chief Rabbit), but we know that he will succeed as he has already learnt how to *behave* like a general: 'Behind him, Pipkin shivered in the damp and he turned and nuzzled him; much as the general, with nothing left to do, might fall to considering the welfare of his servant, simply because the servant happened to be there.'[52] It is passages like this which makes one feel that Adams' discourse on generalship/leadership speaks volumes about his attitude to 'natural' social relationships.

To the author of *Watership Down* any social group without a chain of command is automatically suspect. Early on in their travels Hazel's group meet up with a rabbit called Cowslip who invites them back to his warren. The new rabbit's companions exhibit what are for Adams two manifest signs of decadence: they are sceptical about established religion (the myths of the Prince Rabbit, El-ahrairah) and they have no Chief Rabbit! Moreover, their prized poet is 'a mere youngster', Silverweed (a coy reference to youth culture?) who has a 'wild, desperate air'[53] and whose poems evoke an atmosphere of death and decay (one ought to note that this section is something of a *tour de force*, right down to the dying cadences in Silverweed's poem which convey the feeling of fatalism in Cowslip's warren – a superb touch).

Hazel's band are clearly disturbed by the way in which Cowslip's warren has rejected traditional rabbit lore. Later on we discover that this instinctive reaction has a healthy foundation, as the warren turns out to be a trap in the most literal sense (it is run as a rabbit farm by men and periodically one of Cowslip's companions disappears). Whilst one may not accept Richard Boston's description of this warren as 'a kind of welfare state'(!)[54] the association of an absence of religious belief with a world living on borrowed time is instructive.

It would be naïve in the extreme to claim that *Watership Down* was written solely as a moral tract for young readers. Nevertheless, in interviews Adams does seem to be obsessed with the theme of the 'permissive society', and he looks back nostalgically to a pre-war era which he associates with the simple Christian virtues of family life, and an unquestioning attitude towards those in authority. 'You can't have an army unless you have *courage*. And you can't have a society unless you believe in Christian monogamy. If we haven't got a firm family structure we're completely down the pan. We knew damn well that not all soldiers were brave in battle, but unless someone believes in the standards of the regiment where will we be?'[55]

The last war seems to have been a kind of watershed for Adams. At one point in the text Dandelion (one of Hazel's group) tells a story about the legendary rabbit El-ahrairah who is prepared to go off and risk his life in order to save his people who are threatened by destruction in a war. By the time he arrives back the war is long over, and the generation who have grown up in the meantime despise their parents' attempts to keep the memory alive.

> 'That war lark, old fellow', said the first buck. 'That's all finished now. That's got nothing to do with us.' . . .
> 'My father was in it', said the second buck. 'He gets on about it sometimes. I always go out quick. "They did this and then we did that" and all that caper. Makes you curl up, honest. Poor old geezer, you'd think he'd want to forget about it. I reckon he makes half of it up. And where did it get him, tell me that?'[56]

Clearly an ungrateful generation and one whose pacifism bodes ill for the future! Admittedly, there is a playful side to this passage in the way it parodies the dialogue of the 1950s 'kitchen-sink drama', and Adams maintains that he is 'an entertainer', whose views are 'no better than anyone else's'.[57] But *Watership Down* is not just a light-hearted fantasy, and it does not seem to me that passages such as the above are written in an entirely tongue-in-cheek vein. Moreover, one senses a certain maliciousness in Adams' mimicry of working-class speech. We are reminded of the social attitudes of the pre-war thrillers of Wallace or Sapper, and a world whose margins are inhabited by 'lower orders' who are either comic or surly. (In this connection it is interesting to note how Woundwort is given a decidedly working-class accent in the film version.)

Watership Down is preoccupied with a predominantly male world of adventure. Females are a 'significant absence' for most of the narrative, and when they finally appear they conform to a recognisable stereotype – they are rather unreliable without strong leadership and their main role is to provide a way of propagating the group. Ironically, Adams cannot deny the central role of the does in the life of the warren, as they dig the burrows, while the male only gives token help. In fact, if one looks dispassionately at the roles played by the sexes it is undeniable that the does are the focus for much of the 'social life' of the rabbit. However, this centrality has to be repressed in order to maintain the core of the narrative which is based on the exclusively male community of Hazel's band of warriors.

In an essay on 'Boys' Weeklies', written in the late 1930s, George Orwell made the following comment: 'It is probable that many people who consider themselves extremely sophisticated and "advanced" are actually carrying through life an imaginative background which they acquired in childhood from (for instance) Sapper and Ian Hay.'[58] *Watership Down* was written in the late 1960s, but it is worth reminding ourselves that its author received his education before the war, the period when authors such as Sapper were at the height of their popularity, particularly with a public school readership. Is it surprising, then, that Adams' story reproduces the 'imaginative background' and social attitudes of the pre-war boys' adventure story? Of course, it is possible to show how Adams' fable draws on the 'universal' archetype of the Quest for much of its basic narrative pattern, but the core of the text has far more in common with the imaginative 'universe' of Biggles or Bulldog Drummond than that of Odysseus.

Conclusion

In this chapter I have tried to show that *Watership Down* is more than just a reworking of a timeless myth. Whilst it is possible to draw parallels between Adams' tale and the classical Quest, any analysis which remains on this level is restricting itself to an exceedingly partial account of the text. In fact, the most interesting feature of this particular fantasy is the way in which it differentiates itself from other myths in the process of addressing a specific cultural milieu at a specific moment in time. Thus I want to conclude with a brief examination of the historical 'conjuncture' of the late 1960s, in order to shed some light on the 'mental universe' of its author.

Adams has described his political views as 'those of the great army of ordinary educated middle-class opinion which finds nothing to support it in the trendy media which runs [*sic*] round chasing its tail all the time'.[59] The disaffection and frustration expressed in this statement, which is carried by the overall tone as much as the content, is an important indication of the mood of the 'traditional' middle class at the end of the 1960s.

This was an altogether different – puzzling, contradictory – world for the traditional middle classes, formed in and by an older, more 'protestant' ethic. Advanced capitalism now required not thrift but consumption; not sobriety but style; not postponed gratifications but immediate satisfaction of needs; not goods that last but things that are expendable: the 'swinging' rather than the sober life style. The gospel of work was hardly apposite to a life increasingly focussed on consumption, pleasure and play . . . Naturally, the middle-classes took fright at this erosion of their whole way of life: and when the middle-classes take fright, they conjure up demons from the air. Traditional middle-class life, they imagined, was being undermined by a conspiracy between progressive intellectuals, soft liberals, the pornographers and the counter culture.[60]

In the eyes if Adams and many fellow members of the 'ordinary, educated middle-class', society was experiencing a crisis of 'moral authority', with youth seen as being particularly 'at risk'. The 'alternative' culture, with its non-competitiveness, its stress on egalitarianism rather than unquestioned authority, and its rather ambiguous attitude to established sexual roles, came to symbolise a society which had lost its way. Adams has said that *Watership Down* was written to affirm 'the dignity of the child',[61] and he clearly felt that his young readers were in need of strong moral guidance at this moment of cultural upheaval (in one interview he proclaimed that 'Christianity must offer a last ditch stand against the forces that threaten family life').[62] Hence the reassertion of a tradi tional boys' comic vision of society in which well-bred, intelligent individuals lead a humble rank and file in a 'bracing' adventure. Hence also the contrast between the 'healthy' values represented by Hazel's group and the 'soft', lotus-eating world of Silverweed and company.

In *Fantasy: The Literature of Subversion* Rosemary Jackson argues that a study of fantasy can reveal how a particular culture differentiates itself from other cultures – 'it is the identification, the naming of otherness, which is a telling index of a society's religious and political beliefs'.[63] Drawing on an article by Fredric Jameson ('magical narratives: romance as genre')[64] Jackson points out that this 'naming of otherness' provides a significant clue to the way in which a culture identifies those forces or values which are perceived as posing some kind of threat to its existence. By analysing the way in which this otherness/difference is inscribed in the text we can begin to uncover the 'ideological assumptions of the author and of the culture in which they originate.'[65] As Jameson remarks: 'Any analysis of romance as a mode will then want to come to terms with the intimate and constitutive relationship between the form itself, as a genre and a literary institution, and this deep-rooted ideology which has only too clearly the function of drawing the boundaries of a given social order and providing a powerful internal deterrent against deviancy or subversion'.[66]

Watership Down sets up clear distinctions between what is 'natural' (Hazel and Co.) and what is 'deviant' (Silverweed and Co.). Moreover, the fact that Adams sometimes feels obliged to make quite direct didactic interventions is, perhaps, an indication of the defensive mood of his class fraction at the end of the 1960s.

It would be convenient if we could finish here, having settled accounts with *Watership Down* in this neat manner. Unfortunately, things are never that clear-cut, particularly in the area of cultural analysis. To account for the production of Adams' conservative fantasy in terms of the 'collective consciousness' of the traditional middle class is one thing; to explain the appeal of that text to those who did not necessarily share Adams' world-view is entirely another. The fact that a substantial student/ex-student readership derived pleasure from *Watership Down* indicates that Adams' novel was open to a number of different readings which reflected aesthetic/ideological discourses existing independently of the text. As Tony Bennett has commented, the literary text 'enters back into history – is historically "redetermined" – during the process of its reception, figuring not as the source of *an* effect, but the *site* on which *plural and even contradictory* effects may be produced during the course of its history as a received text'.[67] Thus, on one level it was clearly possible to see *Watership Down* as 'a classic of animal literature' – a reading which simply by-passed the political allegory embedded in the text. Alternatively, Adams' fable, like Tolkien's *Lord of the Rings*, could be enjoyed as a heroic romance which celebrated the victory of a collective of 'little people' over a powerful 'totalitarian' system – an interpretation which seemed to fit in with the 'libertarian' self-image of the student subculture.

Thus it would be wrong to assume that the majority of Adams' readers were necessarily *aware* of the more conservative overtones of the allegory which formed the subtext of *Watership Down*. Adams has to be regarded as, first and foremost, a fabulator of adventure stories and that, combined with an infectious love of the countryside, is undoubtedly the source of his popular appeal. In fact, his writing tends to lose its edge when he takes himself seriously as a mystic – hence the failure of that bizarre fusion of Jung and C. S. Lewis which forms the basis of *Shardik*. However, if the success of *Watership Down* is ultimately attributable to Adams' skill in producing an 'immensely readable story', this 'readability' has certain potential effects. Under the guise of a whimsical pastoralism Adams' narrative inserts the reader into a world where the equation between 'nature' and conservative values is quite direct. Other interpretations of *Watership Down* are possible, as I have shown, but one cannot ignore the fact that Adams' fable is underscored by a 'residual'[68] conservatism. Thus, in its own oblique manner *Watership Down* has contributed to a vein of nostalgia for 'traditional' patterns of life which has played an important part in the reconstitution of English culture over the last decade, and which shows no signs of disappearing in the near future.

NOTES

1. C. Booker, *The Seventies* (Harmondsworth: Penguin, 1980), p. 251.
2. J. Cornwell, 'From Rabbits to Riches', *Observer Magazine* (29 September 1974), p. 44.
3. Booker, *The Seventies*, p. 251.
4. Cornwell, 'Rabbits to Riches', p. 47.
5. Ibid., p. 47.
6. Interview with Adams in *Radio Times* (24 September 1977), p.10.

234 *Popular Fiction and Social Change*

7. See T. Morgan, 'Sharks: The Making of a Best Seller', in R. Atway, *American Mass Media* (New York: Random House, 1978), pp. 140–50.

8. See F. Inglis, 'Spellbinding and Anthropology: The Work of Richard Adams and Ursula Le Guin', in D. Butts (ed.), *Good Writers for Young Readers* (St Albans: Hart-Davis Educational, 1977), pp. 114–28.

9. I take this concept from Lucien Goldmann's work. See especially the essay 'Genetic Structuralism in the Sociology of Literature', in E. and T. Burns (eds), *Sociology of Literature and Drama* (Harmondsworth: Penguin, 1973), pp. 109–23.

10. Ibid., p. 120.

11. Ibid.

12. Inglis, 'Spellbinding and Anthropology', pp. 114–28.

13. Ibid., p. 124.

14. A position associated of course with the early Marx.

15. F. Musgrove, *Ecstacy and Holiness: Counter Culture and the Open Society* (London: RKP, 1974).

16. R. Adams, *Watership Down* (Harmondsworth: Penguin, 1974), p. 159.

17. Musgrove, *Ecstasy and Holiness*, p. 87.

18. Adams, *Watership Down*, p. 138.

19. Ibid., p. 129.

20. R. Williams, *The Country and the City* (St Albans: Paladin, 1975), p. 303.

21. Adams, *Watership Down*, p. 269.

22. Ibid., p. 268.

23. See Raymond Williams' discussion of Arnold in *Culture and Society* (London: Chatto & Windus, 1958).

24. The term is from Raymond Williams' *The Country and the City*, p. 309.

25. Ibid.

26. Ibid.

27. N. Manlove, *Modern Fantasy* (Cambridge University Press, 1975), p. 166.

28. Adams, *Watership Down*, p. 468.

29. For a useful discussion of this theme see R. Giddings and E. Holland, *J. R. R. Tolkien: The Shores of Middle-Earth* (London: Junction, 1981), pp. 130–32.

30. Booker, *The Seventies*, p. 252.

31. Ibid., p. 252.

32. Ibid.

33. Ibid.

34. Ibid.

35. I have borrowed this term from Raymond Williams' *The Long Revolution* (Harmondsworth: Penguin, 1961), Chapter 4.

36. K. Marx, *Grundrisse* (trans. M. Nicolaus) (Harmondsworth: Penguin, 1973), p. 110.

37. Ibid.

38. Booker, *The Seventies*, p. 254.

39. Ibid.

40. Ibid.

41. Ibid., pp. 254–5.

42. Ibid., p. 255.
43. Ibid.
44. J. Cornwell, 'Rabbits to Riches'.
45. R. Boston, 'Trend Setters: *Watership Down*', *Guardian* (6 August 1976).
46. Adams, *Watership Down*, p. 42.
47. Ibid., p. 80.
48. R. Jackson, *Fantasy: The Literature of Subversion* (London: Methuen, 1981), p. 155.
49. See Manlove, *Modern Fantasy*.
50. Adams, *Watership Down*, p. 16.
51. Ibid., p. 67.
52. Ibid., p. 66.
53. Ibid., p. 112.
54. Boston, 'Trend Setters'.
55. Quoted in an interview with John Heilpern, *Observer Magazine* (9 October 1977).
56. Adams, *Watership Down*, p. 286–7.
57. Adams, *Radio Times* interview.
58. G. Orwell, *The Collected Essays, Journalism and Letters*, Vol. 1 (Harmondsworth: Penguin, 1971), p. 528.
59. Adams, *Radio Times* interview.
60. S. Hall and T. Jefferson, *Resistance Through Ritual* (London: Hutchinson, 1975), p. 64.
61. *Observer Magazine* interview with John Heilpern.
62. Ibid.
63. R. Jackson, *Fantasy*, p. 52.
64. F. Jameson, 'Magical Narrative: Romance as Genre', *New Literary History*, 7, No. 1 (Autumn 1975), 133–63.
65. R. Jackson, *Fantasy*, p. 52.
66. Jameson, 'Magical Narrative', p. 140.
67. T. Bennett, 'Marxism & Popular Fiction', *Literature and History*, VII, No. 2 (Autumn 1981), 156.
68. Raymond Williams defines the 'residual' element in a culture as that which 'by definition. has been effectively formed in the past, but . . . is still active in the cultural process, not only and often not at all as an element of the past, but as an effective element of the present'. (Thus the 'residual' is not to be confused with the 'archaic' which is 'wholly recognized as an element of the past, to be observed, to be examined, or even on occasion to be consciously "revived" in a deliberately specializing way'.) Williams argues that 'the idea of rural community is predominantly residual, but is in some limited respects alternative or oppositional to urban capitalism, though for the most part it is incorporated, as idealization or fantasy, or as an exotic – residential or escape – leisure function of the dominant order itself'. (*Marxism and Literature*, Oxford University Press, 1976, p. 122).

Further Reading

The following is not intended to be an exhaustive bibliography of popular fiction. Rather than attempting to cover the whole of the field, I have concentrated on books and essays which have appeared in recent years or 'classics' of criticism which are still in print. In the main I have restricted the list to those texts which deal with popular literature, since that has been the focus of the chapters in this book. However, some of the more recent (and productive) analysis of popular fiction has looked at narrative across a range of media (e.g. the essays by Bennett and Martin), and I have tried to include this work where it has seemed appropriate.

History and Theory of Popular Fiction

Angenot, M., *Le Roman populaire: Recherches en paralittérature* (Montreal: Presses de l'Université du Quebec, 1975). An examination of French popular fiction in the period 1830–1914, but important for Angenot's definition of 'paralittérature'. Not available in English but referred to in Parrinder (see under Science Fiction).

Bennett, T., 'Marxism and Popular Fiction', *Literature and History*, VII, No 2 (Autumn 1981), 138–65. Attacks Marxist criticism for neglecting popular fiction in favour of 'canonic' texts.

Bigsby, C. W., *Approaches to Popular Culture* (London: Edward Arnold, 1976). A reader containing essays from historians, sociologists, linguists and literary critics – of mixed quality.

Bromley, R., 'Natural Boundaries: the Social Function of Popular Fiction', *Red Letters*, No 7 (1978), 34–60. Dense but illuminating application of Gramsci's notion of 'common sense' to the analysis of popular texts.

Bromley, R., 'The Gentry, Bourgeois Hegemony and Popular Fiction', *Literature and History*, VII, No 2 (Autumn 1981), 166–83. Develops the thesis of Bromley's earlier article and applies it to popular romance novels of the 1930s.

Cawelti, J. G., *Adventure, Mystery, and Romance* (Chicago: University of Chicago Press, 1976). Attacks the theory that popular fiction is a degraded literary product and argues that 'formulaic' literature has a different function from that of its 'mimetic' (élite) counterpart. The main weakness of Cawelti's work is the tendency to reduce popular fiction to three ahistorical 'archetypes' (*viz.* adventure, mystery and romance).

Cockburn, C., *Bestseller* (London: Sidgwick & Jackson, 1972). Entertaining though untheorised study of English bestsellers during the period 1900–39.

Escarpit, R., *The Book Revolution* (London: Harrap, 1966). Important work of empirical sociology which offers a definition of the 'bestseller' in terms both of volume and pace of sales (see also Sutherland, below).

Fiedler, L., 'Towards a Definition of Popular Literature', in C. Bigsby (ed.), *Superculture: American Popular Culture and Europe* (London: Paul Elek, 1975). Quirky but useful essay from a maverick of the American literary critical scene.

Hall, S. and Whannel, P., *The Popular Arts* (London: Hutchinson, 1964). One of the earliest to break away from élitist approaches to popular culture. Includes concrete case-studies which are designed for secondary school teachers and is both clear and lively.

James, L., *Fiction for the Working Man 1830–50* (Harmondsworth: Penguin, 1973). Important study of literature and the early urban working class.

Jameson, F., 'Ideology, Narrative Analysis and Popular Culture', *Theory and Society*, No 4 (1977), 543–59. A review of Cawelti (see above) which examines the contributions made by structuralism and marxism to the study of popular narrative. Useful summary of different approaches.

Laing, S., 'Philip Gibbs and the Newsreel Novel', *Literature and History*, VII, No 2 (Autumn 1981), 184–207. Penetrating analysis of one of the most successful 'middlebrow' authors of the interwar years. Highlights the relationship between Gibbs' interpretation of political events and the construction of a national identity in the newsreels of the period.

Leavis, Q. D., *Fiction and the Reading Public* (London: Chatto & Windus, 1930. Available in Penguin). Pioneering survey of the historical development of popular literature and the effects of journalism, advertising and so on on literary language. Marred by an élitist perspective which conflicts with Leavis' assertion that she has adopted an 'anthropological approach' to her subject.

Lowenthal, L., *Literature, Popular Culture and Society* (Pale Alto, California: Pacific Paperback Books, 1968). Covers much the same ground as Leavis' book but is characterised by a more rigorous approach, derived from the work of the Frankfurt School.

Martin, G., *U203 Popular Culture: Unit 13 Readers, Viewers and Texts* (Milton Keynes: Open University Press, 1981). Argues that popular fictions should not be seen as simple imitations of the 'real world', but as a 'reworking of those ideological structures within which we conduct our lives'.

Meyersohn, R. (*et al.*), *Literary Taste, Culture & Mass Communication* (Cambridge: Chadwyck-Healey, 1980). Massive collection of articles, book extracts, etc., in fourteen volumes. Volume 12 includes a section on bestsellers, but it is worth investigating the others as well.

Neuburg, V., *Popular Literature* (Harmondsworth: Penguin, 1977). History of the development of popular literature 'from the beginning of print to the year 1897'.

Rockwell, R., *Fact in Fiction* (London: RKP, 1974). Explores the way in which sociologists can 'use' literature as evidence. Includes an interesting chapter on 'normative values' in spy fiction.

Swingewood, A., *The Myth of Mass Culture* (London: Macmillan, 1977). A good introduction to theories of popular/mass culture. Tries to steer a course between Leavis on the one hand and simplistic Marxism on the other.

Sutherland, J., *Bestsellers: Popular Fiction of the 1970s* (London: RKP, 1981). Surveys a wide variety of British and American novels of the 1970s and highlights the movement towards 'an American kind of book'.

Williams, R., *The Long Revolution* (London: Chatto & Windus, 1961. Available in Penguin). Chapter Four, 'The Analysis of Culture', outlines the hypothesis that much of the fiction of the 1840s offered 'magical resolutions' to the 'real' problems faced by readers in their everyday lives. Useful starting point for the analysis of popular fiction.

Popular Genres

(n.b. this list only deals with the genres which have been the subject of detailed examination in our reader. For introductory reading on other genres such as the Gothic or Western see J. G. Cawelti in Section One.)

SCIENCE FICTION

Aldiss, B., *Billion Year Spree: The History of Science Fiction* (London: Weidenfeld & Nicolson, 1973; Corgi, 1975). Still the best informed general history of the genre – serious and scholarly, but with the enthusiasm and nuanced detail of an insider.

Klein, G., 'Discontent in American Science Fiction', *Science Fiction Studies*, IV, No 1, Part I (March 1977) 3–13. A seminal and influential study which tries to explain the development of post-war American SF in terms of its social base.

Martin, G., *U203 Popular Culture: Unit 27 Science Fiction* (Milton Keynes: Open University Press, 1982). Useful survey of the field that makes informed use of modern frameworks of critical analysis.

Nicholls, P. (ed.), *The Encyclopedia of Science Fiction* (London: Granada, 1981). Massive work of enthusiastic scholarship. Essential for students and fans alike.

Parrinder, P., *Science Fiction: Its Criticism and Teaching* (London: Methuen, 1980). Up-to-date academic survey of the field, with a useful chapter on the sociology of the genre.

Parrinder, P. (ed.), *Science Fiction: A Critical Guide* (London: Longman, 1979). Contains interesting essays by, amongst others, Marc Angenot, Raymond Williams, Tom Shippey and Parrinder himself.

Rose, M. (ed.), *Science Fiction: A Collection of Critical Essays* (Englewood Cliffs, New Jersey: Prentice-Hall, 1976). A valuable collection of scholarly essays, including work by Kingsley Amis, Robert Scholes, Darko Suvin, Stanislaw Lem, Susan Sontag and others.

Scholes, R. and Rabkin, E., *Science Fiction: History, Science, Vision* (New York: Oxford University Press, 1977). An introductory survey, valuable particularly for its historical account of the genre and its sample analysis of classic SF texts.

Science Fiction Studies, IV, Part 3 (November 1977). A special issue on the sociology of science fiction.

Suvin, D., *Metamorphoses of Science Fiction: On The Poetics and History of a Literary Genre* (Yale University Press, 1979). A densely written, but highly rewarding collection of essays on the poetics and history of the genre. Arguably the most significant academic survey of SF yet published.

UTOPIA AND FANTASY

Brooke-Rose, C., *A Rhetoric of the Unreal* (Cambridge University Press, 1975). Exceedingly difficult, but rewarding formalist analyses of a wide range of fantastic narratives, including an excellent chapter on Tolkien.

Clarke, I. F., *The Pattern of Expectation, 1644–2001* (London: Jonathan Cape, 1979). A straightforward descriptive account of the history of utopian and dystopian speculation in futuristic fiction.

Jackson, R., *Fantasy: The Literature of Subversion* (London: Methuen, 1981). Original study, drawing mainly on psychoanalytic perspectives, but with a useful summary of other theoretical approaches.

Levitas, R., 'Dystopian Times? The Impact of the Death of Progress on Utopia', *Theory, Culture and Society*, 1, No 1 (Spring 1982) 53–64. Interesting sociological analysis of popular utopian currents in modern industrial societies, with illustrations from a number of bestselling texts.

Manlove, C. N., *Modern Fantasy: Five Studies* (Cambridge University Press, 1975). Contains useful chapters on Tolkien, C. S. Lewis and Mervyn Peake.

Suvin, D., *Metamorphoses of Science Fiction: On the Poetics and History of a Literary Genre* (Yale University Press, 1979). Included here because it is as much a study of utopianism as of SF. Looks at the relationship between subversive utopianism and conservative escapism from Thomas More to the twentieth century.

Todorov, T., *The Fantastic: A Structural Approach to a Literary Genre* (Cornell University Press, 1975). Seminal structuralist essay on fantasy and illusion in the development of literary genres.

Williams, R., 'Utopias and Science Fiction', in P. Parrinder (ed.), *Science Fiction: A Critical Guide* (London: Longman, 1979). A brief but stimulating article offering a critical typology of Utopian writing and situating its most recent developments in historical perspective.

Zipes, J., *Breaking the Magic Spell* (London: Heinemann, 1979). Draws on the writings of Ernst Bloch, classic Marxist theorist of utopianism, in offering a radical approach to fairy-tales and fantasy.

THRILLERS

Bennett, T., 'James Bond as Popular Hero', in *U203 Popular Culture: Politics, Ideology & Popular Culture, No. 2* (Milton Keynes: Open University Press, 1982). A recent study of the Bond 'phenomenon' which draws on both structuralist and psychoanalytic theory.

Cawelti, J. G., *Adventure, Mystery and Romance* (Chicago: University of Chicago

Press, 1976), Chapters 3–5. Includes excellent case-studies of the detective and 'hard-boiled' genres, whilst attempting to account for the popularity of different types of thriller in terms of changing social attitudes to crime.

Eco, U., 'The Narrative Structure in Fleming', in Waites, B., Bennett, T. and Martin, G. (eds), *Popular Culture: Past and Present* (London: Croom Helm, 1981). An important essay which tries to connect the internal narrative 'machinery' of the Bond stories with the changing ideological context in which they were produced.

Hall, S. and Whannel, P., *The Popular Arts* (London: Hutchinson, 1964). Contains a chapter entitled 'The Avenging Angels' which offers an interesting comparison between Mickey Spillane and Raymond Chandler (the latter is preferred, mainly because of his use of irony).

Keating, H. R., *Whodunit? A Guide to Crime, Suspense and Spy Fiction* (London: Windward, 1982). Introductory guide, mainly devoted to biographies of thriller writers.

Palmer, J., *Thrillers: Genesis and Structure of a Popular Genre* (London: Edward Arnold, 1979). Seminal work which draws on both literary and sociological theory in tracing the origins of the thriller to the mid-nineteenth century.

Porter, D., *The Pursuit of Crime* (Yale University Press 1981), Eclectic but useful guide to theories of 'pleasure' and their application to suspense fiction.

Symons, J., *Bloody Murder* (Harmondsworth: Penguin, 1975). Highly readable introduction to the history of thrillers pre-1970. Thumbnail sketches of a wide range of authors, from Poe to Forsyth.

Watson, C., *Snobbery With Violence* (London: Eyre & Spotiswoode, 1971). Entertaining and astute criticism of British thriller writers, concentrating on the pre-war period.

WOMEN'S ROMANCE

Anderson, R., *The Purple Heart-throbs* (London: Hodder and Stoughton, 1974). An entertaining study of the emergence of romantic fiction as a 'mass' form, with many quotations from Charlotte M. Yonge to Denise Robins and Mills and Boon.

Beauman, N., *A Very Great Profession* (London: Virago, 1983). Examines the 'women's novel' between the two World Wars and includes chapters on sex, romance and love.

Cecil, M., *Heroines in Love, 1750–1974* (London: Michael Joseph, 1974). This is a book of extracts from women's magazines and advice books. Each piece of romantic fiction is introduced with a description of its period context.

De Rougemont, D., *Passion and Society* (London: Faber and Faber, revised edition, 1956). The 'classic' examination of the ideology of courtly love and its contemporary resonances, as traced through key European myths, such as 'Tristan and Iseult'. Also a 'message' book, reminding its readers that the root of 'passion' is, unalterably, 'suffering' . . .

King, J. and Stott, M. (eds), *Is This Your Life?* (London: Virago, 1977). Explores a variety of contemporary media images of women, including those in popular fiction, women's magazines, film and television.

McRobbie, A. and McCabe, T. (eds), *Feminism for Girls* (London: RKP, 1981). Examines the experiences of modern adolescent girls in Britain from a feminist perspective and includes chapters on romance and sexuality and the ideology of the popular teen magazine, *Jackie*.

Miles, R., *The Fiction of Sex* (London: Vision, 1974). Concentrates on the theme of 'sex difference' in the twentieth-century novel and includes a chapter on 'Moral themes and the consolation of romance'.

Sarsby, J., *Romantic Love and Society* (London: Penguin, 1983). Aims to study 'the place' of romantic love 'in the modern world'. However, does offer some useful empirical material on courtship in Britain and girls' attitudes to it; plus a chapter on 'Women's magazine fiction: love ideology for the dependent woman'.

Sullerot, E., *Women on Love* (London: Jill Norman, 1980). A lively, idiosyncratic account of 'eight centuries of feminine writing', with many illustrations and examples, mainly from France.

Women's Studies Group, Centre for Contemporary Cultural Studies, *Women Take Issue* (London: Hutchinson, 1978). Excellent resumé of recent feminist work in the area of cultural studies. Includes chapters on ideologies of femininity and romance and women's magazines. The two collections based on work done by the Birmingham University CCCS in this list (McRobbie and McCabe is the other) are really the only recent examples of attempts to provide properly analytical accounts of romantic fiction and its ideologies. The other contemporary books in this list, while still very useful for their empirical material, tend to remain at the levels of the descriptive, the witty or the idiosyncratic.

Index

244 *Index*